A MAP OF MODERN ENGLISH VERSE

JOHN PRESS

A Map of Modern English Verse

OXFORD UNIVERSITY PRESS
LONDON OXFORD NEW YORK

Oxford University Press

LONDON OXFORD GLASGOW NEW YORK
TORONTO MELBOURNE WELLINGTON CAPE TOWN
IBADAN NAIROBI DAR ES SALAAM LUSAKA ADDIS ABABA
KUALA LUMPUR SINGAPORE JAKARTA HONG KONG TOKYO
DELHI BOMBAY CALCUTTA MADRAS KARACHI

Paperback edition ISBN 0 19 281041 3
Clothbound edition ISBN 0 19 211279 1

First published, simultaneously in clothbound form and as an Oxford University Press paperback, by Oxford University Press, London, 1969. Reprinted with corrections 1971
Third impression 1976

Printed in Great Britain by
Hazell Watson & Viney Ltd
Aylesbury, Bucks

PREFACE

This book consists of a General Introduction, followed by fourteen sections, every one of which is devoted to a poet or a group of poets. These sections all contain a biographical and critical introduction, a number of critical passages, a selection of poems and a bibliography. There is also a general bibliography and a list of sources from which the poems have been taken.

It will be noticed that, in the passages of criticism, I have relied to a great extent on the poets themselves, despite Donald Davie's astringent warning about trusting Yeats as a guide to his own poetry: 'Yeats was not only the man who wrote the poems; he was also, unfortunately, the first and by no means the most intelligent of those who have attempted to explain them.'[1] *A Map of Modern English Verse* is a source book rather than a conspectus of the best critical opinion, and it is partly for this reason that I have given more space to the writings of the poets and their immediate contemporaries than to the exhaustive treatises of academics. But I confess that I would sooner read a page by Shakespeare on *Measure for Measure* than ninety-nine per cent of the Shakespearean criticism written in our day; just as I would sacrifice almost all the commentaries on *The Waste Land* for Eliot's account of that poem's genesis.

Until I began work on this book I did not suspect how many documents essential for a full understanding of modern English verse were inaccessible to all but a few students of poetry. For example, the three volumes of *Some Imagist Poets* (1915–1917) have long been out of print, and the 1917 volume is not held by the British Museum or the other copyright libraries. Ford Madox Ford's *Collected Poems* (1913), with its important Introduction, is seldom to be found outside the great libraries, and the *Collected Poems* (1936), published by OUP, New York, which reprints the Introduction in a slightly different form, appears not to have been distributed in Britain. The first edition of Yeats's *A Vision* (1925) is hard to come by, and the second edition (1937) omits some interesting material, including the superb Dedication. *A Packet for Ezra Pound* (1929) is equally rare; and although most of it is incorporated in *A Vision* (1937), once again there are omissions of several revealing passages. Even the post-war volumes of Yeats's collected prose writings inexcusably omit certain portions of the text without indicating where the cuts have been made.

[1] *An Honoured Guest*, edited by Denis Donoghue and J. R. Mulryne, 1965, p. 79.

Moreover, there are many prefaces, articles, reviews, letters and other fugitive writings which lie forgotten in books now out of print, or in the pages of dead periodicals. It is a chastening experience to pore over the journals of the past fifty years, to stumble on a famous poem or essay next to work by a man whose name is unfamiliar even to specialists, to discover how much intelligent, scholarly writing remains buried in these tomes, to speculate on the fate of one's coevals who now appear so knowledgeable and so clever.

I have usually given the original source of all the critical extracts, and if the passage in question has been reprinted I have indicated where it can most readily be found. This device will, I trust, meet the needs of the student and of the general reader.

I have printed a few passages of verse and of prose which fall on either side of the dates 1909 and 1959. Apart from W. B. Yeats, no poets are included whose verse was published before 1900: this explains the omission of Hardy, Bridges, Housman, and Kipling, all of whom wrote some of their finest poems long after 1909. Nor have I thought it right to count Gerard Manley Hopkins as eligible for inclusion, even though the bulk of his verse remained unpublished until 1918.

Reasons of space and economy have forced me to include only a bare minimum of poems. Since I assume that all readers of this book will have easy access to the works of such major poets as Yeats, Pound, and Eliot, I have given what may seem a disproportionately large space to the poems of minor writers. By the same token I have refrained from printing large chunks of justly famous essays such as Eliot's 'Tradition and the Individual Talent', preferring to find room for less familiar and less accessible passages which are in danger of being undeservedly forgotten.

I have not attempted to discuss the work of poets such as Hugh MacDiarmid whose best poems are in Scots. Lack of space has prevented me from devoting attention to Austin Clarke, Patrick Kavanagh, Thomas Kinsella, and post-Yeatsian Irish verse in general. I regret, too, that it has proved impossible to obtain permission to reproduce a poem by Kathleen Raine and extracts from the critical writings of F. R. Leavis. Some of my other inclusions and omissions may justly be regarded as proof of a partial and fallible judgment. But this is a selective guide, not an encyclopaedia; and I hope that my readers will explore for themselves not only the territory which I have mapped but the regions that stretch beyond its borders.

ACKNOWLEDGEMENTS

For permission to reproduce copyright passages, grateful acknowledgement is made to the publishers and copyright holders of the following:

Richard Aldington, *Collected Poems* (George Allen & Unwin Ltd. and Rosica Colin Ltd.);
W. H. Auden, *Collected Shorter Poems 1927–1957*, *The Dyer's Hand* (Faber & Faber Ltd. and Random House, Inc., New York); *The Collected Poetry of W. H. Auden* (Random House, Inc., New York); *For the Time Being*, Introduction to *A Choice of de la Mare's Verse* (Faber & Faber Ltd.); and *Letters from Iceland* (Curtis Brown Ltd., Faber & Faber Ltd., and Random House, Inc., New York);
George Barker, *Collected Poems 1930–1965* (Faber & Faber Ltd. and October House Inc., New York);
John Betjeman, *Collected Poems* (John Murray Ltd. and Houghton Mifflin Co., Boston);
Thomas Blackburn, *Hospital for Defectives* (Putnam & Co. and the author);
Edmund Blunden, *Poems of Many Years* (William Collins, Sons & Co. Ltd. and A. D. Peters & Co.);
Norman Cameron, *Collected Poems* (Chatto & Windus Ltd., and the Hogarth Press);
Roy Campbell, *Collected Poems*, Vol. 1 (The Bodley Head Ltd. and Henry Regnery Co., Chicago);
Donald Davie, *A Winter Talent* (Routledge & Kegan Paul Ltd. and the author); *Brides of Reason* (Fantasy Press and the author);
W. H. Davies, *Complete Poems* (Jonathan Cape Ltd., Wesleyan University Press, and Mrs H. M. Davies);
H[ilda] D[olittle], *Selected Poems* (André Deutsch Ltd. and the Grove Press Inc., New York);
Keith Douglas, *Collected Poems* (Faber & Faber Ltd. and the Chilmark Press Inc., New York);
Lawrence Durrell, *Collected Poems* (Faber & Faber Ltd. and E. P. Dutton & Co. Inc., New York);
T. S. Eliot, *Collected Poems 1909–1962*, *Notes Towards the Definition of Culture*, *Selected Essays* (Faber & Faber Ltd. and Harcourt, Brace & World, Inc., New York); *To Criticize the Critic*, *On Poetry and Poets* (Faber & Faber Ltd. and Farrar, Straus & Giroux, Inc., New York); *The Use of Poetry* (Faber & Faber Ltd. and Barnes & Noble Inc., New York); Introduction to *Ezra Pound: Selected Poems* (Faber & Faber Ltd., and New Directions Publishing Corporation, New York); *After Strange Gods*, critical note to *Collected Poems of Harold Monro*, and extracts from *The Dial*, *The Egoist*, and *The Tyro* (Faber & Faber Ltd.);
William Empson, *Collected Poems* (Chatto & Windus Ltd., Harcourt, Brace & World, Inc., New York, and the author);
F. S. Flint, extracts from draft article quoted in *The Review* (April 1965) and *The Chapbook* (Mrs Ianthe Price);

Ford Madox Ford, *Collected Poems* (Oxford University Press, Inc., New York and Miss Janice Biala);

Roy Fuller, *Collected Poems* (André Deutsch Ltd., Dufour Editions Inc., Pennsylvania, and the author);

David Gascoyne, *Collected Poems* (Oxford University Press and André Deutsch Ltd.);

Wilfrid Gibson, *Collected Poems 1909–1925* (Macmillan & Co. Ltd.);

Robert Graves, *Collected Poems* (1958), *Collected Poems* (1959), *Collected Poems* (1965), *The Crowning Privilege, Mammon and the Black Goddess,* and *Steps* (Cassell & Co. Ltd., A. P. Watt & Son, Collins-Knowlton-Wing, New York, and the author);

Geoffrey Grigson, *Poetry of the Present* (Phoenix House, David Higham Associates Ltd., and the author);

Thom Gunn, *My Sad Captains* (Faber & Faber Ltd. and University of Chicago Press);

Ivor Gurney, *Poems* (Hutchinson Ltd);

Geoffrey Hill, *For the Unfallen* (André Deutsch Ltd., Dufour Editions Inc., Pennsylvania, and the author);

Ted Hughes, *Lupercal* (Faber & Faber Ltd. and Harper and Row, Publishers, New York);

T. E. Hulme: Alun R. Jones, *The Life and Opinions of T. E. Hulme* (Victor Gollancz Ltd. and The Beacon Press, Boston);

Philip Larkin, *The Less Deceived* (The Marvell Press);

D. H. Lawrence, *Collected Letters,* edited by Harry T. Moore (William Heinemann Ltd., Laurence Pollinger Ltd., the Estate of the late Mrs Frieda Lawrence, The Viking Press Inc., New York, Angelo Ravagli, and C. Montague Weekley); *The Complete Poems,* edited by Vivian de Sola Pinto and F. Warren Roberts (William Heinemann Ltd., Laurence Pollinger Ltd., the Estate of the late Mrs Frieda Lawrence, The Viking Press, Inc., New York, B. W. Huebsch, Inc., and Angelo Ravagli); *Selected Literary Criticism* (William Heinemann Ltd., Laurence Pollinger Ltd., the Estate of the late Mrs Frieda Lawrence, and The Viking Press, Inc., New York);

Alun Lewis, *Selected Poetry and Prose* (George Allen & Unwin Ltd. and Hillary House Publishers, Ltd., New York);

C. Day Lewis, *Collected Poems* (Jonathan Cape Ltd., The Hogarth Press, Harold Matson Co., Inc., New York, and the author); *The Buried Day* (Chatto & Windus Ltd., A. D. Peters & Co., and the author);

Edward Lowbury, *Daylight Astronomy* (Chatto & Windus Ltd., and the author); *New Poems* (Keepsake Press and the author);

Norman MacCaig, *The Sinai Sort* (Chatto & Windus Ltd., The Hogarth Press, and the author);

Louis MacNeice, *Collected Poems* (Faber & Faber Ltd. and Oxford University Press Inc., New York); *The Strings are False* (Faber & Faber Ltd., David Higham Associates Ltd., and Oxford University Press Inc., New York);

Walter de la Mare, *A Choice of de la Mare's Verse* (Faber & Faber Ltd., the author's Literary Trustees, and the Society of Authors);

Edwin Muir, *An Autobiography* (Chatto & Windus Ltd., The Hogarth Press, and Mrs Willa Muir); *Collected Poems* (Faber & Faber Ltd., and Oxford University Press, Inc., New York);

Norman Nicholson, *The Pot Geranium* (Faber & Faber Ltd. and David Higham Associates, Ltd);

Wilfred Owen, *Collected Poems* (Chatto & Windus Ltd., New Directions Publishing Corporation, New York, and Mr Harold Owen);

Ezra Pound, *The ABC of Reading, The Cantos, Literary Essays, Personae, Polite Essays* (Faber & Faber Ltd. and New Directions Publishing Corporation, New York); *Guide to Kulchur, The Spirit of Romance* (Peter Owen and New Directions Publishing Corporation, New York); and extracts from *The English Review* (Faber & Faber Ltd.);

F. T. Prince, *The Doors of Stone* (Rupert Hart-Davis Ltd. and the author);

Michael Riviere, *Poems* (Favill Press and the author);

Isaac Rosenberg, *Collected Works* (Chatto & Windus Ltd., Schocken Books Inc., New York, and the author's Literary Estate);

Siegfried Sassoon, *Collected Poems* (Faber & Faber Ltd., The Viking Press, Inc., New York, and Mr G. T. Sassoon);

Burns Singer, *Still and All* (Martin Secker & Warburg Ltd.);

Edith Sitwell, *Collected Poems* (Macmillan & Co. Ltd., David Higham Associates Ltd., and Vanguard Press, Inc., New York);

Charles Sorley, *Marlborough* (Cambridge University Press);

Bernard Spencer, *Collected Poems* (Alan Ross Ltd. and Dufour Editions Inc., Pennsylvania);

Stephen Spender, *Collected Poems* (Faber & Faber Ltd. and Random House, Inc., New York);

Dylan Thomas, *Collected Poems, Selected Letters* (J. M. Dent & Sons Ltd., David Higham Associates Ltd., and New Directions Publishing Corporation, New York);

Edward Thomas, *Collected Poems* and *Life and Letters* (Faber & Faber Ltd. and Mrs Mifanwy Thomas);

R. S. Thomas, *Pietà* (Rupert Hart-Davis Ltd. and the author); *Poetry for Supper* (Rupert Hart-Davis Ltd., Dufour Editions, Inc., Pennsylvania, and the author);

Charles Tomlinson, *A Peopled Landscape* (Oxford University Press); *Seeing is Believing* (Oxford University Press and Astor-Honor Inc., New York);

Henry Treece, *The Black Seasons* (Faber & Faber Ltd.);

Vernon Watkins, *The Death Bell* (Faber & Faber Ltd.);

W. B. Yeats, *A Packet for Ezra Pound, On the Boiler* (Cuala Press); Introduction to *The Oxford Book of Modern Verse* (Oxford University Press); *The Letters of W. B. Yeats* (Rupert Hart-Davis Ltd. and the Macmillan Co., New York); *A Vision, Autobiographies, Essays and Introductions, Explorations, The Variorum Edition of The Poems* (Macmillan & Co., A. P. Watt & Son, and the Macmillan Co., New York);

Andrew Young, *Collected Poems* (Rupert Hart-Davis Ltd. and the author).

Apologies are offered to those few copyright-holders whom it has proved impossible to locate.

CONTENTS

1

GENERAL INTRODUCTION

It would be ridiculous to suppose that one could single out a decisive moment or event as the origin of modern English verse, but the years 1908 to 1910 have a good claim to be regarded as a crucial phase in the history of English poetry. In the autumn of 1908 Ezra Pound settled in London and was speedily accepted as a brilliant though slightly comic man of letters by a wide circle of writers. In December of that year Ford Madox Ford, the most selfless and perceptive of editors, brought out the first number of his incomparable *English Review*. Towards the end of 1908 T. S. Eliot, having read Arthur Symons's *The Symbolist Movement in Literature* (1899), ordered the works of Laforgue, and during the next two years wrote 'Preludes', 'Portrait of a Lady', and the first draft of 'Prufrock', although none of these poems was printed until Eliot had finally left the States and made his home in London. In March 1909 Pound dined in Soho at the club founded by F. S. Flint and other precursors of Imagism; and a month later published *Personae*. After the death of Swinburne in April 1909 and of Meredith in May, W. B. Yeats remarked 'And now I am King of the Cats', forgetting perhaps that Thomas Hardy was still in the plenitude of his poetical genius. The next year brought to London the first Post-Impressionist Exhibition and Diaghileff's Russian Ballet, two potent agents of a revolution in taste which affected poetry no less than painting and music.

I have summarized these apparently unconnected events to give some idea of which way the wind was blowing towards the end of the Edwardian Age. Apologists of the new poetic have always maintained that the 'situation in poetry in 1909 or 1910 was stagnant to a degree difficult for any young poet of to-day to conceive'.[1] We may take this with a pinch of salt, since poets, like politicians, always exaggerate the corruption or the incompetence of the *régime* which they have superseded. It is true that the fag-end of Victorian Romanticism and Imperialism blighted our poetry, and that a philistine middle-class believed Alfred Austin, Alfred Noyes, Henry Newbolt, and William Watson to be important poets, a delusion fostered by conservative and academic critics. To counterbalance this, we should remember that Thomas Hardy, although in his seventieth year, was still writing poems of undiminished poignancy and force, while Yeats, having recently published his *Collected Works*, was on the threshold of becoming a

[1] T. S. Eliot, Introduction to *Literary Essays of Ezra Pound*, 1954, p. xiii.

major poet. Nor can we afford to despise an epoch which numbered among its established poets Bridges, Housman, and Kipling, and among its rising poets W. H. Davies and Walter de la Mare. With all its faults, literary England was not in 1909 a Pontine Marsh awaiting reclamation at the hands of Pound and Eliot.

The mention of Pound and Eliot may remind us that modern English verse owes much to American poets. Indeed it is sometimes argued that the most vital poetry of the twentieth century in English has been written by Americans, and that it is American rather than English writing which has, over the past fifty or sixty years, displayed linguistic vigour, experimental boldness, and imaginative daring. It would probably be more accurate to say that, at the turn of the century, the upper-middle-class culture of Victorian England was moribund; and that the poetry nurtured by this culture dwindled into feebleness or grew coarsely bombastic. The most original contributions to English verse during this century have been made by Americans living in England (Pound and Eliot), the Anglo-Irish (Yeats and Robert Graves), a Welshman (Dylan Thomas), a man from the Orkneys (Edwin Muir), and English poets belonging to the proletariat or to the lower-middle-class. D. H. Lawrence's father was a miner; Wilfred Owen was born into a family living in straitened circumstances on the border of England and Wales; Isaac Rosenberg, the son of Jewish immigrants, spent almost all his life in the East End of London. The only major English poet of the century born and bred in a prosperous Tennysonian *milieu* is W. H. Auden – and he, after prophesying doom for ten years, packed his bags and emigrated to the United States.

The characteristics of modern, post-symbolist verse are not easy to define in a few words. Ford Madox Ford, a pioneer in his rejection of the Tennysonian, Bardic doctrine that poetry should be noble and confidently assertive, remarked in *Portraits from Life* that poetry should be 'like one's intimate conversation with someone one loved very much'.[2] There have, of course, been some good rhetorical poems written since 1909, but much of the best modern verse fulfils Ford's requirements by combining an easy, conversational diction with a naked intensity of utterance. We may detect also in modern verse a passionate simplicity of emotion coexisting with intellectual complexity and technical sophistication, a blend rarely found in English poetry since the Metaphysicals.

The most fiercely-sustained attack on the theory and practice of the Anglo-American post-symbolists is to be found in Yvor Winters's *In Defense of Reason* (1947). Graham Hough's *Image and Experience* (1960) deploys a further battery of arguments against Imagism and the poetic of Pound and of Eliot, while the most influential poet of the

[2] Cf. the passage from W. H. Auden quoted below, p. 192.

1950s, Philip Larkin, has frequently expressed his distaste for the whole tradition of post-symbolism. C. P. Snow takes up an old left-wing battle cry in *The Two Cultures* (1960), asserting that the dominant artists of the early twentieth century were all politically wicked and anti-social. Even Donald Davie, whom one cannot accuse of prejudice against modernism, declares that there is a 'logical and chronological connection between modernism in the arts and Fascism in politics'.[3]

This charge is, in my judgment, misconceived. It is true that Pound's *Guide to Kulchur* is, in Davie's words, 'an overtly Fascist book', and that he, like his old friend Wyndham Lewis, became an apologist for Fascism. There are strong authoritarian and anti-democratic elements in Yeats and in Eliot; nor should we blind ourselves to the anti-Jewish prejudices of T. E. Hulme, Pound, and Eliot. Yet these prejudices do not spring from their modernist principles: they flourished among traditionalists with equal virulence; and it is disturbing to reflect that the only common ground of sympathy between Hulme, Pound, Eliot, Hilaire Belloc, and Rupert Brooke (who was infected by Belloc) was their anti-Jewish sentiment.

The aberrations of individuals, however distasteful, do not justify us in condemning modernism as a whole, and Davie has recourse to some flimsy arguments to buttress his thesis: 'the Vou club in totalitarian Japan, with which Pound corresponds through Katue Kitasano, is said to have been founded by admirers of Satie.' Hearsay testimony is thus called in to prove guilt by association.

Since Davie specifically refers to the arts and not solely to poetry, one should consider very briefly the record of the best modernist painters and musicians. As far as I am aware, Kandinsky, Munch, Rouault, Stravinsky, and Webern had no truck with Fascism; Schönberg was a refugee from the Nazis, and Bartok escaped to the United States from Fascist Hungary; Picasso declared himself a Communist many years ago. As for the logical connection between modernism and Fascism, it is no accident that Fascism has always denounced modernism in the arts as an offshoot of Jewish, Bolshevik, or plutocratic decadence.

Modern art has indeed been acutely conscious of the nihilism, the violence, and the anguish which permeate our society. Fascism, like Communism, can be regarded as a desperate attempt to give meaning to a world apparently without order or design; and insofar as modern art has also tried to find a pattern in a welter of disorder it shares certain affinities with all forms of totalitarianism, and not merely with Fascism.

In modern English verse the atmosphere of tension and guilt is all-pervasive. The Nietzschean elements in Yeats and in Muir, the obses-

[3] Donald Davie, *Ezra Pound. Poet as Sculptor*, 1965, p. 146.

sion with the pitiless movement of history in Yeats and in Auden, Eliot's rejection of liberal humanitarianism, and Lawrence's awareness in the early 1920s of the darkness incarnate in the forests of Germany are examples of the ways in which an artist may intuitively respond to the potentialities of evil that seethe beneath the surface of all societies.

All these poets have been tormented, as Pascal was in his day, by the infinitesimal size of man in the cosmos. Two world wars, the reintroduction of torture by governments generally reckoned to be civilized, the scientific planning of genocide, the deliberate crushing of the individual by totalitarian states, the eviction of millions of families from their homes, the outbursts of irrational violence and of racial hatred in the great cities of the world, the possibility that *homo sapiens* may destroy himself – all these factors have lent urgency to the question 'What is man?' It is this question which haunts modern English verse.

The decay of faith in Christianity has poisoned one traditional source of strength and consolation. Since we lack the stoicism and the pure hedonism of vigorous pagan civilization, and have lost the hopefulness of a Christian society, death may well appear more terrible to us than to most ages of the past. Much of the best verse written in this century has been concerned with the necessity to assert our awareness of death and our human dignity in the face of death. Yeats's 'Vacillation' III,[4] and Robert Graves's 'Pure Death'[5] are perhaps the two most splendid variations on the dance of death whose strains echo through the corridors of modern poetry.

We may, of course, believe with Robert Graves that 'the foul tidal basin of modernism'[6] is merely an ignoble deviation from the mainstream of English verse. It is conceivable that the course of true poetry in our century descends from Thomas Hardy through Edward Thomas, W. H. Davies, Norman Cameron, and Alun Lewis, to finish in Graves himself; and that modernism, as Philip Larkin has observed, 'is fun no more. Deserted by the tide of taste, the modern movement awaits combing like some cryptic sea-wrack'.[7] Larkin is even more specific: 'May I trumpet the assurance that one reader at least would not wish Hardy's *Collected Poems* a single page shorter, and regards it as many times over the best body of poetic work this century so far has to show?'[8] Hardy's greatness as a poet has been acknowledged, though in less extravagant terms, by writers as diverse as Pound, Auden, Dylan Thomas, and Donald Davie. While sharing this admiration for Hardy

[4] See below, p. 22. [5] See below, p. 183.

[6] *Oxford Addresses on Poetry*, 1962, p. 5.

[7] Review of John Press, *The Chequer'd Shade*, in *The Manchester Guardian*, 18 November 1958.

[8] 'Wanted: Good Hardy Critic', *The Critical Quarterly*, VIII, 2, Summer 1966, p. 179.

I am convinced that the major poetic achievement of the century is the work of the modernist poets, of whom the three major representatives are Yeats, Pound, and Eliot. Nevertheless I have tried to give a fair hearing to what one may call the alternative tradition. The rivalries of contending literary factions are, in the end, irrelevant to the main task and joy of poetry, the struggle to discover truth and to embody it in a form of words:

And what there is to conquer
By strength and submission, has already been discovered
Once or twice, or several times, by men whom one cannot hope
To emulate – but there is no competition –
There is only the fight to recover what has been lost
And found and lost again; and now, under conditions
That seem unpropitious. But perhaps neither gain nor loss.
For us there is only the trying. The rest is not our business.[9]

[9] T. S. Eliot, 'East Coker'.

SELECT BIBLIOGRAPHY

Anthologies

The Oxford Book of Modern Verse, edited by W. B. Yeats, Oxford, 1936.

The Faber Book of Modern Verse, edited by Michael Roberts, London, 1936; 2nd ed., with supplement by Ann Ridler, 1951; 3rd ed., 1965.

The Penguin Book of Contemporary Verse, edited by Kenneth Allott, Harmondsworth, 1950; 2nd ed., 1962.

Criticism

Alvarez, A., *The Shaping Spirit*, London, 1958.

Bayley, John, *The Romantic Survival*, London, 1957.

Blackmur, R. P., *Language as Gesture*, New York, 1952; London, 1954.

Bowra, C. M., *The Heritage of Symbolism*, London, 1943.

—— *The Creative Experiment*, London, 1949.

Brooks, Cleanth, *Modern Poetry and the Tradition*, Chapel Hill, 1939; London, 1948.

Durrell, Lawrence, *Key to Modern Poetry*, London, 1952.

Eliot, T. S., *Selected Essays*, London, 1932; 3rd ed., 1951.

—— *The Use of Poetry and the Use of Criticism*, London, 1933.

Empson, William, *Seven Types of Ambiguity*, London, 1930; 2nd ed., 1947.

Fraser, G. S., *Vision and Rhetoric*, London, 1959.

Graves, Robert, *The Common Asphodel*, London, 1949.

—— *The Crowning Privilege*, London, 1955.

Grubb, Frederick, *A Vision of Reality*, London, 1965.

Hamilton, G. Rostrevor, *The Tell-Tale Article*, London, 1949.

Heller, Eric, *The Hazard of Modern Poetry*, Cambridge, 1953.

Hough, Graham, *Image and Experience*, London, 1960.

Isaacs, J., *The Background of Modern Poetry*, London, 1951.

Jarrell, Randall, *Poetry and the Age*, New York, 1953; London, 1955.

Kermode, Frank, *Romantic Image*, London, 1957.
Leavis, F. R., *New Bearings in English Poetry*, London, 1932; 2nd ed., 1950.
MacNeice, Louis, *Modern Poetry*, London, 1938.
Melchiori, G., *The Tightrope Walkers*, London, 1956.
O'Connor, William Van, *Sense and Sensibility in Modern Poetry*, Chicago, 1948.
Pinto, Vivian de Sola, *Crisis in English Poetry 1880–1940*, London, 1952.
Pound, Ezra, *Literary Essays of Ezra Pound*, edited by T. S. Eliot, London, 1954.
Press, John, *The Chequer'd Shade*, London, 1958.
Read, Herbert, *Collected Essays in Literary Criticism*, London, 1938; 2nd ed., 1951.
—— *The True Voice of Feeling*, London, 1953.
Richards, I. A., *Principles of Literary Criticism*, London, 1924; 2nd ed., 1926.
—— *Practical Criticism*, London, 1929; 2nd ed., 1935.
Riding, Laura, and Graves, Robert, *A Survey of Modernist Poetry*, London, 1927.
Roberts, Michael, *Critique of Poetry*, London, 1934.
Rosenthal, M. L., *The Modern Poets*, New York, 1960.
Sewell, Elizabeth, *The Structure of Poetry*, London, 1951.
Stead, C. K., *The New Poetic*, London, 1964.
Wilson, Edmund, *Axel's Castle*, New York, 1931.
Winters, Yvor, *In Defense of Reason*, Denver, 1947; London, 1960.
—— *The Function of Criticism*, Denver, 1957; London, 1962.
—— *On Modern Poets*, New York, 1959; London, 1960.

2

THE LATER POETRY OF W. B. YEATS

INTRODUCTION

Although W. B. Yeats's reputation rests chiefly upon his lyrical poems they represent only a small proportion of his writings. The 1908 Stratford-upon-Avon edition of his *Collected Works* ran to eight volumes, only one of which was devoted to his non-dramatic verse; after 1908 he continued to be a prolific writer, yet the poems written during the last thirty years of his life fill a mere three hundred pages in his *Collected Poems* (1950). Nevertheless, it is the short poems that entitle him to be ranked as one of the major writers in the language, and he looked on himself as, primarily, a lyric poet.

It is becoming fashionable to blur the distinctions between his earlier and his later poems, to stress the continuity of his art, to emphasize the merits of the early verse. There is some justification for such a view. All through his life Yeats reverts to the same themes, constantly remaking his poems and himself from the old material. And while his early poems may seem to us over-decorative, langorous, shadowy and imprecise, Yeats wished, from the outset, to achieve the very effects which we admire in his later poems. Writing to Katharine Tynan on 14 March 1888, he acknowledged the weakness of his early work: 'it is not the poetry of insight and knowledge, but of longing and complaint – the cry of the heart against necessity – I hope some day to alter that and write poetry of insight and knowledge.'[1] On 6 September 1888 he wrote to her, saying: 'Some day I shall be articulate, perhaps';[2] and on 21 December, in the same year, he again expressed his desire to find some more direct, vigorous mode of utterance: 'I myself have another and kindred need – to substitute the feelings and longings of nature for those of art.'[3]

Even so, we are surely correct in our belief that the later poetry of Yeats is distinct from and greatly superior to his early work. It is impossible to name a precise date and say that this marks the dividing line between his old and his new verse; but one can make some useful generalizations about the development of his art. In an essay dated 1900, Yeats declared:

> we would cast out of serious poetry those energetic rhythms, as of a man running, which are the invention of the will with its eyes always on something to be done or undone; and we would seek out those wavering, medita-

[1] *The Letters of W. B. Yeats*, edited by Allan Wade, 1954, p. 63.

[2] ibid., p. 84. [3] ibid., p. 99.

tive, organic rhythms, which are the embodiment of the imagination that neither desires nor hates, because it has done with time, and only wishes to gaze upon some reality, some beauty.[4]

Within a few years Yeats had begun to study hatred and to feel desire; no longer content to gaze or to contemplate, he plunged into the world of action. Energy, masculinity, strength, common idiom – these watchwords are repeated in his letters, these are the qualities which he aimed to embody in his verse. We find it hard to detect in the work of the Rhymers the syntax of common life: it is touching to observe that Yeats attributes to these companions of his youth the very virtue which he was seeking to cultivate in early middle age: 'Why should men who spoke their opinions in low voices ... live lives of such disorder and seek to rediscover in verse the syntax of impulsive common life?'[5]

We need not seek to ascribe the changes in Yeats's poetry to any single cause, especially as so many different factors all drove him in the same direction. His self-deluding, hopeless dream of marrying Maud Gonne was broken in 1903, when she became the wife of Major John MacBride. Freed from his long thraldom, Yeats resumed his liaison with 'Diana Vernon', who gave him the tenderness and the understanding which Maud Gonne was incapable of offering him. His disillusionment with Irish politics ran parallel with the shattering of his pipedreams about Maud Gonne; and when one night in 1905 some members of the Abbey Theatre audience hissed Maud Gonne after her separation from her husband, Yeats 'felt that never again could he touch popular politics'.[6] The years 1903 to the end of 1908 were a period of harsh dryness for Yeats: he kept no diary, and wrote no autobiographical reminiscences covering this portion of his life; and of the half-dozen poems composed at this time only two are of much merit. Their titles speak for themselves: 'Never Give all the Heart' and 'O Do Not Love Too Long'.

Yeats's involvement with the Abbey Theatre fostered his gifts as a man of business and as a brilliant, if erratic, manipulator of affairs. It also brought him much bitterness, sharpening his contempt for the puritanism and philistinism of priests and hucksters, and feeding his contempt of the mob. His friendship with Synge helped him to understand that the doctrines of Symbolism, as expounded by Arthur Symons, were a threat to the vitality of poetry. By 1906 Yeats had turned away from the esoteric gospel preached in his essay, 'The Autumn of the Body' (1898), and was beginning to celebrate the passionate life of

[4] 'The Symbolism of Poetry'. Reprinted in *Essays and Introduction*, 1961, p. 163.
[5] *Autobiographies*, 1955, p. 304.
[6] Joseph Hone, *W. B. Yeats 1865–1939*, 1943, p. 210. [The title-page was misdated 1942.]

the flesh: 'Art bids us touch and taste and hear and see the world, and shrink from what Blake calls mathematic form, from every abstract thing, from all that is of the brain only, from all that is not a fountain jetting from the entire hopes, memories, and sensations of the body.'[7] Synge faced the extreme consequences of such a belief:

> In these days poetry is usually a flower of evil or good, but it is the timber of poetry that wears most surely, and there is no timber that has not strong roots among the clay and worms. Even if we grant that exalted poetry can be kept successful by itself, the strong things of life are needed in poetry also, to show that what is exalted, or tender, is not made by feeble blood. It may almost be said that before verse can be human again it must learn to be brutal.[8]

The production of his masterpiece, *The Playboy of the Western World*, at the Abbey on 26 January 1907 initiated a week of rioting in the auditorium and in the streets surrounding the theatre. The obloquy which Synge endured, inspired as it was by those elements in Irish life that Yeats most despised, was a source of rage and grief to Yeats. His invigorating friendship with Synge was thus marked by the same misfortune and stress which dogged him in all his activities at this time. Synge's early death deepened his sense of anger and pain. The reluctance of the Dublin city fathers to build a gallery for the paintings that Sir Hugh Lane proposed to give to the city finally confirmed Yeats in his loathing of the narrowness and meanness which infected Irish public life.

There were, moreover, two literary experiences which left their mark upon Yeats's poetry, making it more strong and terse than his early work. He became acquainted in 1910 with Ezra Pound, to whom in 1912 he gave some poems for the recently-founded *Poetry*. Before despatching them to Chicago, Pound impudently altered some of them without informing Yeats, was rebuked and then forgiven by the long-suffering poet. With astonishing humility Yeats asked Pound to go through his writings, and to mark all the abstractions which were, in Pound's view, debilitating. Yeats turned *The Player Queen* from a tragedy into a comedy at Pound's suggestion; and there seems to be no doubt that the younger poet's advice strengthened Yeats's verse. Even as late as 1928 Pound was altering, for the better, Yeats's first draft of 'From the Antigone'.

Secondly, Yeats read with fascination and delight the great edition of Donne published by H. J. C. Grierson in 1912, finding in Donne that fusion of intellectual passion and sensuality which corresponded to his needs.

[7] 'The Thinking of the Body'. Reprinted in *Essays and Introductions*, 1961, pp. 192–3.

[8] Preface to *Poems and Translations*, 1909.

The change of style which was foreshadowed as early as 1902 in 'Adam's Curse', and became apparent with the publication of *The Green Helmet* (1910) was complete by 1914, which saw the publication of *Responsibilities*. When Pound read the final poem, with its bitter ending:

> till all my precious things
> Are but a post the passing dogs defile

he was convinced that Yeats had transformed himself into a truly modern poet.

Richard Ellmann compares Yeats's early work with the art of tapestry and the later with the art of the goldsmith.[9] Almost every critic has acknowledged Yeats's ever-growing technical mastery during the final twenty years of his life. Adverse criticism has concentrated its fire on two seemingly vulnerable points: his political beliefs and his curious metaphysical speculations.

Yeats was undoubtedly in his later years violently opposed to the theory and practice of democracy. To what extent he was a supporter of Fascism is a matter for legitimate debate.[10] His hatred of the mob, which seemed to him the embodiment of democracy, went back to the early years of the century in Dublin. Much as he sympathized with the Easter Rising of 1916, he observed with bitter regret the fanaticism of the Civil War and the deliberate burning of those great houses which had sheltered him, and which his romantic imagination had transformed into the centres of a new Irish civilization comparable with that of the Italian Renaissance. He had not been consulted by those who planned the Rising, nor was he favourably impressed by the character of the newly-founded Irish Free State. Although he was made a Senator he was never wholly at ease in this rôle. It is significant that his most eloquent speech was his most unpopular: an arrogant defence of the Anglo-Irish Protestant minority, occasioned by what he regarded as the illiberal legislation on divorce fostered by his old enemy, the priesthood. Moreover, he distrusted politicians because of 'the desire which every political party has to substitute for life, which never does the same thing twice, a bundle of reliable principles and assertions'.[11] When his friend Kevin O'Higgins, a ruthless politician with authoritarian leanings, was murdered, Yeats turned away from the political scene in disgust. He was filled with contempt for the lower-middle class men who had dragged all greatness down; he disliked De Valera; and

[9] Richard Ellmann, *The Identity of Yeats*, 1954, pp. 20–4.

[10] See Conor Cruise O'Brien's essay, 'Passion and Cunning: An Essay on the Politics of W. B. Yeats', in *In Excited Reverie*, edited by A. Norman Jeffares and K. G. W. Cross, 1965, pp. 207–78. I find this brilliantly-argued essay only partially convincing.

[11] Joseph Hone, *W. B. Yeats 1865–1939*, 1943, p. 194. Hone is summarizing a speech made by Yeats to a theatre audience in October 1903.

for a brief period in the 1930s seemed to have pinned his hopes on O'Duffy and his Blueshirts. Mrs. Yeats, with intuitive shrewdness, held a low opinion of the Blueshirts from the very start, a view which Yeats soon came to share.

There was in Yeats a vein of arrogance and cruelty that sometimes shows in his political utterances, lending a brutal, rancorous tone to conservative sentiments which are not in themselves unreasonable or inhumane. Believing that an age of pitiless autocracy was about to begin, Yeats comes dangerously near to exulting in the approaching triumph of merciless power. Thirty years before, his father had rebuked him for his worship of Nietzschean inhumanity, and age had not taught him compassion. Yet, at his finest, Yeats puts aside the toying with cruelty that dishonours him and speaks out against the brutalities that were degrading Europe. His letter to Ethel Mannin, postmarked 8 April 1936, is the most memorable expression of his concern for the immemorial decencies of civilized life.[12]

It is impossible to separate Yeats's metaphysical beliefs from his political views or from his poetry. Some admirers revere Yeats as a visionary who had access to the immemorial wisdom of the perennial philosophy; sceptical critics stigmatize him as a reactionary snob who shored up a bloody-minded political creed with a ludicrous set of cranky mystical doctrines. There is no need to plump for either of these alternatives: the important fact to remember is that Yeats was a highly intelligent man who was preoccupied throughout his life by the problem of belief, its nature, its function, its relation to life and to poetry. In this, as in so much, he resembled his father, J. B. Yeats, in whose superb letters are foreshadowed many of the speculations which were to exercise the mind of his son.

As early as 1870, in a letter to Edward Dowden, J. B. Yeats remarked that 'the psychological question of the nature of belief lies at the root of the whole of criticism'.[13] In 1915 he reverted to this topic in a letter to W. B. Yeats, declaring that for Blake, as for all artists, 'his mysticism was never the *substance of his poetry, only its machinery*'.[14] An artist needs to hold beliefs, yet must not allow a doctrinaire philosophy to stultify his art: 'To think too curiously would be to invoke the *literal belief* which is fatal to the imaginative mind, and yet *there must be a certain amount of credence*.'[15]

W. B. Yeats, like his father, continually sought a coherent pattern of beliefs that would afford him spiritual certainty without weakening his

[12] *The Letters of W. B. Yeats*, edited by Allan Wade, 1954, pp. 850–1. See below, pp. 20–1.

[13] Quoted by Richard Ellmann, *Yeats: The Man and the Masks*, 1949, p. 17.

[14] Letter to W. B. Yeats, 7 September 1915. *Passages from the Letters of John Butler Yeats*, selected by Ezra Pound, 1917, p. 20.

[15] Letter to W. B. Yeats, 27 August 1915, ibid., p. 10.

imaginative freedom. He could spend years in constructing an elaborate system of beliefs, and yet doubt whether the concept of belief had any validity: 'Some will ask if I believe all that this book contains, and I will not know how to answer. Does the word belief, used as they will use it, belong to our age, can I think of the world as there and I here judging it?'[16]

That there was an element of the *poseur* in Yeats is hard to deny; and some of his dabblings in the occult are difficult to take seriously. It would, however, be wrong to suppose that Yeats was merely a sophisticated unbeliever searching for an aesthetically satisfying philosophy; or that he was, on the other hand, a credulous dupe greedily swallowing the bogus revelations of fraudulent *gurus*.

An early letter to John O'Leary, written in July 1893, suggests that from his youth onwards Yeats genuinely believed in what is sometimes called magic and sometimes the tradition of neo-Platonic mysticism: 'If I had not made magic my constant study I would not have written a single word of my Blake Book, nor would *The Countess Kathleen* have ever come to exist. The mystical life is the centre of all that I do and all that I think and all that I write.'[17]

Nor is there any reason to doubt that the revelations which came to him through his wife's automatic writing profoundly affected his philosophy and his work throughout the last twenty years of his life. We are not obliged to believe that the automatic writing was of supernatural origin, or even to define the term 'supernatural'. We may care to stress the fact that Yeats had long been brooding on the very themes which formed the subject-matter of the mysterious revelations. It is, nevertheless, undeniable that the poems written during these twenty years are his most superb achievement; it is certain that Yeats attributed his increased power and wisdom to the ghostly communicators of *A Vision*. Only a bold, not to say cocksure, critic will affirm that Yeats's insistence on the supreme importance of the revelations was either the self-delusion of a dotard or the charlatanism of a *poseur*.

Part of the fascination exercised by Yeats's personality and poetry alike is that one can never pin them down, never arrange them in neatly-defined categories. Yeats always took care to leave himself a loophole for escape, even if he appeared to be immuring himself in a constricting dogmatic system. Thus, while accepting the spiritual authenticity of the communications of which Mrs. Yeats was the medium, he never renounced the sinewy flexing of his intellectual faculties; and although he offered to spend the remainder of his life 'explaining and piecing together these scattered sentences', the com-

[16] *A Packet for Ezra Pound*, 1929, p. 32. See below p. 19.
[17] *The Letters of W. B. Yeats*, edited by Allan Wade, 1954, p. 211.

municators gave the reply that Yeats must have desired. 'No,' was the answer, 'we have come to give you metaphors for poetry.'[18]

Nor did he passively accept the revelations vouchsafed him. 'The first version of this book, *A Vision* ... fills me with shame',[19] wrote Yeats in his introduction to his recasting of his spiritual testament. Immediately after the publication of the first edition of *A Vision* in 1925 he had set out to remedy his ignorance of philosophy, which had marred the work. Lady Gregory observed that, in the years after 1925, Yeats became a better educated man and more formidable in argument. This change came about because of his hard reading, and not as a result of mysterious communications. Yet the impulse to explore the writings of historians, metaphysicians and mystics sprang directly from the relevations which had moved him so deeply.

It must have seemed to Yeats during the last twenty years of his life that everything he observed, enjoyed and suffered was combining to hammer his thoughts into unity.[20] His marriage had brought him not only emotional fulfilment but a wife endowed with the gift of Sibylline prophecy. His innate authoritarianism and disdain for the mob were reinforced by his experience of Civil War and by the destruction of the great houses which had once appeared the only sure repositories of civilization. The communicators who had revealed esoteric truths had miraculously confirmed what he had long believed: his intuitions were certified by the authority of supernatural visitants. His political prejudices, his study of history, his determinism, his sense of tragic doom all pointed in the same direction. He anticipated, with pitiless relish, a dispensation that 'obeys imminent power, is expressive, hierarchical, multiple, masculine, harsh, surgical'.[21]

He made poetry out of the dialectical conflicts which raged within him. A desire for purity and wisdom was strangely intensified by a delight in witty gossip and in unflagging enjoyment of sexual pleasure that many have thought unbecoming in a public figure of his years and eminence. The longing for immortality implied no renunciation of the sensual world, for in Yeats's paradise we are reborn into a state where we enjoy a heightening of sensuous perception. He believed in the tradition of neo-Platonic wisdom, yet in 'News for the Delphic Oracle' could refer to Pythagoras and Plotinus as 'golden codgers'. Although he moved in the timeless world of magic, in the rarefied atmosphere of esoteric knowledge, he devoted years of his life to the intrigues of the green room and to the chicanery of politics in a provincial backwater. The paradox of his life and work is perfectly exemplified in the rejoinder which he made to a questioner at Oxford who asked: 'Are you not afraid, Sir, that your thoughts will lead you away from the

18 *A Vision*, 1937, p. 8. 19 ibid. p. 19. 20 See below, pp. 19–20.

21 *A Vision*, 1937, p. 263.

realities of life, into some intellectual desert, remote from action?' 'No,' replied Yeats, 'too many of my friends have been shot.'[22]

His zest and his acceptance of life in all its fury and mire informed his work to the very last. He gloried in the paradox that the end of tragedy is joy: his declaration in 'Lapis Lazuli' that 'Hamlet and Lear are gay' broadens out into his valedictory affirmation about the nature of art: 'The arts are all the bridal chambers of joy. No tragedy is legitimate unless it leads some great character to his final joy.'[23] In an age of anxiety and of disintegration he plunged into the sensual whirlpool, yet could still assert the wholeness of life and the integrity of man. He towers above all his contemporaries as the last great poet of the Renaissance, who anticipated, with mingled dread and exultation, the approaching triumph of the Counter-Renaissance.

CRITICISM

(1) *Passages from the Writings of W. B. Yeats*

Your acting seemed to me to have the perfect precision and delicacy and simplicity of every art at its best. It made me feel the unity of the arts in a new way. I said to myself, this is exactly what I am trying to do in writing, to express myself without waste, without emphasis. To be impassioned and yet to have a perfect self-possession, to have a precision so absolute that the slightest inflection of voice, the slightest rhythm of sound or emotion plucks the heart-strings.

Letter to Mrs Patrick Campbell [November 1901], *The Letters of W. B. Yeats*, edited by Allan Wade, 1954, p. 360.[24]

In my *Land of Heart's Desire*, and in some of my lyric verse of that time, there is an exaggeration of sentiment and sentimental beauty which I have come to think unmanly. The popularity of *The Land of Heart's Desire* seems to me to come not from its merits but because of this weakness. I have been fighting the prevailing decadence for years, and I have just got it under foot in my own heart – it is sentiment and sentimental. Let us have no emotions, however abstract, in which there is not an athletic joy.

Letter to George Russell (AE) [? April 1904], *Letters*, pp. 434–5.

I think the whole of our literature as well as our drama has grown effeminate through the over development of the picture-making faculty. The great thing in literature, above all in drama, is rhythm and movement.

Letter to Frank Fay, 4 November 1905, *Letters*, p. 466.

[22] L. A. G. Strong, *A Letter to W. B. Yeats* (1932), p. 25.
[23] *On the Boiler*, 1939, p. 35. Reprinted in *Explorations*, 1962, p. 448.
[24] Hereafter referred to as *Letters*. Dates of letters in square brackets supplied by Allan Wade.

All art is in the last analysis an endeavour to condense as out of the flying vapour of the world an image of human perfection, and for its own and not for the art's sake, and that is why the labour of the alchemists, who were called artists in their day, is a befitting comparison for all deliberate change of style. We live with images, that is our renunciation, for only the silent sage or saint can make himself into that perfection, turning the life inward at the tongue, as though it heard the cry *Secretum meum mihi*; choosing not, as we do, to say all and know nothing, but to know all and say nothing.

Preface to *Poems 1899–1905*, 1906.
Reprinted in *The Variorum Edition of the Poems of W. B. Yeats*, edited by Peter Allt and Russell K. Alspach, 1957, p. 849.

The friends that have it I do wrong
When ever I remake a song,
Should know what issue is at stake:
It is myself that I remake.

Epigraph to *Collected Works in Verse and Prose*, 1908, vol. II.
Reprinted in *The Variorum Edition*, p. 778.

We [artists], on the other hand, are Adams of a different Eden, a more terrible Eden perhaps, for we must name and number the passions and motives of men. There, too, everything must be known, everything understood, everything expressed; there, also, there is nothing uncommon, nothing unclean; every motive must be followed through all the obscure mystery of its logic. Mankind must be seen and understood in every possible circumstance, in every conceivable situation. There is no laughter too bitter, no irony too harsh for utterance, no passion too terrible to be set before the minds of men. The Greeks knew that. Only in this way can mankind be understood, only when we have put ourselves in all the possible situations of life, from the most miserable to those that are so lofty that we can only speak of them in symbols and in mysteries, will entire wisdom be possible.

Speech to the British Association, September 1908.
Richard Ellmann, *The Identity of Yeats*, 1954, p. 245.

In poetry the antithesis to personality is not so much will as an ever growing burden of noble attitudes and literary words. The noble attitudes are imposed upon the poet by papers like the *Spectator* ...

Letter to J. B. Yeats, 16 February 1910, *Letters*, p. 548.

I am speaking of him [Lionel Johnson] very candidly; probably he would not [wish] to be spoken of in this way, but I would wish to be spoken of with just such candour when I am dead. I have no sympathy with the mid-Victorian thought to which Tennyson gave his support, that a poet's life concerns nobody but himself. A poet is by the very nature of things a man who lives with entire sincerity, or rather, the better his poetry the more sincere his life. His life is an experiment in living and those that come after have a right to know it. Above all it is necessary that the lyric poet's life should be known, that we should understand that his poetry is no rootless flower but the speech of man, [that it is no little thing] to achieve anything in any art, to stand alone perhaps for many years, to go a path no other man has gone, to accept one's own thought when the thought of others has the authority of the world behind it ... to give one's life as well as one's words which are so much nearer to one's soul to the criticism of the world.

Unpublished notes for a London lecture on 'Contemporary Poetry' dictated in Dublin in 1910.
Richard Ellmann, *Yeats: The Man and the Masks*, 1949, pp. 5–6.

Your notes [on Donne] tell me exactly what I want to know. Poems that I could not understand or could but understand are now clear and I notice that the more precise and learned the thought the greater the beauty, the passion; the intricacy and subtleties of his imagination are the length and depths of the furrow made by his passion. His pedantry and his obscenity – the rock and the loam of his Eden – but make me the more certain that one who is but a man like us all has seen God.

Letter to J. H. C. Grierson, 14 November [1912], *Letters*, p. 570.

There are always two types of poetry – Keats the type of vision, Burns a very obvious type of the other, too obvious indeed. It is in dramatic expression that English poetry is most lacking as compared with French poetry. Villon always and Ronsard at times create a marvellous drama out of their own lives.

Letter to J. B. Yeats, 5 August 1913, *Letters*, p. 583.

I think with you that the poet seeks truth, not abstract truth, but a kind of vision of reality which satisfies the whole being. It will not be true for one thing unless it satisfies his desires, his most profound desires. Henry More, the seventeenth-century platonist whom I have been reading all summer, argues from the goodness and omnipotence of God that all our deep desires must be satisfied, and that we should reject a philosophy that does not satisfy them. I think the poet reveals truth by revealing those desires.

Letter to J. B. Yeats, 12 September [1914], *Letters*, p. 588.

I separate the rhythmical and the abstract. They are brothers but one is Abel and one is Cain. In poetry they are not confused for we know that poetry is rhythm, but in music-hall verses we find an abstract cadence, which is vulgar because it is apart from imitation. The cadence is a mechanism, it never suggests a voice shaken with joy or sorrow as poetical rhythm does. It is but the noise of a machine and not the coming and going of the breath.

Letter to J. B. Yeats, 14 March [? 1916], *Letters*, p. 608.

One day when I was twenty-three or twenty-four this sentence seemed to form in my head, without my willing it, much as sentences form when we are half-asleep: 'Hammer your thoughts into unity.' For days I could think of nothing else, and for years I tested all I did by that sentence. I had three interests: interest in a form of literature, in a form of philosophy, and a belief in nationality. None of these seemed to have anything to do with the other, but gradually my love of literature and my belief in nationality came together. Then for years I said to myself that these two had nothing to do with my form of philosophy, but that I had only to be sincere and to keep from constraining one by the other and they would become one interest. Now all three are, I think, one, or rather all three are a discrete expression of a single conviction. I think that each has behind it my whole character and has gained thereby a certain newness – for is not every man's character peculiar to himself: – and that I have become a cultivated man.

If I were Four-and-Twenty, 1940.
Reprinted in *Explorations*, 1962, p. 263.
[This essay was written in 1919]

I wrote Leda and the Swan because the editor of a political review asked me for a poem. I thought, 'After the individualistic, demagogic movement, founded by Hobbes and popularized by the Encyclopaedists and the French Revolution, we have a soil so exhausted that it cannot grow that crop again for centuries.' Then I thought, 'Nothing is now possible but some movement from above preceded by some violent annunciation.' My fancy began to play with Leda and the Swan for metaphor, and I began this poem; but as I wrote, bird and lady took such possession of the scene that all politics went out of it, and my friend tells me that his 'conservative readers would misunderstand the poem'.

The Dial, June 1924.
Reprinted in *The Variorum Edition of the Poems of W. B. Yeats*, edited by Peter Allt and Russell K. Alspach, 1957, p. 828.
[See 'Leda and the Swan', below, p. 27]

Every now and then, when something has stirred my imagination, I begin talking to myself. I speak in my own person and dramatize myself, very much as I have seen a mad old woman do upon the Dublin quays, and sometimes detect myself speaking and moving as if I were still young, or walking perhaps like an old man with fumbling steps.

The Bounty of Sweden, 1925.
Reprinted in *Autobiographies*, 1955, p. 532.

I could I daresay make the book richer, perhaps immeasurably so, if I were to keep it by me for another year, and I have not even dealt with the whole of my subject, perhaps not even with what is most important, writing nothing about the Beatific Vision, little of sexual love; but I am longing to put it out of reach that I may write the poetry it seems to have made possible. I can now, if I have the energy, find the simplicity I have sought in vain. I need no longer write poems like 'The Phases of the Moon' nor 'Ego Dominus Tuus', nor spend barren years, as I have done some three or four times, striving with abstractions that substituted themselves for the play that I had planned.

Doubtless I must someday complete what I have begun, but for the moment my imagination dwells upon a copy of Powys Mather's 'Arabian Nights' that awaits my return home. I would forget the wisdom of the East and remember its grossness and its romance. Yet when I wander upon the cliffs where Augustus and Tiberius wandered, I know that the new intensity that seems to have come into all visible and tangible things is not a reaction from that wisdom but its very self. Yesterday when I saw the dry and leafless vineyards at the very edge of the motionless sea, or lifting their brown stems from almost inaccessible patches of earth high up on the cliff-side, or met at the turn of the path the orange and lemon trees in full fruit, or the crimson cactus flower, or felt the warm sunlight falling between blue and blue, I murmured, as I have countless times, 'I have been part of it always and there is maybe no escape, forgetting and returning life after life like an insect in the roots of the grass.' But murmured it without terror, in exultation almost.

Dedication to *A Vision*, 1925, pp. xii–xiii.
Not reprinted in the second edition, 1937.

I think if I could be given a month of Antiquity and leave to spend it where I chose, I would spend it in Byzantium a little before Justinian opened St. Sophia and closed the Academy of Plato. I think I could find in some little wine-shop some philosophical worker in mosaic who could answer all my questions, the supernatural descending nearer to him than to Plotinus even, for the pride of his delicate skill would make what was an instrument of power to princes and clerics, a murderous madness in the mob, show as a lovely flexible presence like that of a perfect human body.

I think that in early Byzantium, maybe never before or since in recorded history, religious, aesthetic and practical life were one, that architects and artificers – though not, it may be, poets, for language had been the instrument of controversy and must have grown abstract – spoke to the multitude and the few alike. The painter, the mosaic worker, the worker in gold and silver, the illuminator of sacred books, were almost impersonal, almost perhaps without the consciousness of individual design, absorbed in their subject-matter and that the vision of a whole people.

A Vision, 1925, pp. 190–1; 1937 edition, pp. 279–80.

[The 1925 edition was privately printed and is very hard to find. The enlarged and revised edition of 1937, reprinted 1962, is readily available.]

Some will ask whether I believe in the actual existence of my circuits of sun and moon. Those that include, now all recorded time in one circuit, now what Blake called 'the pulsaters of an artery', are plainly symbolical, but what of those that fixed, like a butterfly upon a pin, to our central date, the first day of our Era, divide actual history into periods of equal length? To such a question I can but answer that if sometimes, overwhelmed by miracle as all men must be when in the midst of it, I have taken such periods literally, my reason has soon recovered; and now that the system stands out clearly in my imagination I regard them as stylistic arrangements of experience comparable to the cubes in the drawing of Wyndham Lewis and to the ovoids in the sculpture of Brancusi. They have helped me to hold in a single thought reality and justice.

A Vision, 1937, pp. 24–5.

[This passage, which is printed in the section of *A Vision* entitled 'A Package for Ezra Pound', is a recasting of Section XV of *A Package for Ezra Pound* (1929), p. 32. The 1937 version of the passage is more eloquent, elaborate, and evasive.]

The over childish or over pretty or feminine element in some good Wordsworth and in much poetry up to our date comes from the lack of natural momentum in the syntax. This momentum underlies almost every Elizabethan and Jacobean lyric and is far more important than simplicity of vocabulary. If Wordsworth had found it he could have carried any amount of elaborate English. Byron, unlike the Elizabethans though he always tries for it, constantly allows it to die out in some mind-created construction, but is I think the one great English poet – though one can hardly call him great except in purpose and manhood – who sought it constantly.

Letter to H. J. C. Grierson, 21 February [1926], *Letters*, p. 710.

I spend my days correcting proofs. I have just finished the first volume, all my lyric poetry, and am greatly astonished at myself. As it is all speech rather than writing, I keep saying what man is this who in the course of two or three weeks – the improvisation suggests the tune – says the same thing in so many different ways. My first denunciation of old age I made in *The Wanderings of Usheen* (end of part I) before

I was twenty and the same denunciation comes in the last pages of the book. The swordsman throughout repudiates the saint, but not without vacillation. Is that perhaps the sole theme – Usheen and Patrick – 'so get you gone Von Hügel though with blessings on your head'?

Letter to Olivia Shakespear, 30 June [Postmark 1932], *Letters*, p. 798.

Joyce and D. H. Lawrence have however almost restored to us the Eastern simplicity. Neither perfectly, for D. H. Lawrençe romanticises his material, with such words as 'essential fire', 'darkness' etc., and Joyce never escapes from his Catholic sense of sin. Rabelais seems to ecape from it by his vast energy. Yet why not take Swedenborg literally and think we attain, in a partial contact, what the spirits know throughout their being. He somewhere describes two spirits meeting, and as they touch they become a single conflagration. His vision may be true, Newton's cannot be. When I saw at Mrs. Crandon's objects moved and words spoken from some aerial centre, where there was nothing human, I rejected England and France and accepted Europe. Europe belongs to Dante and the witches' sabbath, not to Newton.

Letter to Olivia Shakespear, 9 March [Postmark 1933], *Letters*, p. 807.

Then there is a still more convincing reason why we should not admit propaganda into our lives. I shall write it out in the style of *The Arabian Nights* (which I am reading daily). There are three very important persons (1) a man playing the flute (2) a man carving a statue (3) a man in a woman's arms. Goethe said we must renounce, and I think propaganda – I wish I had thought of this when I was young – is among the things they thus renounce.

Letter to Ethel Mannin, 4 March [? 1935], *Letters*, pp. 831–2.

Do not try to make a politician of me, even in Ireland I shall never I think be that again – as my sense of reality deepens, and I think it does with age, my horror at the cruelty of governments grows greater, and if I did what you want, I would seem to hold one form of government more responsible than any other, and that would betray my convictions. Communist, Fascist, nationalist, clerical, anti-clerical, are all responsible according to the number of their victims. I have not been silent; I have used the only vehicle I possess – verse. If you have my poems by you, look up a poem called *The Second Coming*. It was written some sixteen or seventeen years ago and foretold what is happening. I have written of the same thing again and again since . . .

Forgive me my dear and do not cast me out of your affection. I am not callous, every nerve trembles with horror at what is happening in Europe, 'the ceremony of innocence is drowned'.

Letter to Ethel Mannin [Postmark 8 April 1936], *Letters*, pp. 850–1. [Ethel Mannin and the dramatist Ernst Toller called on Yeats and asked him to recommend for the Nobel Peace Prize the German poet Ossietsky, who was in a Nazi concentration camp. Yeats refused, and gave his reasons in this letter. See 'The Second Coming', below, p. 25]

I detest the Renaissance because it made the human mind inorganic; I adore the Renaissance because it clarified form and created freedom. I too expect the counter-Renaissance, but if we do not hold to freedom and form it will come, not as an inspiration in the head, but as an obstruction in the bowels.

On the Boiler, 1939, p. 27.

[This passage is not reprinted in *Explorations*.]

There are moments when I am certain that art must once again accept those Greek proportions which carry into plastic art the Pythagorean numbers, those faces which are divine because all there is empty and measured. Europe was not born when Greek galleys defeated the Persian hordes at Salamis, but when the Doric studios sent out those broad-backed marble statues against the multiform, vague, expressive Asiatic sea, they gave to the sexual instinct of Europe its goal, its fixed type.

On the Boiler, 1939, p. 37.

Reprinted in *Explorations*, 1962, p. 451. [See 'The Statues', below, pp. 27–8.]

. . . I know for certain that my time will not be long. I have put away everything that can be put away that I may speak what I have to speak, and I find 'expression' is a part of 'study'. In two or three weeks – I am now idle that I may rest after writing much verse – I will begin to write my most fundamental thoughts and the arrangement of thought which I am convinced will complete my studies. I am happy, and I think full of an energy, of an energy I had despaired of. It seems to me that I have found what I wanted. When I try to put all into a phrase I say, 'Man can embody truth but he cannot know it.' I must embody it in the completion of my life. The abstract is not life and everywhere draws out its contradictions. You can refute Hegel but not the Saint or the Song of Sixpence.

Letter to Lady Elizabeth Pelham, 4 January 1939, *Letters*, p. 922.

No longer in Lethean foliage caught
Begin the preparation for your death
And from the fortieth winter by that thought
Test every work of intellect or faith,
And everything that your own hands have wrought,
And call those works extravagance of breath
That are not suited for such men as come
Proud, open-eyed and laughing to the tomb.

from 'Vacillation' III.

(ii) *Passages from the Writings of other Authors*

Art is solitary man, the man as he is behind the innermost, the utmost veils. That is why with the true poet we do not care what are his persuasions, opinions, ideas, religions, moralities – through all these we can pierce to the voice of the essential man if we have the discerning senses. These are no more than the leafy wood out of which the nightingale sings.

J. B. Yeats, Letter to W. B. Yeats, 9 September 1914, *Letters to his son, W. B. Yeats and Others*, edited by J. B. Hone, 1944, p. 193.

All the beliefs, all the creeds that have ever been, are to the artistic mind a machinery and a vehicle for his own *creed*, which is that of all artists that have ever existed, *that he himself exists and that what he wants is more and still more existence.*

J. B. Yeats, Letter to W. B. Yeats, 7 September 1915, *Passages from the Letters of John Butler Yeats*, selected by Ezra Pound, 1917, p. 20.

Mr. Joyce's mind is subtle, erudite, even massive; but it is not like Stendhal's, an instrument continually tempering and purifying emotion; it operates within the medium, the superb current, of his feeling. The basis is pure feeling, and if the feeling of Mr. Yeats were equally powerful, it would also justify his thought. Very powerful feeling *is* crude; the fault of Mr. Yeats's is that it is crude without being powerful. The weakness of his prose is similar to that of his verse. The trouble is not that it is inconsistent, illogical or incoherent, but that the objects upon which it is directed are not fixed; as in his portraits of Synge and several other Irishmen, we do not seem to get the men themselves before us, but feelings of Mr. Yeats projected. It must always be granted that in verse at least Mr. Yeats's feeling is not simply crudeness and egoism, but that it has a positive, individual and permanent quality.

T. S. Eliot, 'A Foreign Mind', review of *The Cutting of an Agate* by W. B. Yeats, *The Athenaeum*, 4 July 1919, pp. 552–3.

Mr. Yeats has once and for all stripped English poetry of its perdamnable rhetoric. He has boiled away all that is not poetic – and a good deal that is. He has become a classic in his own lifetime and *nel mezzo del cammin.* He has made our poetic idiom a thing pliable, a speech without inversions.

Ezra Pound, 'Prolegomena', *The Poetry Review,* II, February 1912, p. 75. Reprinted in *Literary Essays of Ezra Pound,* edited by T. S. Eliot, 1954, pp. 11–12.

There have always been two sorts of poetry which are, for me at least, the most 'poetic'; they are firstly, the sort of poetry which seems to be music just forcing itself into articulate speech, and secondly, that sort of poetry which seems as if sculpture or painting were just forced or forcing itself into words. The gulf between evocation and description, in this latter case, is the unbridgeable difference between genius and talent. It is perhaps the highest function of art that it should fill the mind with a noble profusion of sounds and images, that it should furnish the life of the mind with such accompaniment and surrounding. At any rate Mr. Yeats' work has done this in the past and still continues to do so . . . In the poems on the Irish gallery we find this author certainly at *prise* with things as they are and no longer romantically Celtic, so that a lot of his admirers will be rather displeased with this book. That is always a gain for a poet, for his admirers nearly always want him to 'stay put', and they resent any signs of stirring, of new curiosity or of intellectual uneasiness.

Ezra Pound, 'The Later Yeats', review of *Responsibilities* by W. B. Yeats, *Poetry,* IV, 2 May 1914, pp. 64–8. Reprinted in *Literary Essays of Ezra Pound,* edited by T. S. Eliot, 1954, pp. 378–87.

It is the duty of the poet to reflect his own day as it appears to him, as it has impressed itself upon him. Because I and my friends have, as the saying is, rolled our humps mostly in a landscape that is picked out with the red patches of motor-bus sides, it would be the merest provincialism to say that the author of *Innisfree* should not have sat in the cabins of County Galway or of Connemara, or wherever it is, or that the author of the *Dynasts* should not have wandered about a county called Wessex reading works connected with Napoleon. We should not wish to limit Mr. Yeats' reading to the daily papers, nor indeed do we so limit our own, any more than we should wish to limit the author of that most beautiful impression, the *Listeners,* to the purlieus of Bedford Street where the publishers' offices are.

Ford Madox Ford, Preface to *Collected Poems,* 1913.[25]

25 At this period of his life Ford was known as Ford Madox Hueffer. His *Collected Poems* were published under that name. The date of publication, though shown on the title-page as 1914, was 1913.

There are some poets whose poetry can be considered more or less in isolation, for experience and delight. There are others whose poetry, though giving equally experience and delight, has a larger historical importance. Yeats was one of the latter: he was one of those few whose history is the history of their own time, who are a part of the consciousness of an age which cannot be understood without them. This is a very high position to assign to him: but I believe that it is one which is secure.

T. S. Eliot, 'The Poetry of W. B. Yeats', *Purpose*, xii, 3–4, July–December 1940. Reprinted in *On Poetry and Poets*, 1957, p. 262. [See also W. H. Auden's poem, 'In Memory of W. B. Yeats'.]

POEMS

A Coat

I made my song a coat
Covered with embroideries
Out of old mythologies
From heel to throat;
But the fools caught it,
Wore it in the world's eyes
As though they'd wrought it.
Song, let them take it,
For there's more enterprise
In walking naked.

Under Saturn

Do not because this day I have grown saturnine
Imagine that lost love, inseparable from my thought
Because I have no other youth, can make me pine;
For how should I forget the wisdom that you brought,
The comfort that you made? Although my wits have gone
On a fantastic ride, my horse's flanks are spurred
By childish memories of an old cross Pollexfen,
And of a Middleton, whose name you never heard,
And of a red-haired Yeats whose looks, although he died
Before my time, seem like a vivid memory.
You heard that labouring man who had served my
  people. He said
Upon the open road, near to the Sligo quay –
No, no, not said, but cried it out – 'You have come again,
And surely after twenty years it was time to come.'
I am thinking of a child's vow sworn in vain
Never to leave that valley his fathers called their home.

The Second Coming

Turning and turning in the widening gyre
The falcon cannot hear the falconer;
Things fall apart; the centre cannot hold;
Mere anarchy is loosed upon the world,
The blood-dimmed tide is loosed, and everywhere
The ceremony of innocence is drowned;
The best lack all conviction, while the worst

Are full of passionate intensity.
Surely some revelation is at hand;
Surely the Second Coming is at hand.
The Second Coming! Hardly are those words out
When a vast image out of *Spiritus Mundi*
Troubles my sight: somewhere in sands of the desert
A shape with lion body and the head of a man,
A gaze blank and pitiless as the sun,
Is moving its slow thighs, while all about it
Reel shadows of the indignant desert birds.
The darkness drops again; but now I know
That twenty centuries of stony sleep
Were vexed to nightmare by a rocking cradle,
And what rough beast, its hour come round at last,
Slouches towards Bethlehem to be born?

Sailing to Byzantium

I

That is no country for old men. The young
In one another's arms, birds in the trees
– Those dying generations – at their song,
The salmon-falls, the mackerel-crowded seas,
Fish, flesh, or fowl, commend all summer long
Whatever is begotten, born, and dies.
Caught in that sensual music all neglect
Monuments of unageing intellect.

II

An aged man is but a paltry thing,
A tattered coat upon a stick, unless
Soul clap its hands and sing, and louder sing
For every tatter in its mortal dress,
Nor is there singing school but studying
Monuments of its own magnificence;

And therefore I have sailed the seas and come
To the holy city of Byzantium.

III

O sages standing in God's holy fire
As in the gold mosaic of a wall,
Come from the holy fire, perne in a gyre,
And be the singing-masters of my soul.
Consume my heart away; sick with desire
And fastened to a dying animal
It knows not what it is; and gather me
Into the artifice of eternity.

IV

Once out of nature I shall never take
My bodily form from any natural thing,
But such a form as Grecian goldsmiths make
Of hammered gold and gold enamelling
To keep a drowsy Emperor awake;
Or set upon a golden bough to sing
To lords and ladies of Byzantium
Of what is past, or passing, or to come.

Two Songs from a Play

I

I saw a staring virgin stand
Where holy Dionysus died,
And tear the heart out of his side,
And lay the heart upon her hand
And bear that beating heart away;
And then did all the Muses sing
Of Magnus Annus at the spring,
As though God's death were but a play.

Another Troy must rise and set,
Another lineage feed the crow,
Another Argo's painted prow
Drive to a flashier bauble yet.
The Roman Empire stood appalled:
It dropped the reins of peace and war
When that fierce virgin and her Star
Out of the fabulous darkness called.

Leda and the Swan

A sudden blow: the great wings beating still
Above the staggering girl, her thighs caressed
By the dark webs, her nape caught in his bill,
He holds her helpless breast upon his breast.

How can those terrified vague fingers push
The feathered glory from her loosening thighs?
And how can body, laid in that white rush,
But feel the strange heart beating where it lies?

A shudder in the loins engenders there
The broken wall, the burning roof and tower
And Agamemnon dead.
Being so caught up,
So mastered by the brute blood of the air,
Did she put on his knowledge with his power
Before the indifferent beak could let her drop?

The Statues

Pythagoras planned it. Why did the people stare?
His numbers, though they moved or seemed to move
In marble or in bronze, lacked character.
But boys and girls, pale from the imagined love
Of solitary beds, knew what they were,
That passion could bring character enough,
And pressed at midnight in some public place
Live lips upon a plummet-measured face.

No! Greater than Pythagoras, for the men
That with a mallet or a chisel modelled these
Calculations that look but casual flesh, put down
All Asiatic vague immensities,
And not the banks of oars that swam upon
The many-headed foam at Salamis.
Europe put off that foam when Phidias
Gave women dreams and dreams their looking-glass.

One image crossed the many-headed, sat
Under the tropic shade, grew round and slow,
No Hamlet thin from eating flies, a fat
Dreamer of the Middle Ages. Empty eyeballs knew
That knowledge increases unreality, that
Mirror on mirror mirrored is all the show.
When gong and conch declare the hour to bless
Grimalkin crawls to Buddha's emptiness.

When Pearse summoned Cuchulain to his side,
What stalked through the Post Office? What intellect,
What calculation, number, measurement, replied?
We Irish, born into that ancient sect
But thrown upon this filthy modern tide
And by its formless spawning fury wrecked,
Climb to our proper dark, that we may trace
The lineaments of a plummet-measured face.

SELECT BIBLIOGRAPHY

Works by W. B. Yeats

Collected Poems, London, 1950.

Variorum Edition of the Poems, edited by Peter Allt and Russell K. Alspach, New York, 1957.
A superb edition, containing uncollected poems, variant readings, and notes on the poems by Yeats himself, many of which are unavailable elsewhere. Essential for the student of Yeats.

Autobiographies, London, 1955.

Mythologies, London, 1959.

Essays and Introductions, London, 1961.

Explorations, London, 1962.

A Vision, London, 1962.
A reissue, with corrections, of the 1937 edition.

Letters, edited by Allan Wade, London, 1954.

Some Biographical and Critical Studies

Ellmann, Richard, *Yeats: The Man and the Masks*, London, 1949.

—— *The Identity of Yeats*, London, 1954.

Hall, James and Steinmann, Martin, eds., *The Permanence of Yeats*, New York, 1950.

Henn, T. R., *The Lonely Tower*, London, 1950; 2nd ed. 1965.

Hone, J. M., *W. B. Yeats 1865–1939*, London, 1943; 2nd ed, 1962.
The date of publication of the first edition is incorrectly given on the title-page as 1942.

Jeffares, A. Norman, *W. B. Yeats. Man and Poet*, London, 1949; 2nd ed., 1962.

Kermode, Frank, *Romantic Image*, London, 1957.
Contains some brilliant chapters on Yeats.

Rajan, Balachandra, *W. B. Yeats*, London, 1965.

Stallworthy, Jon, *Between the Lines: Yeats's Poetry in the Making*, Oxford, 1963.

Stock, A. G., *W. B. Yeats: His Poetry and Thought*, Cambridge, 1961.

Ure, Peter, *Yeats*, Edinburgh, 1963.

Wilson, F. A. C., *W. B. Yeats and Tradition*, London, 1958.

—— *Yeats's Iconography*, London, 1960.

Winters, Yvor, *The Poetry of W. B. Yeats*, Denver, 1960.

3

IMAGISM AND THE NEW POETRY

INTRODUCTION

Between 1909 and 1914 English poetry was shaken by a revolution whose consequences are still with us. The new poetic, as it has been called,[1] was not the creation of any one poet or group of poets, although it was closely connected with Imagism, the only poetic movement of the century that has profoundly altered the course of English verse. The history of Imagism and the new poetry has been obscured by the rivalries and squabbles among certain of the leading actors such as Ezra Pound, F. S. Flint, and Amy Lowell. Partisans of T. E. Hulme, who died in 1917, and of Ford Madox Ford have disagreed about the respective significance of these two men's part in the poetic revolution. And since Imagism was an Anglo-American movement, a tincture of nationalistic ardour has left its mark on the controversy about the relative importance of the English and the American contribution to the story. This Introduction is an attempt to trace the outline of the tale clearly and accurately.

The name *Imagiste*, as we shall see, was invented by Ezra Pound in 1912: poems which we may justly term imagist were being written as early as in 1908.[2] A very minor poet, Edward Storer, brought out, towards the end of 1908 or early in 1909, a book of verse called *Mirrors of Illusion*. The first poem in the volume was three lines long and was entitled 'Image':

> Forsaken lovers,
> Burning to a chaste white moon,
> Upon strange pyres of loneliness and drought.

A friend of Storer's, and a considerably more formidable figure, T. E. Hulme, wrote on the back of an hotel bill dated 26 May 1908 another imagist poem, 'Sunset', which was not published in his lifetime. In 1908 Hulme became honorary secretary or treasurer of the Poets' Club, the joint presidents being Henry Simpson and Henry Newbolt. Early in 1909 the Club printed a pamphlet entitled *For Christmas MDCCCCVIII*,

[1] See C. K. Stead, *The New Poetic*, 1964.

[2] For Allen Upward's claim that he was writing 'Imagist' poems in 1900, and for the possibility that Pound had formulated 'Imagist' theories as early as 1902, see K. L. Goodwin, *The Influence of Ezra Pound*, 1966, pp. 3–6.

which contained two imagist poems by Hulme, 'Autumn' and 'A City Sunset'.[3]

F. S. Flint in *The New Age*, February 1909, attacked the 'after dinner ratiocinations' of the group, observing that 'The Poets' Club is Death'. Hulme replied to this attack and soon afterwards the disputants became friends. They founded an unnamed dining club, which first met in Soho on 25 March 1909, numbering among its members Edward Storer and another forgotten poet, Francis Tancred.

In his brief history of Imagism, printed in *The Egoist*, 1 May 1915,[4] F. S. Flint insists that Hulme took the lead in the critical discussions about the necessity of 'absolutely accurate presentation and no verbiage', and that Storer was the main theorizer about the nature and the use of the Image. The essays and jottings by Hulme which were collected in *Speculations* (1924) and in *Further Speculations* (1955) lend support to the view that Hulme anticipated in his writings and in his conversation many of the characteristic innovations and ideals of the new poetic in general and of Imagism in particular.

Flint's article almost certainly underestimates his own part in the story of Imagism. Robert Frost told Professor Isaacs that Flint was the founder of Imagism,[5] an assertion repeated by Edward Dahlberg.[6] Imagism owed much to French symbolism, about which Flint probably knew more than any other English or American poet of the day. Pound's knowledge of contemporary French verse at this time was, compared with Flint's, that of the merest amateur.

In an article called 'This Hulme Business', printed in 1939, Ezra Pound plays down Hulme's contribution to the new poetic and names Ford Madox Ford as the man whose ideas really mattered in pre-war literary London.[7] There can be no question about Ford's superb quality as an editor and as a discoverer of new talent; there is no doubt that Ford was a famous literary figure at a period when Hulme was utterly unknown, except to a tiny circle of friends. It is equally certain that Ford was the major influence in Pound's development at this time, and that his reviews, essays, and prefaces constitute the earliest coherent statements of the principles which animated the new poetic. Yet Ford's direct contribution to the Imagist movement was minimal, compared with that of Hulme, Flint, and Storer. It is true that in his Foreword to

3 Sam Hynes, *Further Speculations*, 1955, says that the second poem was 'Above the Dock'. Mr. Barry Harmer, who is working on the Imagists, has seen a copy of this rare pamphlet and confirms that the second poem is 'A City Sunset', as stated by Alun R. Jones, *The Life and Opinions of T. E. Hulme*, 1960, p. 36 and p. 100. I am grateful to Mr. Harmer for his information about this pamphlet, and have profited from conversation with him about the Imagists.

4 See below, pp. 44–5.

5 J. Isaacs, 'Best Loved of American Poets', *The Listener*, 1 April 1954, pp. 565–7.

6 Edward Dahlberg and Herbert Read, *Truth is More Sacred*, 1961, p. 173.

7 Reprinted in Hugh Kenner, *The Poetry of Ezra Pound*, 1951, p. 307.

the *Imagist Anthology* (1930) Ford claims to be the godfather of the Imagists, but like so many of his best stories this claim needs to be taken with a pinch of salt. In this Foreword he describes Imagism as a by-product of Vorticism. Now, Vorticism was launched on the world by Pound and Wyndham Lewis in the first number of *Blast*, dated 20 June 1914. The name Imagist dates from 1912, and imagist poems, as we have seen, were being written as far back as 1908.

Pound's reasons for minimizing Hulme's rôle can only be conjectured. Hulme was a striking personality, a swaggering amorist with a patriarchal attitude towards women, a blustering self-assurance, a set of violent political and social views, and a bellicosity which was tamed only by a prolonged dose of trench warfare. He must have been a formidable rival to Pound in the literary *salons* of the day. Many years later Pound recalled that Hulme had listened with rapt attention to his discourse on Cavalcanti.[8] It is at least possible that on this occasion Hulme was being elaborately ironical. There is some evidence to show that Hulme did not invariably regard Ezra Pound with admiration or respect, and that Pound was not a particularly welcome guest at Hulme's salon in Frith Street: 'Someone once asked him how long he would tolerate Ezra Pound, and Hulme thought for a moment and then said that he knew already exactly when he would have to kick him downstairs.'[9] According to Richard Aldington, Hulme treated Pound and his Imagism as a joke.[10]

Yet this very form of words suggests that Imagism was, in a sense, Pound's invention or property; and to some extent this was true. It is probable that by about 1910 Hulme had ceased to be interested primarily in poetry or in poetic theory, and that from then until his death in action his main concern was with philosophy, the visual arts, and aesthetics. Pound joined Hulme's dining club on 22 April 1909, when he made the Soho restaurant tremble with his recitation of his own 'Sestina: Altaforte'. He appears to have enjoyed such performances: he is said to have declaimed the same poem on one occasion at the Tour Eiffel in Soho with such vigour that the management placed a screen round the table.[11]

By 1912 Pound had found a name for the kind of verse which Hulme, Flint, and Storer had invented. In a letter to Harriet Monroe, dated 18 August 1912, Pound described one of his own poems as 'an over-elaborate post-Browning "Imagist" affair'.[12] He printed as an appendix

[8] See *Literary Essays of Ezra Pound*, edited by T. S. Eliot, 1954, p. 162.

[9] Jacob Epstein, *An Autobiography*, 1955, p. 60.

[10] Alun R. Jones, *The Life and Opinions of T. E. Hulme*, 1960, p. 33.

[11] Patricia Hutchins, *Ezra Pound's Kensington*, 1965, p. 129. Pound's dining companions were painters and sculptors.

[12] *The Letters of Ezra Pound 1907–1941*, edited by D. D. Paige, 1951, p. 44.

to his own *Ripostes* (1912) five poems by Hulme which he described, with mock solemnity as Hulme's 'Complete Poetical Works'. Pound's prefatory note contains a reference to *Les Imagistes.*[13] Meanwhile, Pound had been impressed by the poems of Richard Aldington and of the American poet Hilda Doolittle (H.D.), who soon afterwards became Aldington's wife. In the summer of 1912 Pound discussed with his two *protégés* the theory of Imagism, convincing them that they were imagist poets. Having expounded his views in the bunshops of Kensington and in his rooms at Church Walk, Pound displayed that exuberant generosity which he invariably showed towards the work of other artists, sending poems by Aldington and by H.D. to *Poetry*, the magazine recently founded by Harriet Monroe. In the November 1912 and the January 1913 issues, Pound described Aldington and H.D. respectively as *Imagistes*. The March 1913 issue printed Pound's famous injunctions, 'A Few Donts',[14] which are sometimes miscalled The Imagist Manifesto. In 1914 he edited anonymously *Des Imagistes,* an anthology containing poems by Aldington, H.D., Flint, Skipwith Cannell, Amy Lowell, William Carlos Williams, James Joyce, Pound, Ford, Allen Upward, and John Cournos. Pound may justly claim to have formulated the principles of Imagism, and to have illustrated his theories by his choice of poems for this anthology.

It is at this juncture that the story becomes muddied by controversy and by the ambitions of rival publicists. For in the summer of 1914 the high-powered, cigar-smoking Amy Lowell descended upon London, determined to meet her fellow *Imagistes* and to weld them into an organized movement. On 17 July 1914 she arranged and paid for an Imagist Dinner at the Dieu Donnes Restaurant, her guests being Aldington, H.D., Cournos, John Gould Fletcher, Flint, Ford, Pound, and Upward. By the time she returned to the States in September she had agreed with five other poets that they should produce three annual Imagist anthologies, which duly appeared under the title *Some Imagist Poets* in 1915, 1916 and 1917.[15] In order to obviate jealousies, nobody was named as editor: the contributors were Aldington, H.D., Fletcher, Flint, D. H. Lawrence, and Amy Lowell.

At this point Ezra Pound parted company with Imagism. It is sometimes suggested that he was inspired by personal dislike of Amy Lowell and by his disinclination to play second fiddle. Pound was always a difficult colleague, but he had good reasons, apart from jealousy and resentment, to dissociate himself from Amy Lowell's schemes. He feared that Imagism, as he understood it, was in danger of losing its

[13] See below, pp. 39–40. [14] See below, pp. 40–1.

[15] Published in Boston by Houghton Mifflin, in London by Constable. For some reason the 1917 volume was not distributed in Britain, and is not to be found in the copyright libraries there.

identity: 'I should like the name "Imagisme" to retain some sort of a meaning. It stands, or I should like it to stand for hard light, clear edges.'[16] Moreover, by the middle of 1914 he had come to believe that the Imagist doctrine of the image was too narrow and over-simplified. His fertile brain had conceived the term 'Vorticism' for the theories which were being expounded somewhat incoherently in Wyndham Lewis's short-lived periodical, *Blast*, founded in June 1914. The connection between Imagism and Vorticism is brought out in a brief passage from Pound's article on Vorticism: 'The image is not an idea. It is a radiant node or cluster; it is what I can, and must perforce, call a VORTEX, from which, and into which, ideas are continually rushing.'[17] Some years later Pound made a remark to Glenn Hughes which epitomizes his relationship with Imagism: 'Imagism was a point on the curve of my development. Some people remained at that point. I moved on.'[18]

Despite Pound's defection, Imagism continued to flourish. The first of the three volumes, *Some Imagist Poets* (1915), was introduced by a preface (unsigned, but almost entirely the work of Richard Aldington) which attempted to summarize the principles of Imagism.[19] This document, like Pound's injunctions of 1913, is sometimes incorrectly referred to as The Imagist Manifesto. The printing in the Imagist number of *The Egoist*, 1 May 1915, of F. S. Flint's article, 'The History of Imagism', led to a bitter quarrel between Flint and Pound, although Flint had toned down his draft for the article, deleting such passages as the following: 'The bottle-green guide(s) who touts for credulous Americans outside the Louvre will [*illegible word deleted*] take you, if you are fool enough, to some odd picture in an out-of-the-way corner and announce with much triumph and mystery that (they are the) he is the only guide who shows you *that*. Mr. Pound's method was the same.'[20]

Despite a reconciliation between the two men in 1921, it seems clear that Flint never forgot or wholly forgave Pound's self-conceit and arrogance. In a tribute to Harold Monro, printed soon after Monro's death in 1932, Flint acknowledged Pound's contribution to the history of Imagism: 'He invented Imagism, and, with Imagism, he changed the direction of and gave new life to American poetry . . . The "image" he took from T. E. Hulme's table talk. The "ism" was suggested to him by the notes on contemporary French poetry which I wrote for Harold

16 Letter to Amy Lowell, 1 August 1914. *The Letters of Ezra Pound 1907–1941*, edited by D. D. Paige, 1951, p. 78. See also *Letters*, p. 45, pp. 84–5, and p. 90.

17 Ezra Pound, 'Vorticism', *The Fortnightly Review*, XCVI, 1914, pp. 469–70.

18 Glenn Hughes, *Imagism and The Imagists*, 1931, p. 38.

19 See below, p. 43.

20 Quoted in Christopher Middleton, 'Documents on Imagism from the Papers of F. S. Flint', *The Review*, 15, April 1965, p. 39. Middleton's article gives a vivid picture of the quarrel between Flint and Pound.

Monro's *Poetry Review*. The collocation of "image" with "ism" came to Pound after I had told him about Fernand Divoire's essay on stratégie littéraire. Pound devised a "stratégie littéraire".'[21] Yet Flint's admiration for Pound's energy and inventiveness could not obliterate his distaste for Pound's apparent trickiness and disloyalty. It rankled with Flint that he and D. H. Lawrence 'were dismissed with contempt by Pound in his letters to Margaret Anderson of the *Little Review*: one of Pound's characteristic treacheries (or honesties, if you like)'.[22]

The Preface to the 1916 volume of *Some Imagist Poets*, again unsigned but this time largely by Amy Lowell, presented Imagism as the literary counterpart of a European revolution in music and painting, exemplified in the work of Debussy, Stravinsky, Gauguin, and Matisse. Amy Lowell stressed the importance in poetry of rhythm and cadence;[23] whereas Hulme had insisted that modern poetry was sculptural rather than musical.[24] John Gould Fletcher's preface to *Irradiations*,[25] which in some ways anticipates the technique of *The Waste Land* and even of *Four Quartets*, drew attention to certain analogies between music and poetry. F. S. Flint, in his experiments with unrhymed cadences, was nearer to Amy Lowell than to Hulme or to Pound.

The motives of the Imagists in contributing to the three volumes of the anthology were as mixed as their literary allegiances. Richard Aldington told Frank MacShane on 17 May 1954 that D. H. Lawrence joined the anthology in 1915 for financial profit.[26] We may choose to discount Aldington's testimony; but we know that at this period of his life Lawrence was, understandably, eager to advance his reputation and that he welcomed the aid of any literary figures of merit who could lend him a helping hand. A letter to Edward Garnett, dated 30 December 1913, reveals his attitude at the time: 'The Hueffer-Pound faction seems inclined to lead me around a little as one of their show-dogs. They seem to have a certain ear in their possession. If they are inclined to speak my name into the ear, I don't care.'[27]

Lawrence certainly owed nothing to the French symbolists so much beloved by Flint, regarding their poems as 'piffling, like lacy valentines'.[28] In May 1929 he laughed about Imagism, declaring to Glenn Hughes that it was all an illusion of Ezra Pound's: 'In the old London days Pound wasn't so literary as he is now. He was more of a mounte-

[21] F. S. Flint, 'Verse Chronicle', *The Criterion*, XI, 45, July 1932, pp. 686–7.

[22] ibid., p. 687.

[23] See below, pp. 43–4.

[24] See below, p. 37.

[25] See below, pp. 45–6.

[26] Frank MacShane, *The Life and Work of Ford Madox Ford*, 1965, p. 101.

[27] *The Collected Letters of D. H. Lawrence*, edited with an Introduction by Harry T. Moore, 2 vols., 1962, vol. I, p. 259.

[28] Quoted in Glenn Hughes, *Imagism and the Imagists*, 1931, p. 170.

bank then. He practiced more than he preached, for he had no audience.'[29] Yet it is worth noting that Lawrence was willing to be represented in the *Imagist Anthology* of 1930, that last parade of the survivors of an old, half-forgotten campaign.

After 1918, Imagism ceased to be an organized literary movement, although its theory and its example permeated English poetry throughout the nineteen-twenties. Lawrence, Pound, and William Carlos Williams went their own poetic ways; Joyce won an international reputation as a novelist; it is likely that their art was permanently enriched and refined by their apprenticeship to the discipline of Imagism. H.D. alone continued to write her exquisite poems in the Imagist manner, until her growing absorption in Egyptian and in Christian mysticism led her to abandon a mode of speech which was no longer adequate for what she had to say. The lesser poetic talents gradually stopped writing or turned to prose: perhaps the saddest figure was F. S. Flint, who after 1920 virtually ceased to write poems, and who published little prose, except translations of historical works from the French and the German. In his 'Verse Chronicle' printed in *The Criterion*, July 1932, Flint confessed that his own verse made him feel physically ill. Talking to Patricia Hutchins in the late nineteen-fifties, he remarked that nobody had taken Imagism very seriously, and that it had all been a joke started by lively young people.[30] Yet insofar as Flint made known the work of the French symbolists to Hulme, to Pound and, indirectly, to other talented poets of that generation; insofar as he helped to found Imagism and to mould the shape of the new poetic, he deserves to be honoured as a pioneer by all who admire the most daring achievements of English poetry in our century.

CRITICISM

What I mean by classical in verse, then, is this. That even in the most imaginative flights there is always a holding back, a reservation. The classical poet never forgets this finiteness, this limit of man. He remembers always that he is mixed up with earth. He may jump, but he always returns back; he never flies away into the circumambient gas.

T. E. Hulme, 'Romanticism and Classicism', *Speculations*, edited by Herbert Read, 1924, pp. 119–20.

When you say a poem or drawing is fresh, and so good, the impression is somehow conveyed that the essential element of goodness is freshness, that it is good because it is fresh. Now this is certainly wrong,

29 ibid., pp. 169–70.

30 Patricia Hutchins, *Ezra Pound's Kensington*, 1965, pp. 135–6.

there is nothing particularly desirable about freshness *per se.* Works of art aren't eggs. Rather the contrary. It is simply an unfortunate necessity due to the nature of language and technique that the only way the element which does constitute goodness, the only way in which its presence can be detected externally, is by freshness. Freshness convinces you, you feel at once that the artist was in an actual physical state. You feel that for a minute. Real communication is so very rare, for plain speech is unconvincing. It is in this rare fact of communication that you get the root of aesthetic pleasure.

ibid., pp. 135–6.

There is a kind of gossamer web, woven between the real things, and by this means the animals communicate. For purposes of communication they invent a symbolic language. Afterwards this language, used to excess, becomes a disease, and we get the curious phenomena of men explaining themselves by means of the gossamer web that connects them. Language becomes a disease in the hands of the counter-word mongers.

T. E. Hulme, 'Cinders', ibid., pp. 217–18.

But the modern is the exact opposite of this [old poetry], it no longer deals with heroic action, it has become definitely and finally introspective and deals with expression and communication of momentary phases in the poet's mind. It was well put by Mr. G. K. Chesterton in this way – that where the old dealt with the Siege of Troy, the new attempts to express the emotions of a boy fishing. The opinion you often hear expressed that perhaps a new poet will arrive who will synthesize the whole modern movement into a great epic, shows an entire misconception of the tendency of modern verse. There is an analagous change in painting, where the old endeavoured to tell a story, the modern attempts to fix an impression . . .

This new verse resembles sculpture rather than music; it appeals to the eye rather than to the ear. It has to mould images, a kind of spiritual clay, into definite shapes.

T. E. Hulme, 'A Lecture on Modern Poetry', *Further Speculations,* edited by Sam Hynes, 1955, pp. 72–5.

Dead Analogies

All styles are only means of subduing the reader.

(i) New phrases made in poetry, tested, and then employed in prose.

(ii) In poetry they are all glitter and new coruscation, in prose useful and not noticed.

(iii) Prose a museum where all thc old weapons of poetry kept.

(iv) Poetry always the advance-guard of language. The progress of language is the absorption of new analogies.

T. E. Hulme, 'Notes on Language and Style', ibid., p. 81.

[It is not easy to date the writings published in *Speculations* and *Further Speculations*. 'A Lecture' was first delivered in 1908 or 1909, and revised for another delivery in 1914. The 'Notes' probably belong to the same period. The extracts quoted from *Speculations* probably date from the years immediately preceding 1914.]

Hulme wasn't hated and loathed by the ole bastards, because they didn't know he was there. The man who did the *work* for English writing was Ford Madox Hueffer (now Ford). The old crusted lice and advocates of corpse language knew that *The English Review* existed.

Ezra Pound, Letter to Michael Roberts, July 1937, *The Letters of Ezra Pound 1907–1941*, edited by D. D. Paige, 1951, pp. 388–9.

My father once wrote of Rossetti that he set down the mind of Dante in the language of Shakespeare. That was clever of my father, but could there have been a greater condemnation of that magic Amateur . . . for what the poet ought to do is to write his own mind in the language of his day . . .

It is for us to get at the new truths or to give new life to such of the old as will appeal *hominibus bonae voluntatis*. Only to do that we must do it in the clear pure language of our own day and with what is clear and new in our own individualities.

Ford Madox Ford, Letter to Lucy Masterman, 23 January 1912, *Critical Writings of Ford Madox Ford*, edited by Frank MacShane, 1964, p. 154.

With regard to more speculative matters. I may really say that for a quarter of a century I have kept before me one unflinching aim – to register my own times in terms of my own times, and still more to urge those who are better poets and better prose-writers than myself to have the same aim . . .

I should say, to put a personal confession on record, that the very strongest emotion – at any rate of this class – that I have ever had was when I first went to the Shepherd's Bush Exhibition and came out on a great square of white buildings all outlined with lights. There was such a lot of light – and I think that what I hope for in Heaven is an infinite clear radiance of pure light! There were crowds and crowds of people – or no, there was, spread out beneath the lights, an infinite moving mass of black, with white faces turned up to the light, moving slowly, quickly, not moving at all, being obscured, reappearing . . .

I remember seeing in a house in Hertford an American cartoon representing a dog pursuing a cat out of the door of a particularly hideous tenement house, and beneath this picture was inscribed the words: 'This is life – one damn thing after another.' Now I think it would be better to be able to put that sentiment into lyric verse than to remake a ballad of the sorrows of Cuchullain or to paraphrase the Book of Job. I do not mean to say that Job is not picturesque; I do not mean to say that it is not a good thing to have the Book of the Seven Sorrows of whom you will in the background of your mind or even colouring your outlook. But it is better to see life in the terms of one damn thing after another, vulgar as is the phraseology or even the attitude, than to render it in terms of withering gourds and other poetic paraphernalia. It is, in fact, better to be vulgar than affected, at any rate if you practise poetry.

Ford Madox Ford, Preface to *Collected Poems*, 1913,[31] pp. 13–20.

For the ten years before I got to England there would seem to have been no one but Ford who held that French clarity and simplicity in the writing of English verse and prose were of immense importance as in contrast to the use of a stilted traditional dialect, a 'language of verse' unused in the actual talk of the people, even of 'the best people', for the expression of reality and emotion . . .

The justification or programme of such writing was finally (about 1913) set down in one of the best essays (preface) that Ford ever wrote.

It advocated the prose value of verse-writing, and it, along with his verse, had more in it for my generation than all the retchings (most worthily) after 'quantity' (i.e., quantitative metric) of the late Laureate Robert Bridges or the useful, but monotonous, in their day unduly neglected, as more recently unduly touted, metrical labours of G. Manley Hopkins.

Ezra Pound, 'Ford Madox (Hueffer) Ford: Obit', *The Nineteenth Century*, CXXVI, August 1939, pp. 178–9.

As for the 'School of Images', which may or may not have existed, its principles were not so interesting as those of the 'inherent dynamists' or of *Les Unanimistes*, yet they were probably sounder than those of a certain French school which attempted to dispense with verbs altogether; or of the Impressionists who brought forth:

Pink pigs blossoming upon the hillside;

or of the Post-Impressionists who beseech their ladies to let down slate-blue hair over their raspberry-coloured flanks.

Ardoise rimed richly – ah, richly and rarely rimed! – with *framboise*.

[31] At this period of his life Ford was known as Ford Madox Hueffer. His *Collected Poems* were published under that name. The date of publication, though shown on the title-page as 1914, was 1913.

As for the future, *Les Imagistes*, the descendants of the forgotten school of 1909, have that in their keeping.

Ezra Pound, Prefatory Note to 'The Complete Poetical Works of T. E. Hulme', printed as an Appendix to Pound's *Ripostes*, 1912.

['The Complete Poetical Works' consisted of five poems. Pound's prefatory note begins: 'In publishing his *Complete Poetic Works* at thirty, Mr. Hulme has set an enviable example to many of his contemporaries who have had less to say.']

Mr. Richard Aldington is a young English poet, one of the 'Imagistes', a group of ardent Hellenists who are pursuing interesting experiments in *verse libre*; trying to attain in English certain subtleties of cadence of the kind which Mallarmé and his followers have studied in French.

'Notes and Announcements', *Poetry*, 1, 2, November 1912, p. 65.

The youngest school here that has the nerve to call itself a school is that of the *Imagistes*.

Ezra Pound, 'Status Rerum', *Poetry*, 1, 4, January 1913, p. 126.

In response to many requests for information regarding *Imagism* and the *Imagists*, we publish this note by Mr. Flint, supplementing it with further exemplification by Mr. Pound. It will be seen from these that *Imagism* is not necessarily associated with Hellenic subjects, or with *vers libre* as a prescribed form.

'Editor's Note', *Poetry*, 1, 6, March 1913, p. 198.

The 'Don'ts' in the following reprint had a plain utilitarian purpose in that they were intended as a rejection slip to be used by a trade paper. They were aimed at the faults most prevalent of poetry as we found it in 1905–12.

Naturally the second clause in the Imagist triad was the first to be avoided. That really did require a little thought and consciousness, and was promptly followed by various more wordy formulae designed to avoid the trouble.

It is not to be expected that a great number of people in any age will be able to maintain an interesting tenseness in verbal manifestation, any more than we are likely to be beset by a large herd of great draughtsmen or an overwhelming swarm of composers capable of great melodic invention.

A RETROSPECT

In the spring or early summer of 1912, 'H.D.', Richard Aldington and myself decided that we were agreed upon the three principles following:

1. Direct treatment of the 'thing' whether subjective or objective.

2. To use absolutely no word that does not contribute to the presentation.

3. As regarding rhythm: to compose in the sequence of the musical phrase, not in sequence of a metronome.

Upon many points of taste and predilection we differed, but agreeing upon these three positions we thought we had as much right to a group name, at least as much right, as a number of French 'schools' proclaimed by Mr. Flint in the August number of Harold Monro's magazine for 1911 ...[32]

I set together a few phrases on practical working about the time the first remarks on imagisme were published. The first use of the word 'Imagiste' was in my note to T. E. Hulme's five poems, printed at the end of my 'Ripostes' in the autumn of 1912. I reprint my cautions from *Poetry* for March, 1913.

A FEW DONT'S

An 'Image' is that which presents an intellectual and emotional complex in an instant of time. I use the term 'complex' rather in the technical sense employed by the newer psychologists, such as Hart, though we might not agree absolutely in our application.

It is the presentation of such a 'complex' instantaneously which gives that sense of sudden liberation; that sense of freedom from time limits and space limits, that sense of sudden growth, which we experience in the presence of the greatest works of art.

It is better to present one Image in a lifetime than to produce voluminous works.

Ezra Pound

[The passages under the headings A Retrospect and A Few Dont's were printed in *Pavannes and Divisions* (1918), in a section that contained a group of early essays and notes. This section was entitled 'A Retrospect'. The three introductory paragraphs are to be found only in *Make it New* (1934), p. 335, in the section entitled 'A Stray Document'.

The whole of 'A Retrospect' from *Pavannes and Divisions* is reprinted in *Literary Essays of Ezra Pound*, edited by T. S. Eliot (1954), pp. 3–14. It is too long to quote in full, but it should be studied in its entirety.]

As to contemporaries, since you ask it, I will, privately, go so far as to say that Lawrence was never an Imagist. He was an *Amy*gist. Ford dug him up and boomed him in *Eng. Rev.* before Imagism was launched. Neither he nor Fletcher accepted the Imagist programme. When the prospect of Amy's yearly outcroppings was by her assured, they agreed

[32] See F. S. Flint's 'Contemporary French Poetry' in *The Poetry Review*, I, viii, August 1912 (not 1911), pp. 355–414.

to something different. This is not an attack on L's ability as a writer but merely to amend the statement in yr. circular.

The name was invented to launch H.D. and Aldington before either had enough stuff for a volume. Also to establish a critical demarcation long since knocked to hell.

T. E. Hulme was an original or pre-.

Bill Williams was as 'original' as cd. be managed by writing from London to N.J. Flint was the next acquisition, tho' really impressionist. He and Ford and one or two others shd. by careful cataloguing have been in another group, but in those days there weren't enough non-symmetricals to have each a farm to themselves. Several others have since faded, Lawrence wasn't asked, and Fletcher declined.

The test is in the second of the three clauses of the first manifesto.

Even this amount of reminiscences bores me exceedingly.

Ezra Pound, Letter to Glenn Hughes, 26 September 1927, *The Letters of Ezra Pound 1907–1941*, edited by D. D. Paige, 1951, p. 288.

The defect of earlier Imagist propaganda was not in mis-statement but in incomplete statement. The diluters took the handiest and easiest meaning, and thought only of the STATIONARY image. If you can't think of imagism or phanopoeia as including the moving image, you will have to make a really needless division of fixed image and praxis or action.

I have taken to using the term phanopoeia to get away from irrelevant particular connotations tangled with a particular group of young people who were writing in 1912.

Ezra Pound, *ABC of Reading*, 1934, p. 36.

Poetry should be burned to the bone by austere fires and washed white with rains of affliction: the poet should love nakedness and the thought of the skeleton under the flesh. But because the public will not pay for poetry it has become the occupation of learned persons, given to soft living among veiled things and unaccustomed to being sacked for talking too much. That is why from the beautiful stark bride of Blake it has become the idle hussy hung with ornament kept by Lord Tennyson, handed on to Stephen Phillips and now supported at Devonshire Street by the Georgian school. But there has arisen a little band who desire the poet to be as disciplined and efficient at his job as the stevedore. Just as Taylor and Gilbreth want to introduce scientific management into industry so the *imagistes* want to discover the most puissant way of whirling the scattered star dust of words into a new star of passion.

Rebecca West, 'Imagisme', *The New Freewoman*, 1, 5, 15 August 1913, p. 86. [On 1 January 1914, this periodical became *The Egoist*.]

The poets in this volume do not represent a clique. Several of them are personally known to the others, but they are united by certain common principles, arrived at independently. These principles are not new; they have fallen into desuetude. They are the essentials of all great poetry, indeed of all great literature, and they are simply these:

1. To use the language of common speech, but to employ always the *exact* word, not the nearly-exact, nor the merely decorative word.

2. To create new rhythms – as the expression of new moods – and not to copy old rhythms, which merely echo old moods. We do not insist upon 'free verse' as the only method of writing poetry. We fight for it as for a principle of liberty. We believe that the individuality of a poet may often be better expressed in free verse than in conventional forms. In poetry, a new cadence means a new idea.

3. To allow absolute freedom in the choice of subject. It is not good art to write badly about aeroplanes and automobiles; nor is it necessarily bad art to write well about the past. We believe passionately in the artistic value of modern life, but we wish to point out that there is nothing so uninspiring nor so old-fashioned as an aeroplane of the year 1911.

4. To present an image (hence the name: 'Imagist'). We are not a school of painters, but we believe that poetry should render particulars exactly and not deal in vague generalities, however magnificent and sonorous. It is for this reason that we oppose the cosmic poet, who seems to us to shirk the real difficulties of his art.

5. To produce poetry that is hard and clear, never blurred nor indefinite.

6. Finally, most of us believe that concentration is of the very essence of poetry.

The subject of free-verse is too complicated to be discussed here. We may say briefly, that we attach the term to all that increasing amount of writing whose cadence is more marked, more definite, and closer knit than that of prose, but which is not so violently nor so obviously accented as the so-called 'regular verse'. We refer those interested in the question to the Greek Melic poets, and to the many excellent French studies on the subject by such distinguished and well-equipped authors as Remy de Gourmont, Gustave Kahn, Georges Duhamel, Charles Vildrac, Henri Ghéon, Robert de Souza, André Spire, etc.

Preface to *Some Imagist Poets*, 1915, pp. vi–viii.

[Written by Richard Aldington, slightly revised by Amy Lowell.]

It is this very fact of 'cadence' which has misled so many reviewers, until some have been betrayed into saying that the Imagists discard rhythm, when rhythm is the most important quality in their technique. The definition of *vers libre* is – a verse-form based upon cadence. Now cadence in music is one thing, cadence in poetry quite another, since we are not dealing with tone but with rhythm. It is the sense of perfect balance of flow and rhythm . . .

The unit in *vers libre* is not the foot, the number of the syllables, the quantity, or the line. The unit is the strophe, which may be the whole poem, or may be only a part. Each strophe is a complete circle: in fact the meaning of the Greek word 'strophe' is simply that part of the poem which was recited while the chorus were making a turn round the altar set up in the centre of the theatre . . . But one thing must be borne in mind: a cadenced poem is written to be read aloud, in this way only will its rhythm be felt. Poetry is a spoken and not a written art.

Preface to *Some Imagist Poets*, 1916, pp. viii–xii.

[Almost entirely written by Amy Lowell.]

At that time [late in 1908], I had been advocating in the course of a series of articles on recent books of verse a poetry in *vers libre*, akin in spirit to the Japanese. An attack on the Poets' Club brought me into correspondence and acquaintance with T. E. Hulme; and, later on, after Hulme had violently disagreed with the Poets' Club and had left it, he proposed that he should get together a few congenial spirits, and that we should have weekly meetings in a Soho restaurant. The first of these meetings, which were really the successors of certain Wednesday evening meetings, took place on Thursday, March 25, 1909 . . . I think that what brought the real nucleus of this group together was a dissatisfaction with English poetry as it was then (and is still, alas!) being written. We proposed at various times to replace it by pure *vers libre*; by the Japanese *tanka* and *haikai*; we all wrote dozens of the latter as an amusement; by poems in a sacred Hebrew form, of which 'This is the House that Jack Built' is a perfect model – by rhymeless poems like Hulme's 'Autumn', and so on. In all this Hulme was ringleader. He insisted too on absolutely accurate presentation and no verbiage; and he and F. W. Tancred, a poet too little known, perhaps because his production is precious and small, used to spend hours each day in the search for the right phrase. Tancred does it still; while Hulme reads German philosophy in the trenches, waiting for the general advance. There was also a lot of talk and practice among us, Storer leading it chiefly, of what we called the Image. We were very much influenced by modern French symbolist poetry.

On April 22, 1909, Ezra Pound . . . joined the group . . . Ezra Pound used to boast in those days that he was

Nil praeter 'Villon' et doctus cantare Catullum,

and he could not be made to believe that there was any French poetry after Ronsard. He was very full of his *troubadours*; but I do not remember that he did more than attempt to illustrate (or refute) our theories with their example . . .

There is no difference, except that which springs from difference of temperament and talent, between an imagist poem of to-day and those written by Edward Storer and T. E. Hulme.

F. S. Flint, 'The History of Imagism', *The Egoist*, II, 5, 1 May 1915, pp. 70–1.

There are at least three stupid things about *Imagisme*: the word itself is stupid; the tables of the law of Imagisme laid down by Mr. Pound in a series of 'Don'ts of an Imagist', published in Poetry (Chicago) in ——, are stupid; and the crowning stupidity of all is Mr. Pound's belief, which he holds strongly, that his was the dynamism that created both the law and the works exemplfying the law which he managed to publish, in 1914, in a book (called) (ungrammatically and) with the silly title of 'Des Imagistes: An Anthology'.

F. S. Flint, Draft of 'The History of Imagism', from 'Documents on Imagism from the Papers of F. S. Flint', by Christopher Middleton, *The Review*, 15, April 1965, pp. 35–51.

[This article traces the bitter quarrel about Imagism between Flint and Pound.]

For all poets, old and new, the poetic act is a sacramental act with its rubric and its ritual. The Victorian poets are Protestant. For them the bread and wine are symbols of Reality, the body and the blood. They are given 'in remembrance'. The sacrament is incomplete. The Imagists are Catholic; they believe in Trans-substantiation. For them the bread and wine are the body and the blood. They are given. The thing is done. *Ita Missa est.* The formula may lead to some very ugly ritual, but that is the fault of the Imagist not of Imagism.

May Sinclair, 'Two Notes', *The Egoist*, II, 5, 1 June 1915, p. 89.

I maintain that poetry is capable of as many graduations in cadence as music is in time. We can have a rapid group of syllables – what is called a line – succeeded by a slow, heavy one; like the swift scurrying-up of the wave, and the sullen dragging of itself away. Or we can gradually increase or decrease our *tempo*, creating *accelerando* and *rallentando* effects. Or we can follow a group of rapid lines with a group of slow ones, or a single slow, or *vice versa.* Finally, we can have a perfectly even and unaltered movement throughout if we desire to be monotonous.

The good poem is that in which all these effects are properly used to convey the underlying emotions of its author, and that which welds all these emotions into a work of art by the use of dominant *motif*, subordinate themes, proportionate treatment, repetition, variation – what in music is called development, reversal of rôles, and return. In short, the good poem fixes a free emotion, or a free range of emotions, into an inevitable and artistic whole.

John Gould Fletcher, Preface to *Irradiations: Sand and Spray*, 1915.

. . . the most interesting verse which has yet been written in our language has been done either by taking a very simple form, like the iambic pentameter, and constantly withdrawing from it, or taking no form at all and constantly approximating to a very simple one. It is this contrast between fixity and flux, this unperceived evasion of monotony, which is the very life of verse . . .

We may therefore formulate as follows: the ghost of some simple metre should lurk behind the arras in even the 'freest' verse; to advance menacingly as we doze, and withdraw as we rouse. Or, freedom is only freedom when it appears against the background of an artificial limitation.

. . . the decay of intricate formal patterns has nothing to do with the advent of *vers libre*. It had set in long before. Only in a closely-knit and homogeneous society, where many men are at work on the same problems, such a society as those which produced the Greek chorus, the Elizabethan lyric, and the Troubador canzone, will the development of such forms ever be carried to perfection. And as for *vers libre*, we conclude that it is not defined by absence of pattern or absence of rhyme, for other verse is without these; that it is not defined by non-existence of metre, since even the *worst* verse can be scanned; and we conclude that the division between Conservative Verse and *vers libre* does not exist, for there is only good verse, bad verse, and chaos.

T. S. Eliot, 'Reflections on *Vers Libre*', *The New Statesman*, VIII, 204, 3 March 1917, pp. 518–19. Reprinted in *To Criticize the Critic*, 1965, pp. 183–9.

POEMS

T. E. HULME (1883–1917)

Above the Dock

Above the quiet dock in midnight,
Tangled in the tall mast's corded height,
Hangs the moon. What seemed so far away
Is but a child's balloon, forgotten after play.

The Embankment

(The fantasia of a fallen gentleman on a cold, bitter night)

Once, in finesse of fiddles found I ecstasy,
In a flash of gold heels on the hard pavement.
Now see I
That warmth's the very stuff of poesy.
Oh, God, make small
The old star-eaten blanket of the sky,
That I may fold it round me and in comfort lie.

Images

Her skirt lifted as a dark mist
From the columns of amethyst.

*

The lark crawls on the cloud
Like a flea on a white body.

*

The after-black lies low along the hills
Like the trailed smoke of a steamer.

F. S. FLINT (1885–1960)

Houses

Evening and quiet:
a bird trills in the poplar trees
behind the house with the dark green door
across the road.

Into the sky,
the red earthenware and the galvanized iron chimneys
thrust their cowls.
The host of the steamers on the Thames is plain.

No wind;
the trees merge, green with green;
a car whirs by;
footsteps and voices take their pitch
in the key of dusk,
far-off and near, subdued.

Solid and square to the world
the houses stand,
their windows blocked with venetian blinds.

Nothing will move them.

EZRA POUND (b. 1885)

Albatre

This lady in the white bath-robe which she calls a peignoir,
Is, for the time being, the mistress of my friend,
And the delicate white feet of her little white dog
Are not more delicate than she is,
Nor would Gautier himself have despised their contrasts in whiteness
As she sits in the great chair
Between the two indolent candles.

Fan-piece for her Imperial Lord

O fan of white silk,
  clear as frost on the grass-blade,
You also are laid aside.

In a Station of the Metro

The apparition of these faces in the crowd;
Petals on a wet, black bough.

Alba

As cool as the pale wet leaves
          of lily-of-the-valley
She lay beside me in the dawn.

FORD MADOX FORD (1873–1939)

from *Antwerp*

II

For there is no new thing under the sun,
Only this uncomely man with a smoking gun
In the gloom . . .
What the devil will he gain by it?
Digging a hole in the mud and standing all day in the rain by it

Waiting his doom,
The sharp blow, the swift outpouring of the blood,
Till the trench of grey mud
Is turned to a brown purple drain by it.
Well, there have been scars
Won in many wars ...
Punic,
Lacedaemonian, wars of Napoleon, wars for faith, war for honour, for love, for possession,
But this Belgian man in his ugly tunic,
His ugly round cap, shooting on, in a sort of obsession,
Overspreading his miserable land,
Standing with his wet gun in his hand ...
Doom!
He finds that in a sudden scrimmage,
And lies, an unsightly lump on the sodden grass ...
An image that shall take long to pass!

RICHARD ALDINGTON (1892–1962)

Sunsets

The white body of the evening
Is torn into scarlet,
Slashed and gouged and seared
Into crimson,
And hung ironically
With garlands of mist.

And the wind
Blowing over London from Flanders
Has a bitter taste.

H.D. (1886–1960)

Heat

O wind, rend open the heat,
cut apart the heat,
rend it to tatters.

Fruit cannot drop
through this thick air –
fruit cannot fall into heat
that presses up and blunts
the points of pears
and rounds the grapes.

Cut the heat –
plough through it,
turning it on either side
of your path.

Oread

Whirl up, sea –
whirl your pointed pines,
splash your great pines
on our rocks,
hurl your green over us,
cover us with your pools of fir.

Lethe

Nor skin nor hide nor fleece
  shall cover you,
nor curtain of crimson nor fine
shelter of cedar-wood be over you,
  nor the fir-tree
  nor the pine.

Nor sight of whin nor gorse
  nor river yew,
nor fragrance of flowering bush,
nor wailing of reed-bird to waken you,
  nor of linnet,
  nor of thrush.

Nor word nor touch nor sight
  of lover, you
shall long through the night but for this:
the roll of the full tide to cover you
  without question,
  without kiss.

Epitaph

So I may say,
'I died of living,
having lived one hour!'

so they may say,
'she died soliciting
illicit fervour;'

so you may say,
'Greek flower; Greek ecstasy
reclaims forever

one who died
following
intricate song's lost measure.'

SELECT BIBLIOGRAPHY

Imagism

Des Imagistes, London and New York, 1914.
Edited by Ezra Pound, although no indication of this is given in the anthology.

Some Imagist Poets, 3 vols, London and Boston, 1915–1917.
In order to emphasize the equality of the poets included in these anthologies, these volumes were edited anonymously.

Imagist Anthology, London and New York, 1930. Instigated by Richard Aldington. Forewords by Ford Madox Ford and Glenn Hughes.

Coffman, Stanley K. Jnr., *Imagism: a Chapter for the History of Modern Poetry*, Norman, 1951.

Hughes, Glenn, *Imagism and the Imagists*, Stanford and London, 1931.

Read, Herbert, *The True Voice of Feeling*, London, 1953.
Contains two important chapters: 'The Isolation of the Image: T. E. Hulme'; 'Ideas in Action: Ezra Pound'.

T. E. Hulme

Hulme, T. E., *Speculations*, edited by Herbert Read, London, 1924; 2nd ed., 1936.

—— *Further Speculations*, edited by Sam Hynes, Minneapolis, 1955.

Jones, Alun R., *The Life and Opinions of T. E. Hulme*, London, 1960. Includes what is likely to be the definitive text of Hulme's poetry.

Roberts, Michael, *T. E. Hulme*, London, 1938.

Ford Madox Ford

Hueffer, Ford Madox, *Collected Poems*, London, 1913.
The date of publication is incorrectly given on the title-page as 1914. At this period of his life Ford was known as Hueffer. The preface to this collection is a remarkable document in the history of modern verse.

Ford, Ford Madox, *Collected Poems*, New York, 1936.
No edition of this book has been published in Britain.
—— *Critical Writings of Ford Madox Ford*, edited by Frank MacShane, Lincoln (Nebraska), 1964.
Contains material hitherto unprinted.
MacShane, Frank, *The Life and Work of Ford Madox Ford*, London, 1965.

Ezra Pound

See below, p. 69.

4

EZRA POUND 1909-1919

INTRODUCTION

Many readers will question the propriety of including Ezra Pound in a survey of modern English verse. Even if we accept the fact that the most original English verse of the century has been written by men who are not English, is it not stretching our categories too far if we allow an invader from the Middle-West of the United States to rank as an English poet? In certain ways Ezra Pound is, by ancestry, education, and temperament, a profoundly American poet: there is a sense in which this nephew of Longfellow has remained, spiritually as well as legally, an American subject, even though, after 1908, his sole period of residence in the United States was during his incarceration there as a man certified mentally unfit to defend himself against a charge of treason.

Yet to ignore Pound's residence in London from 1908 to 1920 is to disqualify oneself from understanding his poetic development and, incidentally, the development of English verse during the past fifty years. Pound deliberately left the United States for London, which he regarded as the indisputable centre of English literature; he acknowledged, at the time and in later years, what London had taught him; he became one of the dominating figures in English literary life for a decade, and did more than any other single man to shape the course of English poetry in our time.

Although Pound has been bitterly attacked by many English and American critics ever since he first began his career as a writer, it would be wrong to suppose that he was greeted in Edwardian London with universal hostility or incomprehension. His first book *A Lume Spento* (1908), brought out by a little-known publisher, was reviewed in *The Evening Standard*. *Personae* (1909) received a notice from R. A. Scott-James in *The Daily News*, and enthusiastic praise from Edward Thomas in the influential *English Review*.[1] Early in 1910 F. S. Flint reviewed favourably, in *The New Age*, Pound's next volume, *Exultations*, although he described 'Sestina: Altaforte' as 'rant'. Admittedly, Pound was handled less kindly in other quarters: to quote one reviewer, 'he affects the eccentric and the obscure; but these qualities do not, in these pages at any rate, leave much room for beauty'.[2]

[1] See below, p. 60. [2] *The Times Literary Supplement*, 27 May 1909.

Nor was it only his young contemporaries who welcomed Pound to London. Then, as now, elder men of letters were kind, even over-indulgent, to young newcomers of promise. It is, perhaps, not to be wondered at that Hulme, Flint, and their fellow-members of the literary dining club should delight in Pound's vitality and gaiety. It is more astonishing that such distinguished writers as Ford Madox Ford and W. B. Yeats should not merely have helped this flamboyant young man, with his flaming hair and his jade ear-ring, but should have allowed him to dominate their lives and their households. We have seen how Yeats asked Pound for his advice about poetry, even after Pound had, without permission, made alterations in some of his poems before sending them to Harriet Monroe for *Poetry*.[3]

Douglas Goldring has given a lively picture of the way in which Pound organized Yeats's Monday evenings at Woburn Buildings, and of how he installed himself as master of ceremonies at the entertainments given by Ford and Violet Hunt in their *ménage* at South Lodge. T. E. Hulme might thoughtfully contemplate the prospect of kicking Ezra Pound downstairs; Ford and Yeats were apparently less irascible or more warm-hearted. Goldring explains why Pound was so much liked by so many people: he was inspired by a passionate, selfless love of literature, and would go to endless trouble to help anybody in whom he detected the tiniest spark of talent.[4]

By the end of 1913 Pound had won for himself an enviable reputation among men of letters in London. Early in 1914 a group of poets visited W. S. Blunt in his house and presented him with a marble statue by Gaudier Brzeska, the young sculptor whose genius Pound was one of the first to recognize. The delegation numbered among its members figures as diverse as Yeats, Sturge Moore, Masefield, Victor Plarr, Frederic Manning, Flint, Aldington, and Pound. It was Pound who was entrusted with the task of making the presentation speech.

Yet even in these early days one can discern the faint outlines of those clouds that were later to become so dark and huge. Pound quarrelled with Arundel del Re over the latter's review of Pound's *Sonnets and Ballate* in *The English Review* of July 1912 and F. S. Flint had to exert himself to effect a reconciliation.[5] This exhibition of literary vanity and touchiness need not be taken too seriously, but it was, unfortunately, a symptom of the dark obsessions, the cantankerous vituperativeness, that were to lead Pound into such murky ways and bring upon him so much tragic punishment and suffering.

As early as 1914 Pound began to indulge in attacks on Jews. The

[3] See above, p. 9.
[4] Douglas Goldring, *South Lodge*, 1943, pp. 47–9.
[5] Flint describes this episode in 'Verse Chronicle', *The Criterion*, XI, 45, July 1932, p. 686.

literary circles in which he moved were not free of anti-Jewish prejudice. Thus, according to Ashley Dukes, T. E. Hulme advocated that all Jews should be forced to wear a distinctive national costume, although he may have spoken in this vein to shock his liberal friends.[6] Pound seems to have found such prejudice congenial. The first number of *Blast*, which appeared on 20 June 1914, included a violent, incoherent tirade by Pound, entitled 'Salutation the Third', which contained the line 'Let us be done with Jews and Jobbery.' In *Personae* (1952) the phrase has been altered to '. . . panders and Jobbery'. Unhappily, 'Salutation the Third' was the precursor of even more unpleasant diatribes in later years.

F. S. Flint, in his quarrel with Pound about Imagism, referred to certain disagreeable traits in Pound's character. John Fenton contributed some 'Contemporary Caricatures' to *The Egoist*, 1 August 1914, among them being a few lines on Ezra Pound:

> His mind is a patch-work of derivations
> Agitated by the wind of Transatlantic snobbery.
> At times really illuminating
> He is too lost in the bog of personal vanity
> To be anything more than the Roosevelt of letters.

His personal vanity; his growing intolerance of everybody who disagreed with him; his conviction that influential people who refused to fall in with all his schemes were moved solely by envy of his superior talent: these and similar characteristics must have become a source of irritation even to those who recognized his devotion to literature and his other abundant virtues. It is, therefore, all the more pleasant to record one friendship that lasted for half a century – his friendship with T. S. Eliot. They first met on 22 September 1914, when Eliot called on Pound and, encouraged by his reception, sent him 'Prufrock' a few days later. Throughout all the vicissitudes of Pound's career their friendship endured, until Pound, in his eightieth year, came to pay tribute to his old comrade at the memorial service held for Eliot in Westminster Abbey. It was the first time that he had revisited for over forty years the city which he had so poignantly recalled in the *Pisan Cantos*:

> and the Serpentine will look just the same
> and the gulls be as neat on the pond
> and the sunken garden unchanged
> and God knows what else is left of our London
>   my London, your London.

Although Pound seldom acknowledged a literary debt to anybody other than Ford Madox Ford, he clearly regarded Eliot as an equal

[6] *Further Speculations*, edited by Sam Hynes, 1955, p. xxx.

partner and collaborator during the first few years of their acquaintance. Eliot, according to Pound,

> displayed great tact, or enjoyed good fortune, in arriving in London at a particular date with a formed style of his own. He also participated in a movement to which no name has ever been given.
>
> That is to say, at a particular date in a particular room, two authors, neither engaged in picking the other's pocket, decided that the dilution of *vers libre*, Amygism, Lee Masterism, general floppiness had gone too far and that some counter-current must be set going. Parallel situation centuries ago in China. Remedy prescribed 'Emaux et Camées' (or the Bay State Hymn Book). Rhyme and regular strophes.
>
> Results: Poems in Mr. Eliot's *second* volume not contained in his first (Prufrock, *Egoist*, 1917), also 'H. S. Mauberley'.
>
> Divergence later.[7]

As we have seen, Pound's revolt against Amygism and his general dissatisfaction even with purer forms of Imagism dated back to the summer of 1914.[8] The development of his own art from Imagism to something more complex and ambitious cannot be easily summarized. We may find a clue to it in a passage from the essay which he wrote as the Preface to the *Poetical Works of Lionel Johnson*, published in 1915: 'We desire the words of poetry to follow the natural order. We would write nothing that we might not say actually in life – under emotion. Johnson's verse is full of inversions, but no one has written purer Imagisme than he has in the line

Clear lie the fields, and fade into blue air.

It has a beauty like the Chinese.'[9] This passage may help us to understand the process by which Pound insensibly moved away from the pure but limited world of Imagism into his new and fruitful admiration for Chinese art and for the values which it incarnated. It is significant that the Preface was published in the same year as *Cathay*, one of Pound's most enduring achievements.

The conservative opposition to Pound grew more bitter and vociferous as time went by. His *Catholic Anthology* (1915) aroused the strong disapproval of Arthur Waugh, who in *The Quarterly* (October 1916), bracketed Pound's anthology with the first two Georgian anthologies and described them as products of 'the new rebellion'. The legend perpetuated by Eliot and by Pound that Waugh stigmatized them as drunken helots is not strictly true.[10]

Hugh Selwyn Mauberley and *Homage to Sextus Propertius* finally

[7] Ezra Pound, 'Harold Monro', *The Criterion*, XI, 45, July 1932, p. 590. Reprinted in *Polite Essays*, 1937, p. 14.

[8] See above, pp. 33–4.

[9] Reprinted in *Literary Essays of Ezra Pound*, edited by T. S. Eliot, 1954, p. 362.

[10] See Pound's 'Drunken Helots and Mr. Eliot', *The Egoist*, IV, 5, June 1917, and T. S. Eliot, *The Use of Poetry*, 1933, p. 71. For Waugh's actual words, see below, p. 110.

destroyed Pound's reputation with academic conservatives, classical scholars and everybody over the past fifty years who wishes that the modern movement in poetry had never been born. The old tale that Pound's 'translation' of Propertius shows him to be a pretentious blunderer who is unable to construe a Latin text should by now be thoroughly discredited, since Donald Davie and J. P. Sullivan have finally demonstrated the absurdity of the charge.[11] Pound's letter to Felix E. Schelling, dated 8 July 1922, should in itself be enough to silence the most thickheaded of his detractors: 'No, I have not done a translation of Propertius. That fool in Chicago took the *Homage* for a translation, despite the mention of Wordsworth and the parodied line from Yeats. (As if, had one wanted to pretend to more Latin than one knew, it wouldn't have been perfectly easy to correct one's divergencies from a Bohn crib.)'[12] Yet, in the face of the evidence, commentators have continued to assert that Pound stumbles from howler to howler, and that his errors would put a fourth-former to shame. Even so robust and humane a scholar as Gilbert Highet, who acknowledges the great merits of Pound's version, does not wholly understand what Pound is setting out to do in his *Propertius.* Highet quotes as an example of Pound's careless ignorance his mistranslation of the phrase '*Cimbrorum . . . minas et benefacta Mari*', which Pound renders as 'Welsh mines and the profits Marius had out of them', instead of the correct version 'the challenge of the Cimbrians and the services of Marius'. Highet remarks that Pound should not have made so ludicrous a howler because he 'should have known that no poet would dream of writing a heroic work about coalmining dividends'.[13]

But this is precisely what Pound is trying to do. Or, to put the matter more accurately, Pound believes that the Roman Empire in the time of Propertius and the British Empire during the First World War had certain features in common, notably their militarism, their corruption, and the stink of usury. It seems improbable that Pound took *Cimbrorum minas* to mean 'Welsh mines': the chances are that he leaped at the chance to incorporate into his poem a reference to capitalism, and to reinforce the parallelism between Imperial Rome and the London of Lloyd George and Horatio Bottomley. Many good poets relish outrageous puns, especially such mistranslations as 'camp-followers' for *hors de combat*, 'in fragrant delight' for *in flagrante delicto*, and 'bum-fiddle' for *ars musica.* Pound may well have enjoyed his mistranslation for its own sake as well as for its poetic fruitfulness. All too many English critics nurtured on the Classics regard Pound as a brash

[11] Donald Davie, *Ezra Pound: Poet as Sculptor*, 1965, pp. 83–91; J. P. Sullivan, *Ezra Pound and Sextus Propertius*, 1965.
[12] *The Letters of Ezra Pound 1907–1941*, edited by D. D. Paige, 1951, p. 245.
[13] Gilbert Highet, *The Classical Tradition*, 1949, p. 70.

American loaded with false erudition, instead of as a superbly intelligent major poet. If they would put aside their prejudices they might recognize *Homage to Sextus Propertius* for what it is: a set of variations on a Roman theme.

Hugh Selwyn Mauberley is, for F. R. Leavis, Pound's masterpiece. It is certainly, except for the *Cantos*, his most elaborate and ambitious poem, whose complexities have been brilliantly elucidated by a variety of critics, notably by J. J. Espey.[14] To what extent the two sequences of which it is composed attain a true poetic unity is a matter for dispute: perhaps the most persuasive judgement is that pronounced by one of Pound's most ardent and intelligent champions:

> the two sequences are much more loosely jointed than they seem to be. Hardly anything is lost, and much is gained, if the poems are read one at a time, as so many poems by Pound, and if the Mauberley persona is dismissed as a distracting nuisance. *Hugh Selwyn Mauberley* thus falls to pieces, though the pieces are brilliant, intelligent always, and sometimes moving (for Gautier repeatedly enabled Pound to surpass himself).[15]

Since Pound left England for good soon after the end of the First World War one may reasonably argue that he severed his direct connection with the development of modern English verse. It is, indeed, tempting to break off these introductory comments at this juncture, thus evading the thorny paths of Pound's subsequent career. The temptation should, nevertheless, be resisted. After all, Pound began to work on the *Cantos* several years before he finally left England; moreover the themes developed and the attitudes adopted in this poem are almost all implicit in the verse and prose composed by Pound during his long residence in London. T. E. Hulme had prophesied that no poet would be able to 'synthesize the whole modern movement into a great epic'.[16] The *Cantos* may be read as an attempt to disprove Hulme's assertion.

Some critics, English and American, seem to resent what they regard as Pound's arrogance and presumptuous folly in undertaking such an enterprise. English writers, comfortably ensconced in their reassuring insularity, smile with condescending irony at Pound's translantic thoroughness in exploring the cultural history of Europe. His compatriots, on the contrary, are mortified at Pound's unAmerican abandonment of his grass-roots, his dissatisfaction with his native traditions. As long ago as 1920, William Carlos Williams attacked Pound on this very point: 'I do not overlook De Gourmont's plea for a meeting of the nations, but I do believe that when they meet Paris will be more than

[14] J. J. Espey, *Ezra Pound's Mauberley*, 1955.
[15] Donald Davie, *Ezra Pound: Poet as Sculptor*, 1965, p. 101.
[16] See above, p. 37.

slightly abashed to find parodies of the middle ages, Dante and Langue d'Oc foisted upon it as the best in United States poetry.'[17]

William Carlos Williams is moved primarily by moral and political disagreements with Pound. Yvor Winters, the most reputable and penetrating of Pound's antagonists, has concentrated his fire upon the weaknesses in Pound's aesthetics and upon Pound's own inadequacies. He shrewdly notes the merits and the limitations of Pound's chosen poetic form: 'Mr. Pound in his versions of Propertius, using the same form as in the *Cantos*, produces coherent comment on formulable themes, or does so part of the time. The change may be due to the genius of Propertius, but it is possible in Mr. Pound's form. The form, however, would not permit of any very rapid or compact reasoning.'[18] Even more serious, according to Winters, is Pound's inability to assimilate into an artistic unity the heterogeneous materials which he has ransacked: 'Pound's relationship to tradition is that of one who has abandoned its method and pillaged its details – he is merely a barbarian on the loose in a museum.'[19] For Pound is, in Winters's view, 'a sensibility without a mind, or with as little mind as is well possible'.[20]

Among the most perceptive judgements ever passed on Pound and on his *Cantos* a few pages of Yeats's *A Packet for Ezra Pound* and of his Introduction to *The Oxford Book of Modern Verse* must rank very high.[21] And there one might leave Pound and his achievement were it not for his behaviour during the war, his arrest, confinement and subsequent history.

It is impossible to deny the terrible folly of his conduct, to defend his intemperate abuse of the Jews or to pretend that his poetry is not flawed by his wild outbursts of obsessive rage. We should, however, think carefully before denouncing him for political wickedness, especially if we approve of the slaughter of citizens in such places as Hamburg, Dresden, Hiroshima, and Nagasaki. Pound supported Mussolini and must therefore bear some responsibility for the conduct of Mussolini's Nazi allies, just as those of us who opposed Hitler must bear some responsibility for the Anglo-American air-raids and for the behaviour of the communist *régimes* in Central and Eastern Europe. There is no evidence that Pound approved of, or even knew about, the torture and massacre of Jews and other prisoners in the Nazi camps. And Pound at least atoned for his pride and errors by undergoing humiliation and

[17] William Carlos Williams, *Kora in Hell*, 1920, p. 28. See Pound's good-humoured rejoinder in *The Letters of Ezra Pound 1907–1941*, edited by D. D. Paige, 1951, pp. 225–6.

[18] Yvor Winters, *Primitivism and Decadence*, 1937. Reprinted in *In Defense of Reason*, 1947, p. 93.

[19] Yvor Winters, *The Anatomy of Nonsense*, 1943. Reprinted in *In Defense of Reason*, 1947, p. 480.

[20] ibid., p. 496. [21] See below, pp. 65–6.

suffering in the Pisan cages, and by enduring the protracted pain of his incarceration in a mental hospital.

The Bollingen Award given to *The Pisan Cantos* was a tribute to Pound's most human poetry, in which he has bound together with consummate art so many diverse strands – autobiographical reflections, lyrical reverie, celebration of the visible world – and revealed himself as a master of such varied tones – humour, playfulness, dignity, tenderness, remorse, and affirmation. The deservedly famous passage about vanity is both the crown of his achievement and the only justification that he needs:

> But to have done instead of not doing
> this is not vanity
> To have, with decency, knocked
> That a Blunt should open
> To have gathered from the air a live tradition
> Or from a fine old eye the unconquered flame
> This is not vanity.
> Here error is all in the not done,
> All in the diffidence that faltered.[22]

CRITICISM

To say what this poet has not is not difficult; it will help to define him. He has no obvious grace, no sweetness, hardly any of the superficial good qualities of modern versifiers; not the smooth regularity of the Tennysonian tradition, nor the wavering, uncertain langour of the new, though there is more in his rhythms than is apparent at first through his carelessness of ordinary effects. He has not the current melancholy or resignation or unwillingness to live; nor the kind of feeling for nature that runs to minute description and decorative metaphor. He cannot be usefully compared with any living writers, though he has read Mr. Yeats. Browning and Whitman he respects, and he could easily burlesque Browning if he liked. He knows mediaeval poetry in the popular tongues, and Villon, and Ossian. He is equally fond of strict stanzas of many rhymes, of blank verse with many unfinished lines, of rhymeless or almost rhymeless lyrics, of Pindarics with or without rhymes. But these forms are not striking in themselves, since all are subdued to his spirit; in each he is true in his strength and weakness to himself, full of personality and with such power to express it that from the first to the last lines of most of his poems he holds us steadily in his own pure, grave, passionate world.

Edward Thomas, review of *Personae of Ezra Pound*, *The English Review*, June 1909, pp. 627–8.

[22] Canto LXXXI, *The Pisan Cantos*.

Poetry is a sort of inspired mathematics, which gives us equations, not for abstract figures, triangles, spheres, and the like, but equations for the human emotions.

Ezra Pound, *The Spirit of Romance*, 1910, p. 5.

CREDO

Rhythm. – I believe in an 'absolute rhythm', a rhythm, that is, in poetry which corresponds exactly to the emotion or shade of emotion to be expressed. A man's rhythm must be interpretative, it will be, therefore, in the end, his own, uncounterfeiting, uncounterfeitable.

Symbols. – I believe that the proper and perfect symbol is the natural object, that if a man uses 'symbols' he must so use them that their symbolic function does not obtrude; so that *a* sense, and the poetic quality of the passage, is not lost to those who do not understand the symbol as such, to whom, for instance, a hawk is a hawk.

Technique. – I believe in technique as the test of a man's sincerity; in law when it is ascertainable; in the trampling down of every convention that impedes or obscures the determination of the law, or the precise rendering of the impulse.

Form. – I think there is a 'fluid' as well as a 'solid' content, that some poems may have form as a tree has form, some as water poured into a vase. That most symmetrical forms have certain uses. That a vast number of subjects cannot be, precisely, and therefore not properly rendered in symmetrical forms.

Ezra Pound, 'Prolegomena', *The Poetry Review*, II, February 1913, p. 73. Reprinted in *Literary Essays of Ezra Pound*, edited by T. S. Eliot, 1954,[23] p. 9.

. . . my sentence of thirty years ago that technique is the test of a writer's sincerity. The writer or artist who is not intolerant of his own defects of technique is a smear.

But the aim of technique is that it establish the totality of the whole.

Ezra Pound, *Guide to Kulchur*, 1938, p. 90.

No good poetry is ever written in a manner twenty years old, for to write in such a manner shows conclusively that the writer thinks from books, convention and *cliché*, and not from life, yet a man feeling the divorce of life and his art may naturally try to resurrect a forgotten mode if he finds in that mode some leaven, or if he thinks he sees in

[23] Hereafter referred to as *Literary Essays*.

it some element lacking in contemporary art which might unite that art again to its sustenance, life.

In the art of Daniel and Cavalcanti, I have seen that precision which I miss in the Victorians, that explicit rendering, be it of external nature, or of emotion. Their testimony is of the eyewitness, their symptoms are first hand.

Ezra Pound, 'Prolegomena', *The Poetry Review*, II, February 1913, p. 75.
Reprinted in *Literary Essays*, p. 11.

As to Twentieth century poetry, and the poetry which I expect to see written during the next decade or so, it will, I think, move against poppy-cock, it will be harder and saner, it will be what Mr. Hewlett calls 'nearer the bone'. It will be as much like granite as it can be, its force will lie in its truth, its interpretative power (of course, poetic force does always rest there); I mean it will not try to seem forcible by rhetorical din, and luxurious riot. We will have fewer painted adjectives impeding the shock and stroke of it. At least for myself, I want it so, austere, direct, free from emotional slither.

Ezra Pound, ibid.
Reprinted in *Literary Essays*, p. 12.

Poetry is a centaur. The thinking, word-arranging, clarifying faculty must move and leap with the energizing, sentient, musical faculties.

I suppose what, in the long run, makes the poet is a sort of persistence of the emotional nature, and, joined with this, a peculiar sort of control...

I think this orderliness in the greatest poetic passages, this quiet statement that partakes of the nature of prose and is yet floated and tossed in the emotional surges, is perhaps as true a test [of genius] as that mentioned by [Aristotle].

Ezra Pound, 'The Serious Artist', *The New Freewoman*, I, 10, 1 November 1913, pp. 194–5.
Reprinted in *Literary Essays*, pp. 51–4.

If Mr. Pound can find a foreign title to a poem, he will do so. Queer exotic hybridity! It would almost be true to say, also, that if Mr. Pound can translate a poem, he will do so, rather than make one . . . is Mr. Pound the instrument, trumpeting the authentic note, or is he the wind in the instrument? . . . Whichever way you look at it, the note is the same, the true note of poetry...

F. S. F[lint], review of *Canzoni*, by Ezra Pound.
The Poetry Review, I, January 1912, pp. 28–9.

He [Pound] is full of the middle ages and helps me to get back to the definite and the concrete away from modern abstractions. To talk over a poem with him is like getting you to put a sentence into dialect. All becomes clear and natural. Yet in his own work he is very uncertain, often very bad though very interesting sometimes. He spoils himself by too many experiments and has more sound principles than taste.

W. B. Yeats, Letter to Lady Gregory, 3 January 1913.
A. Norman Jeffares, *W. B. Yeats: Man and Poet*, 1949, p. 167.

If these are original verses, then Mr. Pound is the greatest poet of this day . . . The poems in *Cathay* are things of supreme beauty. What poetry should be, that they are . . . In a sense they only back up a theory and practice of poetry that is already old – the theory that poetry consists in so rendering concrete objects that the emotions produced by the objects shall arise in the reader – and not in writing about the emotions themselves.

Ford Madox Ford, 'From China to Peru', *Outlook*, XXV, 19 June 1915, pp. 800–1.
Reprinted in David Don Harvey, *Ford Madox Ford 1873–1939: A Bibliography of Works and Criticism*, 1962, p. 207.

Poetry is a composition of words set to music. Most other definitions of it are indefensible, or metaphysical. The proportion or quality of the music may, and does, vary; but poetry withers and 'dries out' when it leaves music, or at least an imagined music, too far behind it. The horrors of modern 'readings of poetry' are due to oratorical recitation. Poetry must be read as music and not as oratory. I do not mean that the words should be jumbled together and made indistinct and unrecognizable in a sort of onomatopaeic paste. I have found few save musicians who pay the least attention to the poet's own music. They are often, I admit, uncritical of his verbal excellence or deficit, ignorant of his 'literary' value or bathos. But the literary qualities are not the whole of our art . . .

It is too late to prevent vers libre. But, conceivably, one might improve it, and one might stop at least a little of the idiotic and narrow discussion based on an ignorance of music. Bigoted attack, born of this ignorance of the tradition of music, was what we had to live through.

Ezra Pound, 'Vers Libre and Arnold Dolmetsch', *The Egoist*, IV, 6, July 1917, pp. 90–1.
Reprinted in *Literary Essays*, p. 437.

. . . there are three 'kinds of poetry': MELOPŒIA, wherein the words are charged over and above their plain meaning, with some musical property, which directs the bearing or trend of that meaning.

PHANOPŒIA, which is a casting of images upon the visual imagination.

LOGOPŒIA, 'the dance of the intellect among words', that is to say, it employs words not only for their direct meaning, but it takes count in a special way of habits of usage, of the context we *expect* to find with the word, its usual concomitants, of its known acceptances, and of ironical play. It holds the aesthetic content which is peculiarly the domain of verbal manifestation, and cannot possibly be contained in plastic or in music. It is the latest come, and perhaps most tricky and undependable mode.

Ezra Pound, 'How to Read', *New York Herald Tribune Books*, V, 17, 18, 19; 13 January, 20 January, 27 January, 1929.
Reprinted in *Literary Essays*, p. 25.

Such a relation [as envisaged by Pound] between poetry and music is very different from what is called the 'music' of Shelley or Swinburne, a music often nearer to rhetoric (or the art of the orator) than to the instrument. For poetry to approach the condition of music (Pound quotes approvingly the dictum of Pater) it is not necessary that poetry should be destitute of meaning. Instead of slightly veiled and resonant abstractions, like

Time with a gift of tears,
Grief with a glass that ran –

of Swinburne, or the mossiness of Mallarmé, Pound's verse is always definite and concrete, because he has always a definite emotion behind it . . .

Words are perhaps the hardest of all material of art: for they must be used to express both visual beauty and beauty of sound, as well as communicating a grammatical statement. It would be interesting to compare Pound's use of images with Mallarmé's; I think it will be found that the former's, by the contrast, will appear always sharp in outline, even if arbitrary and not photographic . . .

The freedom of Pound's verse is rather a state of tension due to constant opposition between free and strict. There are not, as a matter of fact, two kinds of verse, the strict and the free; there is only a mastery which comes of being so well trained that form is an instinct and can be adapted to the particular purpose in hand.

T. S. Eliot, *Ezra Pound: His Metric and Poetry*, 1917, pp. 13–15.

[This essay, which is reprinted in *To Criticize the Critic* (1965), pp. 162–82, was originally published anonymously, because, as Eliot later explained, 'Ezra was then known only to a few and I was so completely unknown that it seemed more decent that the pamphlet should appear anonymously'. *The Cantos of Ezra Pound: Some Testimonies* (1933), p. 16.]

Pound has never been at home in twentieth-century Europe. He can only get life out of books – from the life about him, he can obtain nothing. Something prompts him, therefore, to mock the world he sees, because he hates it; and when he mocks, the vividness utterly abandons him. The smile becomes a leer, the attitude a pose, the dependence on other men's work assumes the dimensions of intolerable pedantry, Technically Pound's later work is even more interesting than his earlier. The *vers libre* experiments of *Ripostes* and *Cathay*, the free, broken blank verse of *Near Perigord* and *Three Cantos*, are fascinating things to study. But except where he follows faithfully some other work, as in *Cathay*, the poems in these last two volumes are almost valueless. They are 'a broken bundle of mirrors', the patchwork and debris of a mind which has never quite been able to find the living beauty it set out to seek. As a pioneer, as a treader in unbroken paths, America can afford to salute the earlier, as it is forced to reject the later Pound; and a whole host of modern American poets could never have done the work they are doing without the inspiration of his influence.

F. S. Flint, 'Some Contemporary American Poets', *The Chapbook*, II, ii, May 1920, p. 25.

One is a harder judge of a friend's work than of a stranger's because one knows his powers so well that his faults seem perversity, or we do not know his powers and think he should go our way and not his, and then all in a moment we see his work as a whole and judge as with the eyes of a stranger. In this book just published in America are all his poems except those Twenty-Seven Cantos which keep me procrastinating, and though I had read it all in the little books I had never understood until now that the translations from Chinese, from Latin, from Provencal, are as much a part of his original work, as much chosen as to theme, as much characterized as to style, as the vituperation, the railing, which I had hated but which now seem a necessary balance. He is not trying to create forms because he believes, like so many of his contemporaries, that old forms are dead, so much as a new style, a new man. Again and again he breaks the metrical form which the work seemed to require, or which, where he is translating, it once had or interjects some anachronism, as when he makes Propertius talk of an old Wordsworthian, that he may pull it back not into himself but into this hard, shining, fastidious modern man, who has no existence, who can never have existence, except to the readers of his poetry . . . Synge once said to me, 'All our modern poetry is the poetry of the lyrical boy', but here, in spite of all faults and flaws – sometimes that exasperation is but nerves – is the grown man, in 'Cathay' his passion and self-possession, in 'Homage to Sextus Propertius' his self-abandonment that recovers itself in mockery, everywhere his masterful curiosity.

W. B. Yeats, *A Packet for Ezra Pound*, 1929, pp. 7–9.
[Most of this book is reprinted in *A Vision* (1937), but this passage is omitted.]

When I consider his work as a whole I find more style than form; at moments more style, more deliberate nobility and the means to convey it than in any contemporary poet known to me, but it is constantly interrupted, broken, twisted into nothing by its direct opposite, nervous obsession, nightmare, stammering confusion; he is an economist, poet, politician, raging at malignants with inexplicable characters and motives, grotesque figures out of a child's book of beasts. This loss of self-control, common among uneducated revolutionists, is rare – Shelley had it in some degree – among men of Ezra Pound's culture and erudition. Style and its opposite can alternate, but form must be full, sphere-like, single. Even where there is no interruption he is often content, if certain verses and lines have style, to leave unbridged transitions, unexplained ejaculations, that make his meaning unintelligible. He has great influence, more perhaps than any contemporary except Eliot, is probably the source of that lack of form and consequent obscurity which is the main defect of Auden, Day Lewis, and their school, a school which, as will presently be seen, I greatly admire. Even where the style is sustained throughout one gets an impression, especially when he is writing in *vers libre*, that he has not got all the wine into the bowl, that he is a brilliant improvisator translating at sight from an unknown Greek masterpiece.

W. B. Yeats, Introduction to *The Oxford Book of Modern Verse*, 1936, pp. xxv–xxvi.

POEMS

Lament of the Frontier Guard

By the North Gate, the wind blows full of sand,
Lonely from the beginning of time until now!
Trees fall, the grass goes yellow with autumn.
I climb the towers and towers to watch out the barbarous land:
Desolate castle, the sky, the wide desert.
There is no wall left to this village.
Bones white with a thousand frosts,
High heaps, covered with trees and grass;
Who brought this to pass?
Who has brought the flaming imperial anger?
Who has brought the army with drums and with kettle-drums?
Barbarous kings.
A gracious spring, turned to blood-ravenous autumn,
A turmoil of wars-men, spread over the middle kingdom,
Three hundred and sixty thousand,
And sorrow, sorrow like rain.
Sorrow to go, and sorrow, sorrow returning.

Desolate, desolate fields,
And no children of warfare upon them,
  No longer the men for offence and defence.
Ah, how shall you know the dreary sorrow at the North Gate,
With Rihoku's name forgotten,
And we guardsmen fed to the tigers.

By Rihaku

from *Hugh Selwyn Mauberley*

IV

These fought in any case,
and some believing,
  pro domo, in any case . . .

Some quick to arm,
some for adventure,
some for fear of weakness,
some from fear of censure,
some for love of slaughter, in imagination,
learning later . . .
some in fear, learning love of slaughter;

Died some, pro patria,
  non 'dulce' non 'et decor' . . .
walked eye-deep in hell
believing in old men's lies, then unbelieving
came home, home to a lie,
home to many deceits,
home to old lies and new infamy;
usury age-old and age thick
and liars in public places.

Daring as never before, wastage as never before.
Young blood and high blood,
fair cheeks, and fine bodies;

fortitude as never before

frankness as never before,
disillusions as never told in the old days,
hysterias, trench confessions,
laughter out of dead bellies.

from *Homage to Sextus Propertius*

VI

When, when and whenever death closes our eyelids,
Moving naked over Acheron
Upon the one raft, victor and conquered together,
Marius and Jugurtha together, one tangle of shadows.

Caesar plots against India,
Tigris and Euphrates shall, from now on, flow at his bidding,
Tibet shall be full of Roman policemen,
The Parthians shall get used to our statuary
        and acquire a Roman religion;
One raft on the veiled flood of Acheron,
   Marius and Jugurtha together.

Nor at my funeral either will there be any long trail,
      bearing ancestral lares and images;
No trumpets filled with my emptiness,
Nor shall it be on an Atalic bed;
   The perfumed cloths shall be absent.
A small plebeian procession.
   Enough, enough and in plenty
There will be three books at my obsequies
Which I take, my not unworthy gift, to Persephone.

You will follow the bare scarified breast
Nor will you be weary of calling my name, nor too weary
      To place the last kiss on my lips
When the Syrian onyx is broken.

        'He who is now vacant dust
        'Was once the slave of one passion:'
Give that much inscription
        'Death why tardily come?'

You, sometimes, will lament a lost friend,
      For it is a custom:
This care for past men,

Since Adonis was gored in Idalia, and the Cytharean
Ran crying with out-spread hair,
      In vain, you call back the shade,
In vain, Cynthia. Vain call to unanswering shadow,
      Small talk comes from small bones.

SELECT BIBLIOGRAPHY

Works by Ezra Pound

Personae: Collected Shorter Poems, New York, 1949; London, 1952.

The Letters of Ezra Pound 1907–1941, edited by D. D. Paige, New York, 1950; London, 1951.

The Translations of Ezra Pound, with an Introduction by Hugh Kenner, London, 1953.

Literary Essays of Ezra Pound, edited with an Introduction by T. S. Eliot, Norfolk (Connecticut) and London, 1954.

ABC of Reading, London, 1934.

Make it New, London, 1934.

Polite Essays, London, 1937.

Guide to Kulchur, London, 1938.

Some Biographical and Critical Studies

Davie, Donald, *Ezra Pound: Poet as Sculptor*, London, 1965.

Dekker, George, *Sailing after Knowledge*, London, 1963.

Eliot, T. S., *Ezra Pound: His Metric and Poetry*, New York, 1917; reprinted in *To Criticize the Critic*, London, 1965.

Espey, John J., *Ezra Pound's Mauberley: a Study in Composition*, Berkeley and London, 1955.

Fraser, G. S., *Ezra Pound*, Edinburgh, 1960.

Hutchins, Patricia, *Ezra Pound's Kensington*, London, 1965.

Kenner, Hugh, *The Poetry of Ezra Pound*, Norfolk (Connecticut) and London, 1951.

Leavis, F. R., *New Bearings in English Poetry*, London, 1932; 2nd ed., 1950. Contains an important essay on Pound.

Norman, Charles, *Ezra Pound*, New York, 1960.

Rosenthal, M. L., *A Primer of Ezra Pound*, New York, 1960.

Stock, Noel, *Poet in Exile: Ezra Pound*, Manchester, 1964.

Sullivan, J. P., *Ezra Pound and Sextus Propertius*, London, 1965.

5

T. S. ELIOT

INTRODUCTION

Although it is far too early for a frank and definitive biography of T. S. Eliot to be written, the outlines of his life and of his development as an artist are already familiar and well documented. His early years in St. Louis, Missouri, and the blossoming of his intellectual powers at Harvard have been chronicled by Herbert Howarth in his *Notes on Some Figures Behind T. S. Eliot* (1965). It seems likely that he inherited from his mother his strong moral sense, his deep, unspectacular piety and his feeling for the arts, particularly for the arts of poetry and drama. Yet there were few indications in his early days that he might transform himself into a major poet. His youthful contributions to *The Harvard Advocate* were accomplished examples of poetic *pastiche* which proved only that their author combined literary knowledge with sensibility in the handling of words and of traditional poetic forms.

It is never easy to trace with any certainty the course of events which have influenced a poet's mind; and Eliot himself has suggested that the process is more complex than is often supposed: 'It is probable that men ripen best through experiences which are at once sensuous and intellectual; certainly many men will admit that their keenest ideas have come to them with the quality of sense-perception; and that their keenest sensuous experience has been "as if the body thought".'[1] In the face of such a warning it may be rash to attribute too much importance to Eliot's reading of a book; yet the influence of Arthur Symons's *The Symbolist Movement in Literature* (1899) may reasonably be regarded as decisive in shaping Eliot's poetic development. A short passage from this work anticipates the course that the new poetry was to follow and summarizes, with prophetic insight, the majestic achievement of Eliot himself:

> Here then, in this revolt against exteriority, against rhetoric, against a materialistic tradition; in this endeavour to disengage the ultimate essence, the soul, of whatever exists and can be realized by the consciousness; in this dutiful waiting upon every symbol by which the soul of things may be made visible; literature, bowed down by so many burdens, may at last attain liberty, and its authentic speech. In attaining this liberty, it accepts a

[1] T. S. Eliot, 'A Sceptical Patrician', review of *The Education of Henry Adams* in *The Athenaeum*, 4647, 23 May 1919, pp. 361–2.

heavier burden; for in speaking to us so intimately, so solemnly, as only religion has hitherto spoken to us, it becomes itself a kind of religion, with all the duties and responsibilities of the sacred ritual.[2]

Eliot read Symons in 1908 and in the Christmas of that year placed an order for the poems of Laforgue, whom Symons had praised as a pioneer of modern sensibility. Up to that date Eliot's poetic models were the writers of graceful early-seventeenth-century lyrics: he has not chosen to preserve any specimens of this apprentice-work in his *Collected Poems*, but he has retained an exercise in the Laforguian mode, 'Conversation Galante', which dates from 1909 and is the earliest poem in the collection.

One thinks of Eliot as an austere sage, an aged eagle, brooding on mystical experience, an ascetic moralist who constantly denied the claims of the flesh. The evidence that we possess about Eliot as a young man suggests that he was delightfully gay and that he was abundantly endowed with the gift of sensuous enjoyment. One of Eliot's oldest friends, Conrad Aiken, has recalled their early days together, and has tantalizingly referred to an unpublished epic about 'that singular and sterling character known as King Bolo, not to mention King Bolo's Queen, "that airy fairy hairy-'un, who led the dance on Golders Green with Cardinal Bessarion".'[3]

Eliot's meeting with Ezra Pound on 22 September 1914 was of decisive importance. It was Pound who first recognized Eliot's poetic genius; it was Pound who brought him to the notice of literary circles in Britain and in the United States; it was Pound who secured him a regular platform in *The Egoist*. Some of Eliot's poems written several years before were printed, thanks to Pound, in *Blast* (July 1915), in Pound's *Catholic Anthology* (1915) and in several numbers of *Poetry* during that same year. One of the poems to appear in *Poetry* was 'Prufrock', which Aiken had brought to England in 1914 and handed over to Pound after failing to persuade English editors of its merits. Even Harold Monro, one of the most intelligent and receptive of contemporary poetry-lovers, seems at first not to have appreciated the revolutionary quality of 'Prufrock'. According to Aiken, 'Monro – though ten years later he was a convert, if this side idolatry – thought Prufrock bordered on insanity.'[4] Monro must speedily have overcome his initial hostility to the poem, for we find Ezra Pound writing to Harriet Monroe in a letter dated 25 September 1915 that Monro had discovered 'Prufrock' on his unaided

[2] Introduction, p. 10.

[3] Conrad Aiken, 'King Bolo and Others', *T. S. Eliot: A Symposium*, compiled by Richard Marsh and Tambimuttu, 1948, p. 22. See also *The Letters of Wyndham Lewis*, edited by W. K. Rose, 1963, p. 66 for references to other ribald poems.

[4] Conrad Aiken, 'King Bolo and Others', *T. S. Eliot: a Symposium*, compiled by Richard Marsh and Tambimuttu, 1948, p. 22.

own'.[5] The poem reached a much wider audience two years after its original appearance in *Poetry*, since in June 1917 the Egoist Press published *Prufrock and Other Observations*, yet even in 1917 Eliot was so little known that he judged it wiser to publish anonymously his short book on Pound.[6]

Between 1917 and 1922 Eliot's reputation among the *cognoscenti* was enhanced by the publication of *Poems* (1920) and by a series of critical essays and reviews contributed to a variety of periodicals, mainly to *The Egoist, The Times Literary Supplement*, and *The Athenaeum.* There is a good case for regarding 1922 as being no less decisive a date in the history of English letters than 1798. For in 1922 Eliot achieved a double triumph: the appearance of *The Waste Land* marked the beginning of Eliot's long reign as the major poetic influence of his time; and his editorship of *The Criterion*, which he assumed in that same year, confirmed his dominating position as poet and critic, an eminence gained in the space of seven years. The old literary order was rapidly disintegrating. A. E. Housman published his *Last Poems* in 1922 and kept for the rest of his life the vow of silence implied by the title. Edward Marsh, tactful as ever, decided that the fifth of his Georgian anthologies also published in 1922 would be the last of the series.

We must, however, beware of exaggerating the extent of Eliot's triumph. George Watson's summary of Eliot's achievement is incontestable, so far as it goes:

> Eliot's success was not only profoundly merited, but was total and instantaneous within the terms it had set itself; the capture of young intellectuals of creative energy in England and the United States in the 1920s. That capture involved, in a very few years, the capture of the seats of literary power, of the London literary journals and of influential younger teachers of literature in the universities.[7]

But it does not go far enough. From the early 1920s until the late 1930s Eliot's work was greeted with incomprehension and even with hostile abuse by representative spokesmen of the middlebrow public, and of the conservative men who occupied leading positions in influential academic and literary circles. As late as 1934, Ivor Brown, who as a dramatic critic, and as an editor of *The Observer*, had been widely read by a literate audience, could refer to *The Waste Land* as 'balderdash', and as 'pretentious bungling with the English language'.[8] J. B. Priestley,

[5] *The Letters of Ezra Pound 1907–1941*, edited by D. D. Paige, 1951, p. 108.

[6] In 1914 or 1915 Eliot had described Pound's verse as 'touchingly incompetent'. See Conrad Aiken, op. cit., p. 23.

[7] George Watson, 'The Triumph of T. S. Eliot', *The Critical Quarterly*, VII, 4, 1965, p. 337; and subsequent correspondence in *The Critical Quarterly*, VIII, 2, 1966, pp. 180–2.

[8] Ivor Brown, *I Commit to the Flames*, 1934, p. 10.

in the same decade, is reported as saying that Eliot was 'donnish, pedantic, cold', and that 'it would have been better for contemporary English literature if Eliot had stayed in Louisville, or wherever he came from'.[9] It was the production of *Murder in the Cathedral* at Canterbury, and not his poetic genius, that made Eliot acceptable to the official and ecclesiastical hierarchy of Britain.

Nor is it true to say that *The Waste Land* was instantly recognized as a masterpiece by enlightened critical opinion. George Watson quotes no unreservedly favourable estimate of that poem earlier than the 1926 edition of I. A. Richards's *Principles of Literary Criticism*. Much more characteristic of the general reaction, even among readers well disposed towards Eliot, was the judgement of *The Times Literary Supplement*, 20 September 1923: 'Here is a poet capable of a style more refined than that of any of his generation, parodying without taste or skill . . . Here is a writer to whom originality is almost an inspiration borrowing the greater number of his best lines, creating hardly any himself.' In two remarkable articles entitled 'The Classical Tradition', printed in *The Adelphi*, III, 9 and 10, in February and March 1926, John Middleton Murry argued that nobody in fifty, or even in ten, years' time would take the trouble to read *The Waste Land*, unless there should occur some revolutionary transformation in Eliot, 'some liberation into a real spontaneity'. *The Hollow Men* was a proof that such a miracle would not take place. The most intelligent response to the poem in England came from Harold Monro, and even he hedged his praise with a cautious qualification: 'The Waste Land seems to me as near to Poetry as our generation is at present capable of reaching . . . The Waste Land is one metaphor with a multiplicity of interpretations.'[10]

Eliot endured abuse and accepted praise with a slightly ironical courtesy. There is no evidence that he was deflected from his course or profoundly affected by either his assailants or his adulators. His integrity, constancy of purpose, and fidelity to his inner vision remained unshaken throughout the fifty years of his life in England. Nor did his conversion to Anglo-Catholicism entail a profound change in his mode of thought or in the temper of his mind. Certain of his convictions grew stronger, certain of his beliefs assumed a new significance, but in essence the Eliot of the late 1920s remained what he had been ten years earlier.

The earliest essays printed in *Selected Essays* date from 1919, although even in the third edition of this book (1951), which corrects the mis-

[9] I. Donnelly, *The Joyous Pilgrimage*, 1935, p. 133.

[10] Harold Monro, 'Notes for a Study of The Waste Land', *The Chapbook*, 34, February 1923, pp. 21–24. Conrad Aiken's 'An Anatomy of Melancholy', printed in *The New Republic*, 7 February 1923, was the earliest American review of the poem which recognized its nature and significance. See *T. S. Eliot: the Man and his Work*, edited by Allen Tate, 1967, pp. 194–202.

dating of several essays, the date of 'Tradition and the Individual Talent' (1919) is still given as 1917. Eliot had, however, begun to contribute articles and reviews to *The Egoist* in 1917; and it is fascinating to observe in these very early writings the characteristics of his later criticism. We find him already occupied in that year with speculations about the nature of tradition: 'All the ideas, beliefs, modes of feeling and behaviour which we have not time or inclination to investigate for ourselves we take second-hand and sometimes call tradition.'[11] The typical note of mocking asperity is present in that sentence, and in the footnote: 'For an authoritative condemnation of theories attaching extreme importance to tradition as a criterion of truth, see Pope Gregory XVI's encyclical *Singularis nos* (July 15, 1834), and the Vatican Council canon of 1870, *Si quis dixerit . . . Anathema sit.*' His later scepticism about progress and about the desirability of social change is anticipated in his review of Ezra Pound's selection from the letters of J. B. Yeats, in which Eliot refers to 'the present time when the dust of Social Reconstruction, Empire Resources Development and other Reform is in our eyes, when England seems drifting towards Americanization'.[12]

Equally characteristic are his comments on the poet's task and on the means whereby he can best perform it. In October 1917 and in the following month Eliot contributed to *The Egoist* some 'Reflections on Contemporary Poetry'. He begins by quoting Hayim Fineman's praise of John Davidson for having erected 'a new dwelling place for the imagination on the basis of things that are real to modern man'. Eliot's comment is in his best manner: 'This is really Davidson's cardinal sin as well as his virtue; he too often is interested in the dwelling-place rather than the tenant, who is the same through all ages.'[13] Again, in his remark about the possibility of innovations, we can detect the scepticism, the urbanity, the caution and the acuteness which make his finest criticism so enjoyable and salutary: 'In literature especially the innovations which we can consciously and collectively aim to introduce are few, and mostly technical. The main thing is to be quite certain what they are.'[14]

Eliot's critical writings from 1917 onwards form a singularly coherent whole, and are the best available introduction to his poetry. He himself has recognized the relation between his verse and his criticism:

> The best of my *literary* criticism – apart from a few notorious phrases which have had a truly embarrassing success in the world – consists of essays on poets and poetic dramatists who had influenced me. It is a by-product of my private poetry-workshop; or a prolongation of the thinking that went into the formation of my own verse.[15]

11 'Reflections on Contemporary Poetry', *The Egoist*, IV, 10, November 1917, p. 151.
12 *The Egoist*, IV, 6, July 1917, p. 89. 13 *The Egoist*, IV, 9, October 1917, p. 134.
14 *The Egoist*, IV, 10, November 1917, p. 151.
15 'The Frontiers of Criticism', *On Poetry and Poets*, 1957, p. 106.

Conversely, his criticism provides extremely valuable clues about the nature of his poetry and about the specific influences that formed his imagination and moulded his style. Eliot often expresses a polite scepticism about critical appraisal of his poetry, nowhere more memorably and devastatingly than in a passage written in 1927:

> I admit that my own experience, as a minor poet, may have jaundiced my outlook; that I am used to having cosmic significances, which I never suspected, extracted from my work (such as it is) by enthusiastic persons at a distance; and to being informed that something which I meant seriously is *vers de société*; and to having my personal biography reconstructed from passages which I got out of books, or which I invented out of nothing because they sounded well; and to having my biography invariably ignored in what I did write from personal experience.[16]

By limiting ourselves to Eliot's own statements about his life and the development of his art we are minimizing the dangers of misinterpreting the significance of his work, although for any full understanding of his achievement we must supplement from other sources the few revelations that he chooses to make public.

There seems little doubt that the experiences of childhood play a vital part in the formation of a poet's imaginative life. Characteristically, Eliot has told us very little about his childhood, but he has made it quite clear that the landscapes of his early days left an ineffaceable mark upon him:

> I feel there is something in having passed one's childhood beside the big river, which is incommunicable to those who have not. Of course my people were Northerners and New Englanders, and of course I have spent many years out of America altogether; but Missouri and Mississippi have made a deeper impression on me than any other part of the world.[17]

He has also reminded us of the second landscape which meant so much to him in childhood:

> In New England I missed the long dark river, the ailanthus tree, the flaming cardinal birds, the high limestone buffs where we searched for fossil shellfish; in Missouri I missed the fir trees, the bay and goldenrod, the song-sparrows, the red granite and the blue sea of Massachusetts.[18]

Some of the most numinous passages in *Four Quartets* derive their poignancy and strength from Eliot's ability to recapture and to evoke the wonder and the awe that he had experienced as a child in New England and in the South.

Yet if, like so many Romantic poets, Eliot had been able to derive

[16] 'Shakespeare and the Stoicism of Seneca', *Selected Essays*, 1951, p. 127.

[17] Communication to a St. Louis paper in 1930. Quoted by F. O. Matthiessen, *The Achievement of T. S. Eliot*, 1958, p. 186.

[18] Preface to Edgar Ansel Mowrer, *This American World*, 1928. Quoted by George Williamson, *A Reader's Guide to T. S. Eliot*, 1955, pp. 207–8.

emotional power only from subjective brooding upon his childhood, he would not have become a major poet. It is his ability to fuse into poetry a multitude of experiences and a wealth of intellectual speculation that gives his verse such range and authority. Few poets of his stature have so deliberately studied their art, and set out to write poetry with such calculation and assurance. We know from his own account the starting-point from which he set out: 'the form in which I began to write, in 1908 or 1909, was directly drawn from the study of Laforgue together with the later Elizabethan drama'.[19] We know also that he was deeply indebted in his later years to Dante, and that another formative influence was Baudelaire. Indeed, Eliot acknowledges his debt to the whole tradition of French Symbolism, and in so doing consciously allies himself with the masters of modern European poetry:

> in the second half of the nineteenth century the greatest contribution to European poetry was certainly made in France. I refer to the tradition which starts with Baudelaire and culminates in Valéry. I venture to say that without this French tradition the work of three poets in other languages – and three very different from each other – I refer to W. B. Yeats, to Rainer Maria Rilke and, if I may, to myself, would hardly be conceivable.[20]

One other name must be added to the list of those who exercised a decisive influence on Eliot's poetry. Ezra Pound did not merely launch Eliot on his career as a reviewer and essayist and badger editors into printing his early verse; he also subjected that verse to a radical and detailed criticism. Eliot allowed Pound to perform drastic critical surgery on *The Waste Land*, the exact nature of which it will soon be possible to discuss in detail, since in the autumn of 1968 it was announced that the first draft of this poem, long believed to have been lost or destroyed, had been lying in the New York Public Library for many years among the papers of John Quinn. Eliot's awareness of his debt to Pound is unequivocally acknowledged in his review of the American edition of Pound's collected poems published in 1928 under the title *Personae*: 'I have in recent years cursed Mr. Pound often enough; for I am never sure that I can call my verse my own; just when I am most pleased with myself, I find that I have caught up some echo from a verse of Pound's.'[22]

To explain precisely how a poet turns his diverse experiences into poetry is beyond the resource of any critic. We cannot tell how Eliot's childhood experiences, his first marriage, and his study of Laforgue, Baudelaire, and Dante gave *The Waste Land* and *Four Quartets* their

[19] T. S. Eliot, Introduction to *Ezra Pound: Selected Poems*, 1928, p. viii.
[20] *Notes towards the Definition of Culture*, 1948, p. 112.
[21] See T. S. Eliot, Introduction to *Ezra Pound: Selected Poems*, 1928, p. xxi.
[22] T. S. Eliot, 'Isolated Superiority', *The Dial*, LXXXIV, 1, January 1928, pp. 4–7. Quoted by F. R. Leavis, *New Bearings in English Poetry*, 1932, p. 133.

peculiar structure and quality. Even Eliot's account of the way in which 'a poet's work may proceed along two lines on an imaginary graph' must not, he tells us, be applied too literally. All we can say is that, at times, the two lines may converge to produce a masterpiece: 'That is to say, an accumulation of experience has crystallised to form material of art, and years of work in technique have prepared an adequate medium; and something results in which medium and material, form and content, are indistinguishable.'[23]

Some commentators have delved so deep for influences on Eliot's poetry, and have discovered or fabricated such recondite significances in apparently simple phrases, that the poetry has been buried alive beneath a mound of scholarship. The best introduction to Eliot's verse is F. O. Matthiessen's *The Achievement of T. S. Eliot*, which was first published in 1935. Matthiessen constantly stresses the fact that the difficulties of Eliot's poems are no greater and no less than those presented by Milton's 'Lycidas'. The greater our knowledge of the allusions in the verse of these two masters, the more refined and profound will be the pleasure and understanding which they yield; but the prime need is to listen receptively to the melodic pattern of the lines before attempting to decipher their prose meaning, or to search for something which is not there:

> I am also thankful that my first introduction to Eliot's poetry came through my friends, the poets Phelps Putnam and Maxwell Evarts Foster, who made me listen to it read aloud, thus enabling me to feel from the outset its lyric sound and movement, instead of letting me begin by losing the poetry in a tortuous effort to find a logical pattern in its unfamiliar structure.[24]

Eliot himself always emphasizes the value of what he calls 'the auditory imagination'.[25] In his review of Ezra Pound's *Personae* he observes that 'a man who devises new rhythms is a man who extends and refines our sensibility; and that is not merely a matter of "technique"'. Eliot's sensitivity to the importance of rhythm leads him to see connections between poetry and our environment which would not be apparent to most readers: 'perhaps the conditions of modern life (think how large a part is now played in our sensory life by the internal combustion engine!) have altered our perception of rhythms'.[26]

Good critics recognized from the start that Eliot's verse has more affinities with musical compositions than with prose discourse.[27] It is

23 T. S. Eliot, Introduction to *Ezra Pound: Selected Poems*, 1928, p. xx.

24 F. O. Matthiessen, *The Achievement of T. S. Eliot*, 1958, p. xv.

25 See below, pp. 84–5.

26 T. S. Eliot, Introduction to *Savonorola*, 1926, a dramatic poem by Eliot's mother, Charlotte Eliot.

27 See I. A. Richards, *Principles of Literary Criticism*, 1926, pp. 289–90, and F. R. Leavis, *New Bearings in English Poetry*, 1932, p. 103.

relevant to our understanding of *The Waste Land* to know that in the months before the composition of this poem Eliot had immersed himself in Wagner's *Ring*. It is probable that *Four Quartets* owes something to the string quartets of Beethoven and of Bartok. I doubt whether one can correlate precisely the music and the poems, although one critic suggests that *Four Quartets* is indebted structurally to Bartok's Sixth Quartet,[28] whereas another critic, with equal confidence, announces that the key to the sequence is Beethoven's Quartet in A minor, op. 132.[29] All we can be sure of is that the music and the poetry belong to the same order of genius and that they are alike in drawing strength and poignancy from an acceptance of suffering.

An anthology of critical assaults on Eliot from 1915 onwards would make instructive reading. Ignoring the almost incoherent abuse with which frothing conservative men of letters saluted his early verse, one may discern two lines of attack upon his achievement – reasoned criticism of Eliot's literary theory and poetic practice; and criticism, sometimes reasoned, sometimes savagely unfair, of his political and social principles.

As long ago as 1920, Emanuel Morgan, in a number of satirical jottings about his contemporaries, affixed to Eliot the following label:

> The wedding cake
> Of two tired cultures.[30]

More seriously and formidably, Yvor Winters has surveyed the whole range of Eliot's writings, and subjected it to some damaging comments. His description of *The Waste Land* as 'broken blank verse interspersed with bad free verse and rimed doggerel'[31] reveals so crippling an insensitivity to the texture and the rhythm of verse that one is tempted to disregard any judgement on poetry that he may choose to deliver. Yet his demonstration of the inconsistencies and weaknesses of Eliot's criticism is, in places, disconcertingly shrewd; nor can one wholly dismiss his accusation that *The Waste Land* breaks down into lyrical fragments and is flawed by fragmentary didacticism.[32] It was, after all, one of Eliot's admirers who, in a circular printed early in 1922, described *The Waste Land* as a series of poems: 'Last winter [Eliot] broke down and was sent off for three months' rest. During that time he wrote *Waste Land*, a series of poems, possibly the finest that the modern movement in English has produced.'[33]

28 Genesius Jones, *Approach to the Purpose*, 1964, p. 263.
29 Herbert Howarth, *Notes on Some Figures Behind T. S. Eliot*, 1965, p. 279.
30 Emanuel Morgan, 'Pins for Wings', *The Chapbook*, 13, July 1920, p. 25.
31 Yvor Winters, *In Defense of Reason*, 1947, p. 500.
32 ibid., p. 143. Cf. Donald Davie's judgement on *Hugh Selwyn Mauberley*, above, p. 58.
33 John Rodker, Circular for 'Bel Esprit', *The Letters of Ezra Pound 1907–1941*, edited by D. D. Paige, 1951, p. 241, footnote.

Graham Hough, in *Image and Experience* (1960), has developed Winters's observations into a more general onslaught upon the modernist movement in English poetry, Frank Kermode has argued that Eliot's theory about 'dissociation of sensibility' is unsupported by historical evidence, however potent a weapon it may have been in the hands of the apologists for post-symbolist critical theory.[34]

This kind of criticism, acute and salutary though it may be, is scarcely likely to damage Eliot's reputation. He has, however, been savagely assailed by a number of writers for his pronouncements on political questions and for the social implications of his poetry.

I suggested that Eliot's conversion to Christianity entailed no dramatic reversal of his earlier beliefs, but many of his admirers were shocked and alienated when he proclaimed his adherence to Anglo-Catholicism, Royalism, and Classicism. The author of 'Prufrock', 'The Hippopotamus' and *The Waste Land* was now transformed into a renegade, whose disavowal of agnosticism was comparable with Wordsworth's abandonment of his youthful revolutionary principles. Something of this uncomprehending bitterness envenoms a verse polemic by W. T. Nettlefold, entitled 'Fan Mail for a Poet':

HOW NICE for a man to be clever,
So famous, so true;
So sound an investment; how EVER
So nice to be YOU.

To peer into basements, up alleys,
A nose for the search.
To challenge with pertinent sallies,
And then JOIN the church.

First comes Prufrock, then Sweeney, and then
Thomas à Becket.
How frightfully nice of the good men
In cloth to forget it.

And so on, for another five stanzas of jibing and flyting. Not content with denouncing Eliot's rejection of scepticism, liberalism, and humanitarianism, some of his opponents have accused him of espousing Fascism and anti-Semitism.

There is not a scrap of evidence to support the charge that Eliot was ever a Fascist or a sympathizer with Fascism, unless one stigmatizes as such anybody who regards with ironical distaste the claims of democracy and socialism to be the salvation of mankind. Christopher Logue attempted to revive this old *canard* by quoting part of an editorial by Eliot from *The Criterion*, to the effect that the aims set forth in the

34 Frank Kermode, *Romantic Image*, 1957, pp. 138–61.

statement of policy of a Fascist manifesto were 'wholly admirable'.[35] Eliot's reply proved beyond doubt that the phrase wrenched from its content by Logue was part of a careful argument designed to prick the bubble of Fascist rhetoric.[36]

Eliot was by temperament as well as by conviction ill-qualified to sympathize with the aspirations of a modern industrial society. He tended to exaggerate the vices of such a society, to emphasize its rootless, shifting quality, to deplore its vulgarity, to lament its irreligion, to hanker after the values of a conservative, agrarian, hierarchical society grounded in the Christian faith. If forced to choose between a Communist state and a Fascist state which did not overtly attack the church, he would probably have regarded the latter as the lesser of two evils. But unless we are prepared to rig the evidence or to twist the meaning of words, we cannot say that Eliot was a Fascist.

The charge of anti-Semitism is better founded. Eliot never advocated the persecution of Jews, and he recognized the wicked folly of blaming one group or one race for the evils inherent in all human societies. Yet he is guilty of referring to Jews in terms of contempt in both his verse and his prose. It is arguable that in poems such as 'Gerontion' and 'Burbank' Eliot is speaking as a lyrical dramatist and not in his own person. One cannnot, however, defend along these lines the following phrase from his prose: '. . . reasons of race and religion combine to make any large number of free-thinking Jews undesirable.'[37] Eliot believed that usury and free-thinking corrupt society, and this is a legitimate, though illiberal, contention. But he gives the impression that Jewish usurers and free-thinkers are more reprehensible than their Gentile counterparts.

We must remember that in the circles where Eliot grew up a genteel prejudice against Jews was fairly common; that some of his first English friends sported a similar prejudice; and that he found intellectual justification for this attitude in some of the Continental writers and political thinkers whom he most admired. Unhappily, his conversion to Christianity did nothing to chasten his predisposition to nurture anti-Jewish sentiments. The history of the Church is stained by so many savage persecutions of heretics and Jews that Eliot is able to gloze the barbarous cult of anti-Semitism with a traditional veneer of Catholic respectability. There is a case for holding that even Pound's demented raving about Jews is preferable to the sanctimonious tones of the pious Catholic apologists who justify the cruelty of their Church towards the race that gave birth to Jesus Christ. The more one admires Eliot's work

[35] Letter to *The Times Literary Supplement*, 6 September 1957, p. 533.

[36] Letter to *The Times Literary Supplement*, 13 September 1957, p. 547.

[37] *After Strange Gods*, 1934, p. 20. It is worth recalling that Eliot never allowed this book to be reprinted.

the more one must grieve that it is to some extent tainted by one of the ugliest and most virulent diseases of our time.

There are some readers who, while acknowledging Eliot's genius, find his verse remote, impersonal, and arid. For others, his greatness lies not only in the superb technical assurance of his poetry but in the emotional power, the vulnerability to pain, the disciplined love of created things, which vibrate beneath its flawless surface. I should like to end with a prose quotation from Eliot's introduction to an edition of the *Pensées* of Pascal which was published in 1931:

> I can think of no Christian writer, not Newman even, more to be commended than Pascal to those who doubt, but who have the mind to conceive, and the sensibility to feel, the disorder, the futility, the meaninglessness, the mystery of life and suffering, and who can only find peace through a satisfaction of the whole being.[38]

CRITICISM

Passages from the Writings of T. S. Eliot

The substance of poetry, Mr. Yeats says, is 'truth seen in passion'. To most readers this will fall into memory – for it is an easy phrase to remember – along with something said by Matthew Arnold, or Wordsworth, or Professor Saintsbury, but Mr. Yeats means what he says. He is quite literal, too, when he says: 'In every great poet is a Herbert Spencer', or 'the poet does not seek to be original, *but the truth*, and to his dismay and consternation, it may be, he finds the original, thereby to incur hostility and misunderstanding.'

Mr. Yeats understands poetry better than anyone I have ever known who was not a poet, and better than most of those who have the reputation of poets. This last quotation, in fact, is a thought which takes very deep roots; it strikes through the tangle of literature direct to the subsoil of the greatest – to Shakespeare and Dante and Æschylus. Ordinary writers of verse either deal in imagination or in 'ideas'; they escape from one to the other, but neither one nor the other nor both together is truth in the sense of poetic truth. Only old ideas 'part and parcel of the personality' are of use to the poet. (This is worth repeating to our American contemporaries who study Freud.)

Review of *Passages from the Letters of John Butler Yeats*, selected by Ezra Pound, *The Egoist, IV*, 6, July 1917, p. 90.

England puts her Greater Writers away securely in a Safe Deposit Vault, and curls to sleep like Father. There they go rotten; for if our predecessors cannot teach us to write better than themselves, they will surely teach us to write worse; because we have never learned to criticize

[38] *Selected Essays*, 1951, p. 416.

Keats, Shelley, and Wordsworth (poets of assured though modest merit), Keats, Shelley, and Wordsworth punish us from their grave with the annual scourge of the Georgian Anthology.

We must insist upon the importance of intelligent criticism . . . I mean the ceaseless employment of criticism by men who are engaged in creative work. It is essential that each generation should reappraise everything for itself. Who, for instance, has a first-hand opinion of Shakespeare? Yet I have no doubt that much could be learned by a serious study of that semi-mythical figure.

I have seen the forces of death with Mr. Chesterton at their head upon a white horse. Mr. Pound, Mr. Joyce and Mr. Lewis write living English; one does not realize the awfulness of death until one meets with the living language.

'Observations', *The Egoist*, V, 5, May 1918, p. 69.

We insist in the face of a hostile majority that reading, writing, and ciphering does not complete the education of a poet. The analogy to science is close. A poet, like a scientist, is contributing toward the organic development of culture: it is just as absurd for him not to know the work of his predecessors or of men writing in other languages as it would be for a biologist to be ignorant of Mendel or De Vries. It is exactly as wasteful for a poet to do what has been done already, as for a biologist to rediscover Mendel's discoveries. The French poets in question [Corbière, Laforgue, Rimbaud and other French poets anthologized in *The Little Review*, February 1918] have made 'discoveries' in verse of which we cannot afford to be ignorant, discoveries which are not merely a concern for French syntax. To remain with Wordsworth is equivalent to ignoring the whole of science subsequent to Erasmus Darwin.

'Contemporanea', *The Egoist*, V, 6, June–July 1918, p. 84.

The poet's mind is in fact a receptacle for seizing and storing up numberless feelings, phrases, images, which remain there until all the particles which can unite to form a new compound are present together.

If you compare several representative passages of the greatest poetry you see how great is the variety of types of combination, and also how completely any semi-ethical criterion of 'sublimity' misses the mark. For it is not the 'greatness', the intensity, of the emotions, the components, but the intensity of the artistic process, the pressure, so to speak, under which the fusion takes place, that counts . . .

Poetry is not a turning loose of emotion, but an escape from emotion; it is not the expression of personality, but an escape from personality.

But, of course, only those who have personality and emotions know what it means to want to escape from these things.

'Tradition and the Individual Talent', *The Egoist*, VI, 4, September–October 1919, pp. 54–5, and VI, 5, November–December 1919, pp. 72–3. Reprinted in *Selected Essays*, 3rd ed. 1951, pp. 13–22. All references to *Selected Essays* are to this edition.

[This essay should be studied in its entirety.]

The only way of expressing emotion in the form of art is by finding an 'objective correlative'; in other words, a set of objects, a situation, a chain of events which shall be the formula of that *particular* emotion; such that when the external facts, which must terminate in sensory experience, are given, the emotion is immediately evoked.

'Hamlet and his Problems', *The Athenaeum*, 4665, 26 September 1919. Reprinted, and retitled 'Hamlet', in *Selected Essays*, p. 145.

Immature poets imitate; mature poets steal; bad poets deface what they take, and good poets make it into something better, or at least something different. The good poet welds his theft into a whole of feeling which is unique, utterly different from that from which it was torn; the bad poet throws it into something which has no cohesion.

'Philip Massinger', *The Times Literary Supplement*, 27 May 1920, p. 325. Reprinted in *Selected Essays*, p. 206.

Tennyson and Browning are poets, and they think; but they do not feel their thought as immediately as the odour of a rose. A thought to Donne was an experience; it modified his sensibility. When a poet's mind is perfectly equipped for its work, it is constantly amalgamating disparate experience; the ordinary man's experience is chaotic, irregular, fragmentary. The latter falls in love, or reads Spinoza, and these two experiences have nothing to do with each other, or with the noise of the typewriter or the smell of cooking; in the mind of the poet these experiences are always forming new wholes . . .

It is not a permanent necessity that poets should be interested in philosophy, or in any other subject. We can only say that it appears likely that poets in our civilization, as it exists at present, must be *difficult*. Our civilization comprehends great variety and complexity, and this variety and complexity, playing upon a refined sensibility, must produce various and complex results. The poet must become more and more comprehensive, more allusive, more indirect, in order to force, to dislocate if necessary, language into his meaning . . .

Those who object to the 'artificiality' of Milton or Dryden sometimes tell us to 'look into our hearts and write'. But that is not looking deep enough; Racine or Donne looked into a good deal more than the heart.

One must look into the cerebral cortex, the nervous system, and the digestive tracts.

'The Metaphysical Poets', *The Times Literary Supplement*, 20 October 1921, pp. 669–70. Reprinted in *Selected Essays*, pp. 281–91. The three passages quoted above occur respectively on p. 287, p. 289, and p. 290.

Whatever words a writer employs, he benefits by knowing as much as possible of the history of these words, of the *uses to which they have already been applied*. Such knowledge facilitates his task of giving to the word a new life and to the language a new idiom. The essential of tradition is in this; in getting as much as possible of the whole weight of the history of the language behind his word.

'The Three Provincialities', *The Tyro*, II, 1922, p. 13.
Reprinted in *Essays in Criticism*, I, i, 1951, pp. 38–41.

I think that from Baudelaire I learned first, a precedent for the poetical possibilities, never developed by any poet writing in my own language, of the more sordid aspects of the modern metropolis, of the possibility of fusion between the sordidly realistic and the phantasmagoric, the possibility of the juxtaposition of the matter-of-fact and the fantastic. From him, as from Laforgue, I learned that the sort of material that I had, the sort of experience that an adolescent had had, in an industrial city in America, could be the material for poetry; and that the source of new poetry might be found in what had been regarded hitherto as the impossible, the sterile, the intractably unpoetic. That, in fact, the business of the poet was to make poetry out of the unexplored resources of the unpoetical; that the poet, in fact, was committed by his profession to turn the unpoetical into poetry.

'Talk on Dante', *The Adelphi*, First Quarter 1951, p. 107. Reprinted, and retitled 'What Dante Means to Me', in *To Criticize the Critic*, 1965, p. 126.

The artist, I believe, is more *primitive*, as well as more civilized, than his contemporaries, his experience is deeper than civilization, and he only uses the phenomena of civilization in expressing it. Primitive instincts and the acquired habits of ages are confounded in the ordinary man. In the work of Mr. Lewis we recognize the thought of the modern and the energy of the cave-man.

Review of *Tarr*, by Wyndham Lewis, *The Egoist*, V, 8, September 1918, p. 106.

What I call the 'auditory imagination' is the feeling for syllable and rhythm, penetrating far below the conscious levels of thought and feeling, invigorating every word; sinking to the most primitive and forgotten, returning to the origin and bringing something back, seeking the beginning and the end. It works through meanings, certainly, or not without meanings in the ordinary sense, and fuses the old and obliterated and the trite, the current, and the new and surprising, the most ancient and the most civilized mentality.

The Use of Poetry and the Use of Criticism, 1933, pp. 118–19.

For Kipling the poem is something which is intended to *act* – and for the most part his poems are intended to elicit the same response from all readers, and only the response which they can make in common. For other poets – at least, for some other poets – the poem may begin to shape itself in fragments of musical rhythm, and its structure will first appear in terms of something analogous to musical form; and such poets find it expedient to occupy their conscious mind with the craftsman's problems, leaving the deeper meaning to emerge from a lower level. It is a question then of what one chooses to be conscious of, and of how much of the meaning, in a poem, is conveyed direct to the intelligence and how much is conveyed indirectly by the musical impression upon the sensibility – always remembering that the use of the word 'musical' and of musical analogies, in discussing poetry, has its dangers if we do not constantly check its limitations: for the music of verse is inseparable from the meanings and associations of words.

Introduction to *A Choice of Kipling's Verse*, 1941, p. 18. Reprinted in *On Poetry and Poets*, 1957, p. 238.
[See also 'The Music of Poetry', *On Poetry and Poets*, 1957, pp. 26–38.]

I know, for instance, that some forms of ill-health, debility or anaemia, may (if other circumstances are favourable) produce an efflux of poetry in a way approaching the condition of automatic writing – though, in contrast to the claims sometimes made for the latter, the material has obviously been incubating within the poet, and cannot be suspected of being a present from a friendly or impertinent demon ... To me it seems that at these moments, which are characterized by the sudden lifting of the burden of anxiety and fear which presses upon our daily life so steadily that we are unaware of it, what happens is something *negative*: that is to say, not 'inspiration' as we commonly think of it, but the breaking down of strong habitual barriers – which tend to re-form very quickly ...

Organization is necessary as well as 'inspiration'. The re-creation of word and image which happens fitfully in the poetry of such a poet as Coleridge happens almost incessantly with Shakespeare. Again and again, in his use of a word, he will give a new meaning or extract a latent one; again and again the right image, saturated while it lay in the depths of Shakespeare's memory, will rise like Anadyomene from the sea ...

Why, for all of us, out of all that we have heard, seen, felt, in a lifetime, do certain images recur, charged with emotion, rather than others? The song of one bird, the leap of one fish, at a particular place and time, the scent of one flower, an old woman on a German mountain path, six ruffians seen through an open window playing cards at night at a small French railway junction where there was a water-mill: such memories may have symbolic value, but of what we cannot tell, for they come to represent the depths of feeling into which we cannot peer. We might just as well ask why, when we try to recall visually some period in the past, we find in our memory just the few meagre arbitrarily chosen set of snapshots that we do find there, the faded poor souvenirs of passionate moments.

The Use of Poetry and the Use of Criticism, 1933, pp. 144–8.

But if the word 'inspiration' is to have any meaning, it must mean just this, that the speaker or writer is uttering something which he does not wholly understand, – or which he may even misinterpret when the inspiration has departed from him. This is certainly true of poetic inspiration: and there is more obvious reason for admiring Isaiah as a poet than for claiming Virgil as a prophet. A poet may believe that he is expressing only his private experience; his lines may be for him only a means of talking about himself without giving himself away; yet for his readers what he has written may come to be the expression both of their own secret feelings and of the exultation or despair of a generation. He need not know what his poetry will come to mean to others; and a prophet need not understand the meaning of his prophetic utterance.

'Virgil and the Christian World', *The Listener*, 14 September 1951, pp. 411–12. Reprinted in *On Poetry and Poets* (1957), pp. 122–3.

It is the poet's business to be original, in all that is comprehended by 'technique', only so far as is absolutely necessary for saying what he has to say; only so far as is indicated, not by the idea – for there is no idea – but by the nature of that dark embryo within him which gradually takes on the form and speech of a poem.

Critical note to *Collected Poems of Harold Monro*, edited by Alida Monro, 1933.

What, asks Herr Benn in this lecture [*Problem der Lyrik*], does the writer of such a poem, 'addressed to no one', start with? There is first, he says, an inert embryo or 'creative germ' (*ein dumpfer schöpferischer Keim*) and, on the other hand, the Language, the resources of the words at the poet's command. He has something germinating in him for which he must find words; but he cannot know what words he wants until he has found the words; he cannot identify this embryo until it has been transformed into an arrangement of the right words in the right order. When you have the words for it, the 'thing' for which the words had to be found has disappeared, replaced by a poem. What you start from is nothing so definite as an emotion, in any ordinary sense; it is still more certainly not an idea; it is – to adapt two lines of Beddoes to a different meaning – a

> bodiless childful of life in the gloom
> Crying with frog voice, 'what shall I be?'

I agree with Gottfried Benn, and I would go a little further. In a poem which is neither didactic nor narrative, and not animated by any other social purpose, the poet may be concerned solely with expressing in verse – using all his resources of words, with their history, their connotations, their music – this obscure impulse. He does not know what he has to say until he has said it; and in the effort to say it he is not concerned with making other people understand anything. He is not concerned, at this stage, with other people at all: only with finding the right words or, anyhow, the least wrong words. He is not concerned whether anybody else will ever listen to them or not, or whether anybody else will ever understand them if he does. He is oppressed by a burden which he must bring to birth in order to obtain relief. Or, to change the figure of speech, he is haunted by a demon, a demon against which he feels powerless, because in its first manifestation it has no face, no name, nothing; and the words, the poem he makes, are a kind of form of exorcism of this demon. In other words again, he is going to all that trouble, not in order to communicate with anyone, but to gain relief from acute discomfort; and when the words are finally arranged in the right way – or in what he comes to accept as the best arrangement he can find – he may experience a moment of exhaustion, of appeasement, of absolution, and of something very near annihilation, which is in itself indescribable. And then he can say to the poem: 'Go away! Find a place for yourself in a book – and don't expect *me* to take any further interest in you.'

The Three Voices of Poetry, 1953, pp. 17–18.
Reprinted in *On Poetry and Poets*, 1957, pp. 97–8.

In using myth, in manipulating a continuous parallel between contemporaneity and antiquity, Mr. Joyce is pursuing a method which others must pursue after him. They will not be imitators, any more than the scientist who uses the discoveries of an Einstein in pursuing his own independent, further investigations. It is simply a way of controlling, of ordering, of giving a shape and a significance to the immense panorama of futility and anarchy which is contemporary history. It is a method already adumbrated by Mr. Yeats, and of the need for which I believe Mr. Yeats to have been the first contemporary to be conscious.

It is, I seriously believe, a step forward making the modern world possible in art . . . Psychology (such as it is, and whether our reaction to it be comic or serious), ethnology and *The Golden Bough* have concurred to make possible what was impossible even a few years ago. Instead of narrative method, we may now use the mythical method.

'Ulysses, Order and Myth', *The Dial*, LXXV, 5, November 1923, p. 483.

It is an advantage to mankind in general to live in a beautiful world; that no one can doubt. But for the poet is it so important? We mean all sorts of things, I know, by Beauty. But the essential advantage for a poet is not, to have a beautiful world with which to deal: it is to be able to see beneath both beauty and ugliness; to see the boredom, and the horror, and the glory.

The Use of Poetry and the Use of Criticism, 1933, p. 106.

This speaks to me of that at which I have long aimed, in writing poetry; to write poetry which should be essentially poetry, with nothing poetic about it, poetry standing naked in its bare bones, or poetry so transparent that we should not see the poetry, but that which we are meant to see through the poetry, poetry so transparent that in reading it we are intent on what the poem *points at*, and not on the poetry, this seems to me the thing to try for. To get *beyond poetry*, as Beethoven, in his later works, strove to get *beyond music*. We never succeed, perhaps, but Lawrence's words mean this to me, that they express to me what I think that the forty or fifty original lines that I have written strive towards.

[Unpublished lecture on 'English Letter Writers' – primarily on Keats and Lawrence – which was delivered in New Haven, Conn., during the winter of 1933. Quoted by F. O. Matthiessen, *The Achievement of T. S. Eliot* (3rd ed. 1958), p. 90. Eliot was referring to the passage in one of Lawrence's letters which runs: 'The essence of poetry with us in this age of stark and unlovely actualities is a stark directness, without a shadow of a lie, or a shadow of deflection anywhere. Everything can go but this stark, bare, rocky directness of statement, this alone makes poetry, to-day.'[39]]

POEMS

from *Preludes*

I

The winter evening settles down
With smell of steaks in passageways.
Six o'clock.
The burnt-out ends of smoky days.

[39] Letter to Catherine Carswell, ? 11 January 1916. *The Collected Letters of D. H. Lawrence*, edited with an Introduction by Harry T. Moore, 1962, vol. i, p. 413.

And now a gusty shower wraps
The grimy scraps
Of withered leaves about your feet
And newspapers from vacant lots;
The showers beat
On broken blinds and chimney-pots,
And at the corner of the street
A lonely cab-horse steams and stamps.
And then the lighting of the lamps.

Gerontion

Thou hast nor youth nor age
But as it were an after dinner sleep
Dreaming of both.

Here I am, an old man in a dry month,
Being read to by a boy, waiting for rain.
I was neither at the hot gates
Nor fought in the warm rain
Nor knee deep in the salt marsh, heaving a cutlass,
Bitten by flies, fought.
My house is a decayed house,
And the Jew squats on the window sill, the owner,
Spawned in some estaminet of Antwerp,
Blistered in Brussels, patched and peeled in London.
The goat coughs at night in the field overhead;
Rocks, moss, stonecrop, iron, merds.
The woman keeps the kitchen, makes tea,
Sneezes at evening, poking the peevish gutter.
I an old man,
A dull head among windy spaces.

Signs are taken for wonders. 'We would see a sign!'
The word within a word, unable to speak a word,
Swaddled with darkness. In the juvescence of the year
Came Christ the tiger

In depraved May, dogwood and chestnut, flowering judas,
To be eaten, to be divided, to be drunk
Among whispers; by Mr. Silvero
With caressing hands, at Limoges
Who walked all night in the next room;

By Hakagawa, bowing among the Titians;
By Madame de Tornquist, in the dark room
Shifting the candles; Fraülein von Kulp
Who turned in the hall, one hand on the door. Vacant shuttles
Weave the wind. I have no ghosts,
An old man in a draughty house
Under a windy knob.

After such knowledge, what forgiveness? Think now
History has many cunning passages, contrived corridors
And issues, deceives with whispering ambitions,
Guides us by vanities. Think now
She gives when our attention is distracted
And what she gives, gives with such supple confusions
That the giving famishes the craving. Gives too late
What's not believed in, or if still believed,
In memory only, reconsidered passion. Gives too soon
Into weak hands, what's thought can be dispensed with
Till the refusal propagates a fear. Think
Neither fear nor courage saves us. Unnatural vices
Are fathered by our heroism. Virtues
Are forced upon us by our impudent crimes.
These tears are shaken from the wrath-bearing tree.

The tiger springs in the new year. Us he devours. Think at last
We have not reached conclusions, when I
Stiffen in a rented house. Think at last
I have not made this show purposelessly
And it is not by any concitation
Of the backward devils.
I would meet you upon this honestly.
I that was near your heart was removed therefrom
To lose beauty in terror, terror in inquisition.
I have lost my passion: why should I need to keep it
Since what is kept must be adulterated?
I have lost my sight, smell, hearing, taste and touch:
How should I use them for your closer contact?

These with a thousand small deliberations
Protract the profit of their chilled delirium,
Excite the membrane, when the sense has cooled,
With pungent sauces, multiply variety
In a wilderness of mirrors. What will the spider do,
Suspend its operations, will the weevil

Delay? De Bailhache, Fresca, Mrs. Cammel, whirled
Beyond the circuit of the shuddering Bear
In fractured atoms. Gull against the wind, in the windy straits
Of Belle Isle, or running on the Horn,
White feathers in the snow, the Gulf claims,
And an old man driven by the Trades
To a sleepy corner.

Tenants of the house,
Thoughts of a dry brain in a dry season.

Marina

Quis hic locus, quae
regio, quae mundi plaga?

What seas what shores what grey rocks and what islands
What water lapping the bow
And scent of pine and the woodthrush singing through the fog
What images return
O my daughter.

Those who sharpen the tooth of the dog, meaning
Death
Those who glitter with the glory of the hummingbird, meaning
Death
Those who sit in the sty of contentment, meaning
Death
Those who suffer the ecstasy of the animals, meaning
Death

Are become unsubstantial, reduced by a wind,
A breath of pine, and the woodsong fog
By this grace dissolved in place

What is this face, less clear and clearer
The pulse in the arm, less strong and stronger –
Given or lent? more distant than stars and nearer than the eye

Whispers and small laughter between leaves and hurrying feet
Under sleep, where all the waters meet.
Bowsprit cracked with ice and paint cracked with heat.

I made this, I have forgotten
And remember.
The rigging weak and the canvas rotten
Between one June and another September.
Made this unknowing, half conscious, unknown, my own.
The garboard strake leaks, the seams need caulking.
This form, this face, this life
Living to live in a world of time beyond me; let me
Resign my life for this life, my speech for that unspoken,
The awakened, lips parted, the hope, the new ships.

What seas what shores what granite islands towards my timbers
And woodthrush calling through the fog
My daughter.

SELECT BIBLIOGRAPHY

Works by T. S. Eliot
Collected Poems, London, 1963.
Selected Essays, London, 1932; 3rd ed., 1951.
The Use of Poetry and the Use of Criticism, London, 1933.
On Poetry and Poets, London, 1957.
To Criticize the Critic, London, 1965.

Some Biographical and Critical Studies
Braybrooke, Neville, ed., *T. S. Eliot: A Symposium for his Seventieth Birthday*, London, 1958.
Frye, Northrop, *T. S. Eliot*, Edinburgh, 1963.
Gardner, Helen, *The Art of T. S. Eliot*, London, 1949.
Jones, Genesius, *Approach to the Purpose*, London, 1964.
Kenner, Hugh, *The Invisible Poet: T. S. Eliot*, New York, 1959; London, 1960.
Leavis, F. R., *New Bearings in English Poetry*, London, 1932; 2nd ed., 1950.
Contains an important essay on Eliot.
Marsh, Richard, and Tambimuttu, eds., *T. S. Eliot: a Symposium*, London, 1948.
Matthiessen, F. O., *The Achievement of T. S. Eliot*, New York and London, 1935; 3rd ed., with a chapter on Eliot's later work by C. L. Barber, 1958.
Smith, Grover, *T. S. Eliot's Poetry and Prose*, Chicago, 1956; Cambridge, 1957.
Stead, C. K., *The New Poetic*, London, 1964.
Contains two stimulating chapters on Eliot.
Tate, Allen, ed., *T. S. Eliot: The Man and his Work*, London, 1967.

6

D. H. LAWRENCE

INTRODUCTION

Although it is generally recognized that D. H. Lawrence is one of the major writers of our century, many people still either brush his poetry aside, or reluctantly concede that it has certain merits of an unorthodox kind. Even those who admit that Lawrence was essentially a poet are apt to maintain that his poetic impulses manifested themselves more satisfactorily in the stories and short novels than in verse. It is even suggested that Lawrence's poems are clumsy vessels into which he poured the emotions that overflowed from his works of fiction.

It is sometimes forgotten that Lawrence practised the art of poetry regularly and passionately throughout his career. One stresses the phrase *the art of poetry*. For despite the speed with which he drafted his poems, and despite the fragmentary, trivial character of his feeblest verse, Lawrence usually took considerable pains in the reshaping and rewriting of his drafts. Like Robert Graves, Dylan Thomas and other believers in the Muse, the daimon, or poetic inspiration, Lawrence worked hard at his craft. Nor should the apparent freedom and irregularity of his verse mislead us into supposing that he was indifferent to the formal qualities of poetry. Every poet has his own personal rhythm, however faint and blurred it may be. Lawrence's main contribution to poetry was his extraordinary skill in discovering and embodying in verse the rhythm that would correspond exactly with the subtle yet overwhelmingly powerful rhythm of his sensual perceptions and emotional life. If we are incapable of recognizing this basic fact, we shall remain deaf to the merits of his poetry.

The sheer variety and resourcefulness of his poetry are often ignored. Even before the outbreak of the First World War, Ezra Pound had saluted Lawrence as a master of low-life narrative who had raised verse to the level of contemporary prose.[1] He was right to castigate Lawrence for writing pre-raphaelitish slush, particularly about sex, yet even among his early poems there are achievements of a high order. The opening lines of 'End of Another Home Holiday' are remarkable for their combination of potent suggestiveness with precise description:

> When shall I see the half-moon sink again
> Behind the black sycamore at the end of the garden?
> When will the scent of the dim white phlox
> Creep up the wall to me, and in at my open window?

[1] See below, p. 99.

The rhythmical hesitation is perfectly attuned to the ebb and flow of the poet's fluctuating emotional life.

Or take another early poem, which is comparatively unfamiliar, 'Troth with the Dead':

> The moon is broken in twain, and half a moon
> Beyond me lies on the low, still floor of the sky;
> The other half of the broken coin of troth
> Is buried away in the dark where the dead all lie.

Employing this symbol of the broken moon, Lawrence proceeds to examine without evasion or distortion a painful, troubling human relationship, to evoke and explore a turbulent emotional state by using poetic images and poetic speech.

A poet who can achieve these kinds of success is not technically incompetent or careless. Lawrence frequently chooses to abandon the conventional metrical habits of most English poets because they are not adequate for his purposes, although he is fully capable of writing in normal forms. 'Giorno Dei Morti', which consists of four stanzas of four lines apiece, rhyming in couplets, demonstrates his easy mastery of metre and rhyme, although with characteristic disregard for academic propriety he places it among the *Unrhyming Poems* in his *Collected Poems*. He is always happiest when, trusting his intuitive response to the emotional demands of his theme, he sets his words dancing to an inner music, unconstrained by the rules of prosody. 'Piano', one of his indubitable triumphs, is remarkable for the assurance with which Lawrence varies the length of his lines and places his rhymes in order to make a poem out of disturbingly complex material.[2] Only a poet of uncommon technical cunning could avoid the pitfalls of sentimentality and convey with such immediacy the sensuous impact of the song heard in the dusk, the way in which the music arouses and is interfused with memories of childhood and of a woman singing to her family. In the space of twelve lines Lawrence has contrived to explore the nature of memory, the tension caused by the conflicting forces of maturity and the longing to regain the lost security of childhood, the tremendous range of emotions that music can command, and the final release accorded to the poet by his surrender – a surrender which he recognizes for what it is:

> The glamour
> Of childish days is upon me, my manhood is cast
> Down in the flood of remembrance. I weep like a child for the past.

The combination of delicacy and power in this poem is characteristic of his best work.

[2] See below, p. 102.

Lawrence, though permitting himself to be represented in the Georgian as well as in the Imagist anthologies, remained entirely Lawrentian. *Look! We Have Come Through* is supposed to have elicited from Bertrand Russell the comment, 'They may have come through, but I see no reason why I should look.' This sequence represents a bold attempt to make poetry out of material better suited to fiction or autobiography; it exemplifies one of Lawrence's weaknesses noted by Ezra Pound – his tendency to discuss his disagreeable sensations instead of transforming them into the necessary impersonality of poetry. The sequence of poems entitled *Birds, Beasts and Flowers* is, on the other hand, a triumphant ordering of themes not hitherto explored in English poetry. Lawrence enjoyed with the denizens of the natural world the kind of pure relationship which he failed to establish with human beings. The flame of love and sympathy which burned so fiercely in Lawrence was all too often extinguished in his dealings with men and women, who seemed corrupted by so many distortions and perversions – intellectual sterility, the malevolent will, class attitudes, clinging to money and possessions. Animals and flowers are not endowed with the vices and virtues of human beings, they do not threaten the naked individuality of the man who confronts them. Thus Lawrence was able to love and understand without fear the essential flow of life within these creatures, the divine beauty and energy of these unfallen inhabitants of Eden.

The mastery and originality of *Birds, Beasts and Flowers* are acknowledged even by those who deny that Lawrence is a major poet. Once again, the technical perfection of the poems resides in the appropriateness of the rhythmical variations and repetitions, the marvellous fidelity of the movement of the verse to the states of being evoked by Lawrence's contemplation of this other world, a world totally unlike ours yet interacting with ours so powerfully and intimately.

To have made poetry of high quality from a detailed, unsentimental observation of working-class life, from complicated and painful emotional involvements, and from the strange, inhuman world of nature would be a lifetime's work for most poets. Lawrence excelled in two further modes of verse – the stinging, flyting pieces called *Pansies* and the meditations on mortality which are the theme of *Last Poems*, published by Richard Aldington after Lawrence's death.

The feeblest of the *Pansies*, and the puerile verses entitled *Nettles*, must be ranked among the worst things Lawrence ever wrote. Nevertheless a few of his savage observations on sex, class, social history, money, literary fashion, intellectual snobbery, and English hypocrisy hit the mark with unerring accuracy. The poem, 'Nottingham's New University', sums up, in its ribald near-doggerel, a pile of sociological tracts, indignant novels and earnest autobiographies:

Little I thought, when I was a lad
and turned my modest penny
over on Boots' cash counter,
that Jesse, by turning many

millions of similar honest pence
over, would make a pile
that would rise at last and blossom out
in grand and cakey style

into a university
where smart men would dispense
doses of smart cash-chemistry
in language of common-sense! ...

From this I learn, though I knew it before
that culture has her roots
in the deep dung of cash, and lore
is a last offshoot of Boots.

That mordant satire, and poems such as 'Work', 'Wages', 'Dont's', and 'Now it's Happened' demonstrate the quickness and sharpness of Lawrence's intelligence, the shrewdness of his social observation, his disconcerting ability to penetrate to the reality beneath the jargons and the shams of moralists, educationalists, and men of letters.

Last Poems alone would ensure Lawrence a place among the major poets of our time. They refute the contention advanced by R. P. Blackmur in a celebrated essay that Lawrence's poems are 'the ruins of great intentions.[3] It is precisely their emotional integrity and wholeness, their perception of life in death, their sense of mortality impregnated with immortality, that make them fully achieved works of art, formally superb because they have passed beyond academic formalism. Critical ingenuity and scholarly exegesis are unnecessary in the presence of these poems: the jeering, rancorous irritability which mars some of the later *Pansies* and *Nettles* has been burned away, leaving Lawrence's pure genius illuminated by a radiant glow. Richard Aldington's phrase about 'The Ship of Death' is applicable to all these poems, in which 'suffering and the agony of departure are turned into music and reconciliation'.[4] One can only marvel at their energy and tranquillity and at the means whereby a restless wanderer in search of an unattainable peace found the strength to celebrate his impending death:

[3] 'D. H. Lawrence and Expressive Forms', *Language as Gesture*, 1952, pp. 286–300.
[4] Richard Aldington, Introduction to *Last Poems*, 1933.

then I must know that still
I am in the hands of the unknown God,
he is breaking me down to his own oblivion
to send me forth on a new morning, a new man.

CRITICISM

I think you will find my verse smoother – not because I consciously attend to rhythms, but because I am no longer so crissy-crossy in myself. I think, don't you know, that my rhythms fit my mood pretty well, in the verse. And if the mood is out of joint, the rhythm often is. I have always tried to get an emotion out in its own course, without altering it. It needs the finest instinct imaginable, much finer than the skill of the craftsmen. That Japanese Yone Noguchi tried it. He doesn't quite bring it off. Often I don't – sometimes I do. Sometimes Whitman is perfect. Remember skilled verse is dead in fifty years – I am thinking of your admiration of Flecker.

D. H. Lawrence, Letter to Edward Marsh, 18 August 1913.
The Collected Letters of D. H. Lawrence, edited by Harry T. Moore, vol. 1, 1962, p. 221.

It all depends on the *pause* – the natural pause, the natural *lingering* of the voice according to the feeling – it is the hidden *emotional* pattern that makes poetry, not the obvious form.

Ĭ hăve fŏrgŏt much, Cynară, gone wĭth thĕ wind.

It is the lapse of the feeling, something as indefinite as expression in the voice carrying emotion. It doesn't depend on the ear, particularly, but on the sensitive soul. And the ear gets a habit, and becomes master, when the ebbing and lifting emotion should be master, and the ear the transmitter. If your ear has got stiff and a bit mechanical, *don't* blame my poetry. That's why you like *Golden Journey to Samarkand* – it fits your habituated ear, and your feeling crouches subservient and a bit pathetic. 'It satisfies my ear,' you say. Well, I don't write for your ear. This is the constant war, I reckon, between new expression and the habituated, mechanical transmitters and receivers of the human constitution.

D. H. Lawrence, Letter to Edward Marsh, 19 November 1913.
ibid., pp. 243–4.

The poetry of the beginning and the poetry of the end must have that exquisite finality, perfection which belongs to all that is far off. It is in the realm of all that is perfect. It is of the nature of all that is complete and consummate. This completeness, this consummateness, the finality and the perfection are conveyed in exquisite form: the perfect symmetry, the rhythm which returns upon itself like a dance where the hands link and loosen and link for the supreme moment of the end ...

But there is another kind of poetry: the poetry of that which is at hand: the immediate present. In the immediate present there is no perfection, no consummation, nothing finished ...

From the foregoing it is obvious that the poetry of the instant present cannot have the same body or the same motion as the poetry of the before and after. It can never submit to the same conditions. It is never finished. There is no rhythm which returns upon itself, no serpent of eternity with its tail in its own mouth. There is no static perfection, none of that finality which we find so satisfying because we are so frightened.

Much has been written about free verse. But all that can be said, first and last, is that free verse is, or should be, direct utterance from the instant, whole man. It is the soul and the mind and body surging at once, nothing left out. They speak all together. There is some confusion, some discord. But the confusion and the discord only belong to the reality, as noise belongs to the plunge of water ...

But in free verse we look for the insurgent naked throb of the instant moment. To break the lovely form of material verse, and to dish up the fragments as a new substance, called *vers libre*, this is what most of the free-versifiers accomplish. They do not know that free verse has its own *nature*, that it is neither star nor pearl, but instantaneous like plasm.

D. H. Lawrence, Introduction to *New Poems*, 1918.

A young man is afraid of his demon and puts his hand over the demon's mouth sometimes and speaks for him. And the things the young man says are very rarely poetry. So I have tried to let the demon say his say, and to remove the passages where the young man intruded.

D. H. Lawrence, Note to *Collected Poems*, 1928.

Anyhow, I offer a bunch of pansies, not a wreath of *immortelles*. I don't want everlasting flowers, and I don't want to offer them to anybody else. A flower passes, and that perhaps is the best of it. If we can take it in its transience, its breath, its maybe mephistophelian, maybe palely ophelian face, the look it gives, the gestures of its full bloom, and the way it turns upon us to depart – that was the flower, we have had it, and no *immortelle* can give us anything in comparison. The same with the pansy poems; merely the breath of the moment, and one eternal moment easily contradicting the next eternal moment. Only don't nail the pansy down. You won't keep it any better if you do.

D. H. Lawrence, Foreword to *Pansies*, 1929.

[The prefatory notes to *New Poems* (1918), *Collected Poems* (1928), and *Pansies* (1929) are reprinted in *The Complete Poems of D. H. Lawrence*, edited by Vivian de Sola Pinto and Warren Roberts, 2 vols. (1964).]

The *Love Poems*, if by that Mr. Lawrence means the middling-sensual erotic verses in this collection, are a sort of pre-raphaelitish slush, disgusting or very nearly so. The attempts to produce the typical Laurentine line have brought forth:

I touched her and she shivered like a dead snake

which was improved by an even readier parodist, to

I touched her and she came off in scales.

Jesting aside, when Mr. Lawrence ceases to discuss his own disagreeable sensations, when he writes low-life narrative, as he does in *Whether or Not* and in *Violets*, there is no English poet under forty who can get within shot of him . . .

Mr. Lawrence has attempted realism and attained it. He has brought contemporary verse up to the level of contemporary prose, and that is no mean achievement.

Ezra Pound, Review of *Love Poems and Others*, by D. H. Lawrence, *Poetry*, II, 4, July 1913. Reprinted in *Literary Essays of Ezra Pound*, edited by T. S. Eliot, 1954, pp. 387–8.

There is an admirable formalist criticism of Lawrence's poetry by R. P. Blackmur.[5] From its own point of view it leaves nothing more to be said. Yet at the end the essence of Lawrence's poetry is no more discernible than it was at the beginning . . .

When poetry succeeds formally its quality can be fully exposed by formal criticism; all has been manifested in form. When poetry partly fails from a formal point of view, yet something impressive remains, formal criticism can never be enough. There is something lingering beyond the threshold of realization. The purist may regard it as inadmissible because, in fact, it has not succeeded in gaining admission; yet by a more generous interpretation of the critic's duty, it ought as far as possible to be examined, its relation to what has been fully realized should be made plain. And for that we must abandon the purely formal

[5] 'D. H. Lawrence and Expressive Form', *Language as Gesture*, 1952, pp. 286–300.

procedure and admit expressive and biographical aims to some share of our consideration.

Graham Hough, *The Dark Sun*, 1956, pp. 192–3.

Reading Lawrence's early poems, one is continually struck by the originality of the sensibility and the conventionality of the expressive means. For most immature poets, their chief problem is to learn to forget what they have been taught poets are supposed to feel; too often, as Lawrence says, the young man is afraid of his demon, puts his hand over the demon's mouth and speaks for him. On the other hand, an immature poet, if he has real talent, usually begins to exhibit quite early a distinctive style of his own; however obvious the influence of some older writer may be, there is something original in his manner or, at last, great technical competence. In Lawrence's case, this was not so; he learned quite soon to let his demon speak, but it took him a long time to find the appropriate style for him to speak in. All too often in his early poems, even the best ones, he is content to versify his thoughts; there is no essential relation between what he is saying and the formal structure he imposes upon it.

W. H. Auden, 'D. H. Lawrence', *The Dyer's Hand*, 1963, p. 285.

Most of Lawrence's finest poems are to be found in the volume *Birds, Beasts, and Flowers*, begun in Tuscany when he was thirty-five and finished three years later in New Mexico. All of them are written in free verse.

The difference between formal and free verse may be likened to the difference between carving and modeling; the formal poet, that is to say, thinks of the poem he is writing as something already latent in the language which he has to reveal, while the free verse poet thinks of language as a plastic passive medium upon which he imposes his artistic conception. One might also say that, in their attitude towards art, the formal verse writer is a catholic, the free verse writer a protestant. And Lawrence was, in every respect, very protestant indeed. As he himself acknowledged, it was through Whitman that he found himself as a poet, found the right idiom of poetic speech for his demon.

ibid., p. 287.

The poems in *Birds, Beasts and Flowers* are among Lawrence's longest. He was not a concise writer and he needs room to make his effect. In his poetry he manages to make a virtue out of what in his prose is often a vice, a tendency to verbal repetition. The recurrence of identical or slightly varied phrases helps to give his free verse a structure; the phrases themselves are not particularly striking, but this is as it should be, for their function is to act as stitches.

ibid., p. 290.

POEMS

Violets

Sister, tha knows while we was on th' planks
Aside o' t' grave, an' th' coffin set
On th' yaller clay, wi' th' white flowers top of it
Waitin' ter be buried out o' th' wet?

An' t' parson makin' haste, an' a' t' black
Huddlin' up i' t' rain,
Did t' 'appen ter notice a bit of a lass way back
Hoverin', lookin' poor an' plain?

—How should I be lookin' round!
An' me standin' there on th' plank,
An' our Ted's coffin set on th' ground,
Waitin' to be sank!

I'd as much as I could do, to think
Of im' bein' gone
That young, an' a' the fault of drink
An' carryin's on!—

Let that be; 'appen it worna th' drink, neither,
Nor th' carryin' on as killed 'im.
—No, 'appen not,
My sirs! But I say 'twas! For a blither
Lad never stepped, till 'e got in with your lot.—

All right, all right, it's my fault! But let
Me tell about that lass. When you'd all gone
Ah stopped behind on t' pad, i' t' pourin' wet
An' watched what 'er 'ad on.

Tha should ha' seed 'er slive up when yer'd gone!
Tha should ha' seed 'er kneel an' look in
At th' sloppy grave! an' 'er little neck shone
That white, an' 'er cried that much, I'd like to begin

Scraightin' mysen as well. 'Er undid 'er black
Jacket at th' bosom, an' took out
Over a double 'andful o' violets, a' in a pack
An' white an' blue in a ravel, like a clout.

An' warm, for th' smell come waftin' to me. 'Er put 'er face
Right in 'em, an' scraighted a bit again,
Then after a bit 'er dropped 'em down that place,
An' I come away, acause o' th' teemin' rain.

But I thowt ter mysen, as that wor th' only bit
O' warmth as 'e got down theer; th' rest wor stone cold.
From that bit of a wench's bosom; 'e'd be glad of it,
Gladder nor of thy lilies, if tha maun be told.

Piano

Softly, in the dusk, a woman is singing to me;
Taking me back down the vista of years, till I see
A child sitting under the piano, in the boom of the tingling strings
And pressing the small, poised feet of a mother who smiles as she sings.

In spite of myself, the insidious mastery of song
Betrays me back, till the heart of me weeps to belong
To the old Sunday evenings at home, with winter outside
And hymns in the cosy parlour, the tinkling piano our guide.

So now it is vain for the singer to burst into clamour
With the great black piano appassionato. The glamour
Of childish days is upon me, my manhood is cast
Down in the flood of remembrance, I weep like a child for the past.

Bavarian Gentians

Not every man has gentians in his house
in Soft September, at slow, sad Michaelmas.

Bavarian gentians, big and dark, only dark
darkening the day-time, torch-like with the smoking blueness of Pluto's
    gloom,
ribbed and torch-like, with their blaze of darkness spread blue
down into flattening points, flattened under the sweep of white day
torch-flower of the blue-smoking darkness, Pluto's dark-blue daze,
black lamps from the halls of Dis, burning dark blue,
giving off darkness, blue darkness, as Demeter's pale lamps give off light,
lead me then, lead the way.

Reach me a gentian, give me a torch!
let me guide myself with the blue, forked torch of this flower
down the darker and darker stairs, where blue is darkened on blueness
even where Persephone goes, just now, from the frosted September
to the sightless realm where darkness is awake upon the dark
and Persephone herself is but a voice
or a darkness invisible enfolded in the deeper dark
of the arms Plutonic, and pierced with the passion of dense gloom,
among the splendour of torches of darkness, shedding darkness on the
    lost bride and her groom.

Shadows

And if tonight my soul may find her peace
in sleep, and sink in good oblivion,
and in the morning wake like a new-opened flower
then I have been dipped again in God, and new-created.

And if, as weeks go round, in the dark of the moon
my spirit darkens and goes out, and soft strange gloom
pervades my movements and my thoughts and words
then I shall know that I am walking still
with God, we are close together now the moon's in shadow.

And if, as autumn deepens and darkens
I feel the pain of falling leaves, and stems that break in storms
and trouble and dissolution and distress
and then the softness of deep shadows folding, folding
around my soul and spirit, around my lips
so sweet, like a swoon, or more like the drowse of a low, sad song
singing darker than the nightingale, on, on to the solstice
and the silence of short days, the silence of the year, the shadow,
then I shall know that my life is moving still
with the dark earth, and drenched
with the deep oblivion of earth's lapse and renewal.

And if, in the changing phases of man's life
I fall in sickness and in misery
my wrists seem broken and my heart seems dead
and strength is gone, and my life
is only the leavings of a life:

and still, among it all, snatches of lovely oblivion, and snatches of renewal
odd, wintry flowers upon the withered stem, yet new, strange flowers
such as my life has not brought forth before, new blossoms of me –

then I must know that still
I am in the hands [of] the unknown God,
he is breaking me down to his own oblivion
to send me forth on a new morning, a new man.

SELECT BIBLIOGRAPHY

Works by D. H. Lawrence

The Complete Poems of D. H. Lawrence, edited by Vivian de Sola Pinto and Warren Roberts, 2 vols., London, 1964.
Contains various prefatory notes by D. H. Lawrence to individual volumes; Richard Aldington's Introduction to *Last Poems*, 1933; uncollected poems; four appendices; and a valuable introductory essay by Vivian de Sola Pinto.

The Collected Letters of D. H. Lawrence, edited with an Introduction by Harry T. Moore, 2 vols., London, 1962.

Selected Literary Criticism, edited by Anthony Beal, London, 1956.

Some Biographical and Critical Studies

Alvarez, A., *The Shaping Spirit*, London, 1958.
Contains a perceptive essay on Lawrence's poetry.

Auden, W. H., *The Dyer's Hand*, New York, 1962; London, 1963.
Contains a penetrating essay on Lawrence's poetry.

Blackmur, R. P., *Language as Gesture*, New York, 1952; London, 1954.
The essay on Lawrence's poetry is the most intelligent and damaging attack yet made on Lawrence's theory and practice as a poet.

Hough, Graham, *The Dark Sun*, London, 1956.
The chapter on the poems is an admirable rejoinder to Blackmur.

'Lawrence the Poet. Achievement and Irrelevance', *The Times Literary Supplement*, 26 August 1965, pp. 725–7.
A brilliant review of *The Complete Poems*.

7
THE GEORGIANS

INTRODUCTION

Who were the Georgians? No two critics would agree on the reply to such a seemingly plain question, and perhaps it admits of no simple factual answer. Some writers who dislike all the connotations of the word Georgian are at pains to deny this title to any poet of merit who flourished between 1912 and 1922, the years spanned by Edward Marsh's anthologies. Robert Graves, we are assured, was not a Georgian, nor were D. H. Lawrence, Edward Thomas, Siegfried Sassoon, Wilfred Owen, Isaac Rosenberg, and Edmund Blunden. Whether or not they appeared in *Georgian Poetry* is, according to such critics, totally irrelevant. What matters is the quality of their work: if it is good it cannot be Georgian; if it is Georgian it must, *ipso facto,* be feeble.

In the face of such ingenious sophistry one is tempted to go to the other extreme, to impose a mechanical, external test, to declare that all the poets chosen by Marsh are Georgian, and that they alone can lay claim to the title. Like Dr. Thwackum's definition of religion, this procedure has the merits of simplicity and precision, but there is little else to commend it. A. E. Housman once remarked that to class him as a poet of the nineties would be as technically accurate and as essentially misleading as to number Lot among the Sodomites. It would be equally injudicious to rely upon *Georgian Poetry* as an infallible test of a man's right to be called a Georgian. Marsh's anthologies should be regarded as the personal choice of a single individual rather than as an official telephone directory of subscribers to the Georgian tradition.

Difficult though it would be to give a brief, satisfactory definition of the terms 'Georgian' and 'Georgianism', we can distinguish certain features which may enable us to identify a man as a Georgian. We should, however, remember that all such schematic accounts of poetry are no more than useful introductory guides to the study of poems, every one of which is a unique work of art. Bearing this in mind, we may hazard a description rather than a definition of the Georgians. They were poets who began to publish verse during the first two decades of the present century; they were content to employ the conventions of diction and the forms of verse favoured by almost all English poets from Wordsworth to Hardy; they looked for guidance to Milton, the major Romantics, and the Victorians rather than to Donne, the Metaphysicals, Dryden and Pope; they felt an intuitive sympathy with the specifically English elements of English poetry rather than with its European aspects; they remained ignorant, indifferent or hostile to the revolution in sensibility and technique inaugurated by Pound and Eliot.

The fact that many of these poets were assembled by Marsh in *Georgian Poetry* is of secondary importance. Yet there are certain advantages in beginning a survey of the Georgians by considering these anthologies. In the first place it may help us to distinguish the poets chosen by Marsh in the early days of Georgianism from those whom J. C. Squire enlisted in the pages of *The London Mercury* after Marsh had retired from the field in 1922. Secondly, it may focus our attention on a remarkable man whose generous patronage of poets and painters deserves to be commemorated.

It is all too easy to make fun of Marsh, to despise him for scurrying from one country-house to the next, to dismiss him as an elegant *dilettante* who, for all his fostering of minor talents, was incapable of recognizing the major poets of his time. Marsh was aware of his limitations. He wrote to Christopher Hassall in April 1943 that a bookseller, after praising C. E. Raven's *Science, Religion, and the Future,* remarked that it probably wouldn't appeal to him: '"No," I said, "those are the three subjects which interest me least." I said it as a joke, but thinking it over afterwards realized that it was at least a half-truth—how disgraceful.'[1] While acknowledging Eliot's gifts, he never responded wholeheartedly to his poetry, mainly because he was uncompromisingly hostile to what he regarded as unnecessary obscurity in the arts. Even so, he had the intelligence and the grace to admit that he might be in the grip of an unreasoning prejudice. Writing to Hassall in May 1943, he observed that 'if . . . I look upon Aeschylus as a supreme poet, what business have I to complain of my contemporaries for obscurity? A poser.'[2] Again, he failed to estimate Rosenberg's 'Dead Man's Dump' at its true worth, objecting to its mixture of measured and freely cadenced verse. Since it violated his canons of taste he refused to print it in *Georgian Poetry*; yet he went to the trouble of copying it out for fear that it might be lost.

Marsh's kindness and generosity were lavished not only on men who were congenial to him but on those who violently opposed the values by which he lived. He gave help and money to writers as diverse as Rosenberg, Joyce, Lawrence, and Middleton Murry; although he was deeply wounded when in 1919 Murry reviewed the fourth volume of *Georgian Poetry* in *The Athenaeum* with mocking savagery, he bore him no malice. When Katherine Mansfield died, Marsh wrote Murry a letter of condolence, which ended 'Ever your affectionate friend', and

[1] *Ambrosia and Small Beer,* arranged by Christopher Hassall, 1964, p. 252.
[2] ibid., p. 254.

Murry knew that this was the truth. In his stoical courage, his sagacity as a man of affairs, his regard for breeding, his love of a bawdy tale, Marsh was an eighteenth-century figure, who brought to his patronage of poets a touch of eighteenth-century dignity and munificence.

The genesis of *Georgian Poetry* was a luncheon party given by Marsh in his rooms at Gray's Inn on 20 September 1912, at which the guests were Rupert Brooke, John Drinkwater, W. W. Gibson, Harold Monro, and Arundel del Re. The first anthology bearing this title came out before the end of the year, an example of Marsh's administrative efficiency and decisiveness of mind. Encouraged by the large sales of *Georgian Poetry 1911–1912* – 15,000 were sold – Marsh determined to carry on with his project. He produced four more collections, in 1915, 1917, 1919, and 1922 respectively, forty poets in all being represented in the five collections.[3] Most of these poets conform to the description of the typical Georgian poet which I tried to sketch. A second glance, however, will demonstrate not only the catholicity of Marsh's taste but the undesirability of equating the Georgian poets with the names of those included in *Georgian Poetry*. Even by stretching the meaning of the term, one can scarcely regard Isaac Rosenberg, D. H. Lawrence or the youthful Peter Quennell as Georgians, yet they found shelter beneath Marsh's capacious roof. Conversely, at least four poets whom one may legitimately count as Georgians—Charles Sorley, Edward Thomas, Wilfred Owen, and Andrew Young – were never represented in Marsh's collections.[4]

In the 1920s and 1930s Georgianism became, for many young poets and critics, synonymous with tepidity, escapism, provincial respectability, conservative academicism, and vapid musings about the English countryside. The disciples of Eliot and the left-wing admirers of Auden had their own reasons for belittling the Georgians. In his influential *Faber Book of Modern Verse* (1936), Michael Roberts omitted every poet, except Graves and Owen, whom one could possibly associate with Georgianism. Although he specifically named de la Mare, Blunden, and Sorley as good poets whom he felt obliged to ignore because they had made no notable advances in technique, this slightly contemptuous saving clause made little impression on his readers; and a generation nurtured on this anthology assumed that the Georgians were a stagnant creek far from the main current of English poetry.

This propaganda has been so successful that even today a distorted version of the literary history of the years immediately before 1914 is still widely and uncritically accepted. It is generally believed that

[3] Forty, by my reckoning and by Marsh's. James Reeves, *Georgian Poetry*, 1962, p. 13, gives the number as thirty-six.

[4] Sorley and Owen are considered in the section on 'Poets of the First World War'. Robert Graves, another Georgian, is considered in the section on 'Edwin Muir and Robert Graves'.

Marsh and the Georgians were the current literary Establishment, and that the most significant young writers of the day, such as Pound, Hulme and the Imagists were violently opposed to the conservative Georgians. The Georgians themselves are held to have been amateur men-of-letters, civil servants or journalists, whose knowledge of the countryside was limited to week-end excursions from London. They stand accused of a narrow English provincialism, and of indifference to both the wider culture of Europe and the social realities of their time. Marsh himself is represented as a stickler for gentlemanly good taste, always careful to flatter the prejudices of the respectable upper-middle class.

There is scarcely any truth in these legends. In the two or three years before the outbreak of the War, the Imagists and the Georgians alike were in revolt against the fag-end of Victorian rhetoric and the entrenched forces of literary conservatism led by such men as Newbolt, Noyes, Alfred Austin and William Watson. Stephen Phillips reproved Robert Bridges and his young Georgian followers for their determination at all costs to be 'original'.[5] A similar situation prevailed across the Atlantic: in June 1913 Rupert Brooke found to his amazement that everybody in New York thought Alfred Noyes a bigger poet than Yeats or Bridges.[6]

The career of Harold Monro suggests how fantastic it is to divide the young pre-war poets into two mutually hostile groups – conservative Georgians against daring innovators. He was one of the six men present at Marsh's luncheon which led to the founding of *Georgian Poetry*; he published the anthologies; and his Poetry Bookshop at 50 Devonshire Place may be regarded as the headquarters of Georgianism. Yet he was, at the same time, the English publisher of Pound's anthology *Des Imagistes* and one of the first readers to admire Eliot's 'Prufrock'. In 1922 he published the fifth and final volume of *Georgian Poetry* and, in *The Chapbook* for September 1922, printed Osbert Sitwell's *The Jolly Old Squire or Way Down in Georgia*, a rollicking satire on the Georgians. While admiring the *The Waste Land*, he believed that there was still a place for *Georgian Poetry*, vainly urging Marsh to edit a sixth volume.

Or consider the relationship of T. E. Hulme with his contemporaries. Although he did not greatly care for Rupert Brooke, they spent ten days together in Berlin in November 1912, going to exhibitions and theatres, or sitting outside the Café des Westens discussing poetry and aesthetics. Hulme lived for a while above the Poetry Bookshop, and always remained on good terms with Marsh, Monro and other Georg-

[5] See below, p. 117. Herbert Palmer, *Post Victorian Poetry*, 1938, pp. 76–8, makes some interesting remarks on what he calls the Georgian revolt.

[6] Christopher Hassall, *Rupert Brooke*, 1964, p. 403.

ians who frequented the *salon* which he organized in Mrs. Kibblewhite's house at 67 Frith Street. He was, moreover, one of the judges who awarded *The Poetry Review*'s prize to Brooke's 'Grantchester', the other judges being Marsh, Monro, Newbolt, Edward Thomas, and Ernest Rhys – an unlikely crew.

What of Lawrence, Pound and Eliot? Although I have refused to count Lawrence as a Georgian he was a contributor to *Georgian Poetry* as well as to *Some Imagist Poets*. Of three poems by Lawrence printed in these anthologies – 'Snapdragon', 'Ballad of Another Ophelia', and 'Cruelty and Love' – it would not be easy to determine which is a 'Georgian' and which an 'Imagist' poem. Lawrence's review of *Georgian Poetry 1911–1912*, in *Rhythm*, March 1913,[7] makes it clear that for him Georgianism was a liberating movement, a breath of fresh air in the stuffy atmosphere of pre-war literary England. Strangely enough, he got on splendidly with Rupert Brooke, the two poets laughing and talking animatedly one day in the summer of 1914.[8]

Ezra Pound was gratified when Marsh asked him for contributions to the first volume of *Georgian Poetry*. Marsh eventually decided not to include any American poets, a decision which entailed dropping Pound and Frost, two of his original choices. In these early days there was no question of any hostility between Pound and the Georgians. Edward Thomas wrote an enthusiastic review of Pound's *Personae*,[9] while Brooke's review of the same volume in *The Cambridge Review*, 2 December 1910, though criticizing some of the poems as being 'blatant, full of foolish archaisms, obscure through awkward language not subtle thought, and formless', recognized Pound's latent gifts: 'When he has passed from stammering to speech, and when he has more clearly recognized the nature of poetry, he may be a great poet.'[10] On one occasion at Hulme's *salon* Marsh sat on the floor between Pound and Brooke.

Eliot, though he was one of the Georgian's most acute and damaging critics, did not harry them in pursuit of a domestic literary squabble. Measuring them against the major writers of Europe, he found them wanting, nor could he ever accept them as the leaders of a poetic renaissance. Yet it is unhistorical to believe that he was deliberately reacting against them in his early poems; even 'Prufrock', which reads like a mockery of Georgian conventions, was completed by 1911, a year before the notion of *Georgian Poetry* was conceived.

The only contemporary to draw a sharp line of demarcation between Imagists and Georgians was the very youthful Rebecca West.[11] Much more typical of the prevailing literary opinion was a lecture delivered

[7] See below, p. 117. [8] Christopher Hassall, *Rupert Brooke*, 1964, p. 450.
[9] See above, p. 60. [10] Quoted by Christopher Hassall, *Rupert Brooke*, 1964, p. 210.
[11] See above, p. 42.

at Cambridge in October 1912 by Harold Monro, in which he defined the Contemporary Poet as one who 'had caught the spirit of Darwinism'. He spoke of a group whom he called Impressionists, their chief being Ezra Pound, his disciples including James Elroy Flecker, W. W. Gibson, and Rupert Brooke.[12] Arthur Waugh's review of the first two volumes of *Georgian Poetry* and of Pound's *Catholic Anthology* throws a revealing light upon the tastes and beliefs of a conservative man of letters.[13] After quoting some remarks by Ezra Pound and describing him as one of the champions of Georgian Poetry, Waugh takes Marsh's anthologies to be an example of the new rebellion against all traditions and standards, and criticizes some of the poets for their coarse realism. Finally, after warning his readers that 'cleverness is the pitfall of the New Poetry', Waugh comments adversely on certain passages from Eliot and Pound, and concludes with an anecdote which has given rise to the story that he called Eliot and Pound 'drunken helots'. It is significant that Waugh addresses his admonition to the new Georgians: 'It was a classic custom in the family hall, when the feast was at its height, to display a drunken slave among the sons of the household, to the end that they, being ashamed at the ignominious folly of the gesticulations, might determine never to be tempted into such a pitable condition themselves.'

Other conservative reviewers took a similar line. Edmund Gosse, writing in *The Morning Post*, 27 January 1913, remarked that the poets represented in *Georgian Poetry 1911–1912* 'exchange the romantic, the sentimental, the fictive conceptions of literature, for an ingenuousness, sometimes a violence, almost a rawness in the approach to life itself'. The reviewer of the anthology, in *The Times Literary Supplement*, 27 February 1913, spoke of the poets' 'affected and self-conscious brutality', praised Brooke for being the only one of them who had not eschewed 'emotional simplicity', and referred to the intellectual quality of the verse printed in the volume: 'A poet who is afraid to use his brains seems nowadays to be as rare as was a poet twenty years ago who trusted anything but his sensibilities.'[14] Twenty years afterwards it was the poets of the thirties who were generally regarded as intellectuals, while the Georgians were held to be the poets of sensibility. Indeed, the charges of ugliness, brutality, crudity, and sordid naturalism which were levelled against the poets of the thirties were precisely the offences with which the Georgians were charged by their conserva-

[12] Christopher Hassall, *Rupert Brooke*, 1964, p. 365.

[13] Arthur Waugh, 'The New Poetry', *The Quarterly Review*, 449, October 1916, pp. 365–86. He anticipated some academic critics by declaring that D. H. Lawrence's poems displayed 'a degree of self-abandonment which is so invertebrate as to be practically abnormal'.

[14] The reviews by Gosse and by the *TLS* are quoted in Christopher Hassall, *Edward Marsh: a Biography*, 1959, pp. 684–6.

tive critics. Arthur Waugh condemned W. H. Davies's 'The Bird of Paradise' as a piece of 'sheer ugliness', a description equally applicable to W. W. Gibson's 'Geraniums'. Even in the jingoistic atmosphere of war-time England Marsh had the courage to print Siegfried Sassoon's 'They', with its reference to a British soldier's contracting syphilis.

The Georgians were not versifying pet-lambs. Nor were they comfortably-off townsmen surveying an idealized rural England from the shelter of a weekend cottage. Edmund Blunden wrote about country life because he had grown up in a village, and not in obedience to the dictates of a literary theory. In the Preface to his *Poems 1914–1930* (1930), he refers a little ruefully to those who think of him as 'a pastoral archaism', and remarks how the War has moulded and coloured his poetry. Edward Thomas knew at first hand the dispiriting effects of rural poverty, while W. H. Davies had a more intimate knowledge of urban squalor, dosshouses and slums than any left-wing poet of the 1930s.

Moreover, the literary culture of the Georgians was far less provincial and complacently English than one is sometimes led to believe. Flecker made some good translations of French poetry; Sturge Moore, a man of wide reading and acute intelligence, more than held his own with Yeats in their correspondence on literary and philosophical matters; Brooke was acquainted with the poetry of Stefan George; Sorley knew not only the works of Goethe and Hölderlin in the original but also the poems of Rilke; Edward Thomas, besides being steeped in English literature, had read a fair amount of French and German works. The more one studies the Georgians the less inclined one is to write them off as the mediocre upholders of a stale poetic tradition.

This introductory essay is not the place for a revaluation of Lascelles Abercrombie, Gordon Bottomley, W. H. Davies, Walter de la Mare, Sturge Moore, and other leading Georgians. I propose to consider briefly only two poets, Rupert Brooke and Edward Thomas – the first because he is usually held to be the Georgian poet *par excellence*, the second because his relationship with the Georgians is still a matter of debate.

For some years after his death Rupert Brooke was widely regarded as a cross between Sir Philip Sidney and John Keats, a heroic soldier-poet whose early death robbed English literature of a major writer. The inevitable reaction followed; and it was left to Christopher Hassall's long biography, *Rupert Brooke* (1964), to restore the balance and to present a figure much more interesting, tough, neurotic, and complex than the legend had portrayed.

It must be conceded that his war sonnets are inferior rhetorical pieces, yet his poetic gifts were by no means negligible. T. S. Eliot praised some lines from 'The Fish' as showing 'a really amazing felicity and command of language'.[15] Little though he cared for Brooke's 'begloried sonnets', Isaac Rosenberg described 'Clouds' as 'magnificent'.[16] Nor was he regarded by his elders as a safe, decorous poet. Newbolt referred to him as 'a frank polygamist, and rather cynical about it';[17] some of Brooke's friends, including Frances Cornford, accused his poetry of being too allusive and complex; Newbolt likened him to Donne, and Eliot may well have detected in 'The Fish' a note of Metaphysical intensity. Brooke himself, with his love of Elizabethan vitality and of the Jacobean drama, was trying at all costs to avoid prettiness and was determined to express, however crudely, what he believed to be the truth about the world.

Brooke was blessed (or cursed) with the kind of precocious literary talent that wins a poet immediate recognition. The regularity with which he gained prizes in the poetry competitions of *The Westminster Gazette* suggests that he had a facile ability to write graceful verse unsupported by any strong or coherent emotional experience. T. E. Hulme's letter to Edward Marsh, probably written in July or August 1915, describes Brooke's method of composition: 'He said that with him, in writing, the first *direct* step (of crystallisation, as it were, as distinct from mere thought about a subject) was to get hold of one finished line with a *definite* rhythm, that set the mould for the rest.'[18] This procedure aroused irreverent mirth among Brooke's friends, inspiring Jacques Raverat to ask, 'Have you seen Rupert's note-books, with all the first drafts of sonnets with blanks left for the Oh Gods?'[19]

In May 1912, while staying in Berlin, Brooke wrote one of his most celebrated poems, 'The Old Vicarage, Grantchester'. It is the kind of showpiece which young ladies recite at verse-speaking competitions, and not until one has heard it rendered aloud does one fully comprehend how feeble a poem it is. In fairness to Brooke, we should remember that he originally called it 'The Sentimental Exile', and that he was persuaded by Marsh to alter the title. Brooke's own account of the poem's genesis is contained in a letter to Frances Cornford: 'I scrawled in a café a very long poem about Grantchester, that seemed to me to have pleasant silly passages.'[20]

Despite Brooke's high spirits and capacity for enjoyment, he was a prey to a despair and a self-loathing which it is difficult to account for or to analyse, although it seems likely that they were sexual in origin.

[15] 'Reflections on Contemporary Poetry', *The Egoist*, IV, 8, September 1917, p. 118.
[16] *Collected Works*, edited by Gordon Bottomley and Denys Harding, 1937, p. 313.
[17] *The Later Life and Letters of Sir Henry Newbolt*, edited by Margaret Newbolt, 1942, p. 207.
[18] Alun R. Jones, *The Life and Opinions of T. E. Hulme*, 1960, p. 210.
[19] Christopher Hassall, *Rupert Brooke*, 1964, p. 280.
[20] ibid., p. 343.

The extracts quoted by Christopher Hassall from Brooke's letter of August 1912 to Ka Cox testify to his self-disgust, and to his fear that he was incapable of any fruitful sexual relationship: 'My dear, it's nothing to do with you – I'm somehow rotten. And I guess it'll be better if I don't leave children – people like me – behind.'[21] His tormented love-affair with Ka Cox ended in his suffering a nervous breakdown, from which Jacques Raverat believed he never recovered: 'I still really think he died of it, in a way'.[22] Probably the closest that he came to sexual fulfilment was in Tahiti, where he found brief happiness with a girl called Taatamata, the girl whom he addresses as Mamua in 'Tiare, Tahiti'. Yet during the war he was shaken by a dream in which he went back to Tahiti and learned that she had killed herself.[23] A little later, he received a letter from her, full of misspellings in French, and English; he read it and 'gulped a good deal'.[24] His article about the Samoans contains an almost Lawrentian diagnosis of a spiritual sickness from which Brooke himself was probably suffering. A European living among the Samoans, he says, 'soon learns to *be* his body (and his true mind) instead of using it as a stupid convenience for his personality, a moment's umbrella against the world'.[25]

Viewed in the light of what we now know about Brooke, his war sonnets can no longer be read as a simple clarion call to arms: they are a desperate attempt by a tormented man to find emotional relief from a morbid self-disgust. His outburst against intellectuals – 'dehumanized, disgusting people. They are mostly pacific and pro-Germans. I quarrel with them twice a day.'[26] – is symptomatic of his irritability, and of his refusal to consider the possibility that the war was not an heroic endeavour. A letter to Raverat towards the end of 1914 sounds an hysterical note: 'I really think that large numbers of male people don't want to die. Which is odd. I've been praying for a German raid.'[27] His natural humanity and good sense reasserted themselves when he saw for himself the miseries inflicted by the war on the refugees pouring out of Antwerp. And a letter written soon after the outbreak of war rings truer than the heroics of the war sonnets, the efforts to convince himself that there was a meaning in his life: 'I'm so uneasy – subconsciously. All the vague perils of the time – the world seems so dark – and I'm vaguely frightened.'[28]

After Brooke had visited Yeats and Pound to drink coffee at Woburn Place on 22 January 1913, Yeats wrote to St. John Ervine to express the hope that Brooke would get rid of his 'languid sensuality' and acquire

[21] Christopher Hassall, *Rupert Brooke*, 1964, p. 355.
[22] ibid, p. 522. [23] ibid., p. 476.
[24] ibid., p. 480. [25] ibid., p. 460.
[26] ibid., p. 460. [27] ibid., p. 473.
[28] Rupert Brooke, *Collected Poems*, with a Memoir [by Edward Marsh], 1918, p. cxxiv.

'robust sensuality'.[29] Arthur Waugh, though reproving Brooke for his 'modern melancholy', believed that, had he survived the war, 'its cleansing fire would have lighted him to achievements both in life and poetry far greater than had yet been dreamed of by a philosophy so disillusioned and so disintegrate.'[30] It is kinder to Brooke's memory to suppose that he would have reacted like Wilfred Owen to the cleansing fire of the Somme and Passchendaele. When he lay dying, his friend Denis Browne came to his cabin to tell him that Dean Inge had praised 'The Soldier' in his Easter Day sermon at St. Paul's. Brooke had already received a newspaper cutting from Marsh which quoted both Inge's praise, and his qualifying clause: 'And yet it fell somewhat short of Isaiah's vision and still more of the Christian hope.' Brooke murmured to Browne that he was sorry the Dean didn't think him quite so good as Isaiah. These were his last coherent words. It was fitting that so complex and intelligent a man should have regarded with amused scepticism the kind of fulsome praise that was to be lavished on him after his death.

Nobody has ever questioned the propriety of calling Brooke a Georgian. There is no such general agreement about Edward Thomas's affinities with that group. Unlike F. R. Leavis, who declined to associate Thomas with the Georgians,[31] Thomas associated himself with them from the inception of the movement until his death. He was on terms of friendship with several Georgians, and admired the work of Lascelles Abercrombie, Sturge Moore, Bottomley, de la Mare, and Davies; he was, as we have seen, one of the judges who awarded a prize to Brooke's 'Grantchester'; and when, late in his literary career, he began to write poetry it was to the Georgians that he turned for criticism and recognition.

Since pride and sensitivity forbade him to submit his poems to editors under his own name, he sent them out under the pseudonym of Edward Eastaway. It is much to the discredit of these editors that no periodical, except an obscure quarterly called *Form*, accepted any of his poems. *The Times* failed even to return his manuscripts. *Blackwood* objected to a phrase from 'Lob':

> That Mother Dunch's Buttocks should not lack
> Their name was his care

and refused to be mollified even when Thomas, in mingled amusement and exasperation, altered the offending phrase to 'Happersnapper Hanger', the most outlandish name he could find on his ordnance survey maps.[32]

29 Christopher Hassall, *Rupert Brooke*, 1964, p. 374.
30 'The New Poetry', *The Quarterly Review*, 449, October 1916, p. 379.
31 F. R. Leavis, *New Bearings in English Poetry*, 1932, pp. 68–9.
32 John Moore, *The Life and Letters of Edward Thomas*, 1939, p. 222.

It is often suggested that the Georgians failed to recognize Thomas's gifts, and that his exclusion from *Georgian Poetry* is proof of their indifference to his poetry. The facts do not bear out this contention. It is true that Harold Monro was totally blind to the quality of Thomas's verse, a strange lapse for a man of such discernment. When, without revealing their authorship, Thomas showed some of his early poems to W. H. Davies, the latter remarked that they must be by Robert Frost, and ever afterwards blamed himself for his obtuseness. Unhappily, this incident confirmed Thomas in his fears that he lacked a strongly individual voice.[33]

Yet apart from his close friend, James Guthrie, nobody did more than the Georgians to make Thomas's poems widely known. Bottomley showed some of his first poems to two prominent fellow-Georgians, Lascelles Abercrombie and R. C. Trevelyan, who were 'deeply interested', and who printed eighteen of them in *An Annual Anthology* (1917).[34] Although Marsh's first meeting with Thomas on 5 March 1913 was not a success, it is unfair to blame Marsh for excluding him from *Georgian Poetry*. Thomas did not begin writing verse until 1914, nor did he compose any of his best poems until the winter of 1914–1915. Thus it would scarcely have been feasible to include him even in the second anthology, let alone the first. In 1917 de la Mare, John Freeman and W. J. Turner urged Marsh to put Thomas in the forthcoming anthology, de la Mare offering to stand down in his favour. Marsh, however, felt unable to relax his rule of not printing the posthumous work of any poet unless he had been previously represented in the series.

When, prompted in part by Robert Frost (whose peculiar merits he had immediately recognized), Thomas began to write poems, it was as though he had suddenly discovered the one medium in which his intelligence and sensibility could move unfettered. As he told Eleanor Farjeon, in the winter of 1914–1915, 'If I am consciously doing anything, I am trying to get rid of the last rags of rhetoric and formality which left my prose so often with a dead rhythm.'[35] The virtues of Thomas's poetry are by now so well appreciated that it would be pointless to rehearse them. It is less often remarked that they are precisely the virtues which most of the Georgians aimed at, but seldom achieved. For, as Walter de la Mare wrote in his Foreword to the Faber Library edition of Thomas's *Collected Poems* (1936), 'There is nothing precious, elaborate, brilliant, esoteric, obscure in his work. The feeling is never "fine", the thought never curious, or the word far-fetched.' It was, presumably, because his work lacked these qualities, and because it was devoid of any apparent social or political relevance, that Michael

[33] Richard J. Stonesifer, *W. H. Davies: a Critical Biography*, 1963, p. 116.
[34] John Moore, *The Life and Letters of Edward Thomas*, 1939, p. 238.
[35] ibid., p. 220.

Roberts saw no necessity even to apologize for his exclusion from *The Faber Book of Modern Verse*. Yet much as we may deplore this failure to acknowledge the intuitive subtlety and skill of Thomas's art, we may think it appropriate that Roberts should have swept him away into the lumber-room with the other Georgians. At least he perceived where Thomas's affinities lay.

The Georgians were the last influential group of English poets to be totally unaffected by the modernism of Hulme, Pound, and Wyndham Lewis. It is not a coincidence that they were the last group of young poets to enjoy the esteem of the ordinary reading public. If we are tempted to dismiss them as very minor songsters warbling away in a provincial backwater, it is salutary to recall that all but a handful of poets in every generation are very minor jackdaws decked out in fashionable feathers. Whatever the limitations of *Georgian Poetry* may be, these five volumes contain many more good poems than the various Imagist anthologies or the Sitwellian *Wheels*. And if we admit that Wilfred Owen and Edward Thomas were, in essentials, Georgian poets (though never appearing in Marsh's volumes), then the Georgian achievement begins to look more formidable than most critics of twentieth-century verse have been willing to concede.[36]

CRITICISM

This volume is issued in the belief that English poetry is now once again putting on a new strength and beauty.

Few readers have the leisure or the zeal to investigate each volume as it appears; and the process of recognition is often slow. This collection, drawn entirely from the publications of the past two years, may if it is fortunate help the lovers of poetry to realize that we are at the beginning of another 'Georgian period' which may take rank in due time with the several great poetic ages of the past.

E[dward]. M[arsh]., Prefatory Note, *Georgian Poetry 1911–1912*, 1912.

I may add one word bearing on my aim in selection. Much admired modern work seems to me, in its lack of inspiration and its disregard of form, like gravy imitating lava. Its upholders may retort that much of the work which I prefer seems to them, in its lack of inspiration and its comparative finish, like tapioca imitating pearls. Either view – possibly both – may be right. I will only say that with an occasional exception for some piece of rebelliousness or even levity which may

[36] I read Robert H. Ross's *The Georgian Revolt: Rise and Fall of a Poetic Ideal 1910–1922*, 1967, after I had written this section of the book.

have taken my fancy. I have tried to choose no verse but such as in Wordsworth's phrase

> The high and tender Muses shall accept
> With gracious smile, deliberately pleased.

E[dward]. M[arsh]., Prefatory Note, *Georgian Poetry 1920–1922*, 1922.

This collection is like a big breath taken when we are waking up after a night of oppressive dreams. The nihilists, the intellectual, hopeless people – Ibsen, Flaubert, Thomas Hardy – represent the dream we are waking from. It was a dream of demolition. Nothing was, but was nothing...

But we are awake again, our lungs are full of new air, our eyes of morning. The first song is nearly a cry, fear and the pain of remembrance sharpening away the pure music. And that is this book.

D. H. Lawrence, Review of *Georgian Poetry 1911–1912*, *Rhythm*, II, March 1913, Literary Supplement, pp. xvii–xx. Reprinted in *D. H. Lawrence: Selected Literary Criticism*, edited by Anthony Beal, 1956, p. 72.

We have therefore as the official representative of English verse the patron-saint of what one may call 'the bloodless school' of modern poetry. The representatives of this school are a large class of the younger men who call themselves Georgian poets, and as their leader is Dr. Bridges, so their prophet is Sir Arthur Quiller-Couch. Their business in verse is chiefly that of the present Laureate, a clever cold carpentry of metre and an intense determination to be 'original'. But it may be pointed out that, as in the verse of Dr. Bridges, this technical originality has rather the effect of irritation than inspiration; it is fidgety rather than fiery, and the fact is ignored that what is called the great 'technique' of verse is rather the result of an overpowering emotion and sense of glory than a toying with the inanimate.

Stephen Phillips, 'The Appointment to the Laureateship', *The Poetry Review*, III, 3, September 1913, p. 137.

... the American shows his too quick susceptibility to foreign influence; the Englishman his imperviousness. For contemporary English verse has borrowed little from foreign sources; it is almost politically English; the Georgian poets insist upon the English countryside, and are even positively patriotic. When, therefore, they turn to the common object, to the animal or flower or hearth-rug, it is in the mood, not of Dostoevski but of Wordsworth. Because of this Wordsworthian strain I have called their attention trivial (not invidiously) rather than accidental. Both methods or manners, the Wordsworth and the Dostoevski, may be distinguished from another which is more universal: it is universally human to attach the strongest emotions to definite tokens. Only, while with the Russian the emotion dissolves in a mass of sensational detail, and while with Wordsworth the emotion is of the object and not of human life, with certain poets the emotion is definitely human, merely seizing the object in order to express itself . . .

In the Georgian poets we observe the same [Wordsworthian] attitude. The emotion is derived from the object, and such emotions must either be vague (as in Wordsworth) or, if more definite, pleasing. Thus, it is not unworthy of notice how often the word 'little' occurs; and how this word is used, not merely as a necessary piece of information, but with a caress, a conscious delight . . .

The Georgian Love of Nature is on the whole less vague than Wordsworth's, and has less philosophy behind it: for Wordsworth had a philosophy, though ill apprehended from foreign teachers; the Georgian plays more delicately with his subject, and in his style has often more in common with Stevenson. On the other hand, not having abstractions to fall back upon, the modern poet, when he diverts his attention from birds, fields, and villages, is subject to lapses of rhetoric from which Wordsworth, with his complete innocence of other emotions than those in which he specialized, is comparatively free.

T. S. E[liot]., 'Reflections on Contemporary Poetry', *The Egoist*, IV, 8, September 1917, pp. 118–19.

Verse stands in constant need of what Samuel Butler calls a cross. The serious writer of verse must be prepared to cross himself with the best verse of other languages and the best prose of all languages. In Georgian poetry there is almost no crossing visible; it is inbred. It has developed a technique and a set of emotions all of its own . . . What nearly all the writers have in common is the quality of pleasantness. There are two varieties of pleasantness: (1) The insidiously didactic, or Wordsworthian (a rainbow and a cuckoo's song); (2) the decorative, playful or solemn, minor-Keatsian, too happy, happy brook, or lucent sirops. In either variety the Georgians caress everything they touch . . . Another variety of the pleasant, by the way, is the unpleasant (*sc.* Rupert Brooke on sea-sickness, and Masefield on various subjects).

'Apteryx', 'Verse Pleasant and Unpleasant', review of *Georgian Poetry, 1916–1917. The Egoist*, V, 3, March 1918, p. 43.

['Apteryx' was a pseudonym of T. S. Eliot's.]

Georgianism was an English dead movement contemporary with Imagism and politically affiliated with the then dominant Liberal party. Although not so highly organized, it had a great vogue between the years 1912 and 1918 and was articulate chiefly upon questions of style. The Georgians' general recommendations were the discarding of archaistic diction such as 'thee' and 'thou' and 'floweret' and 'whene'er' and of poetical constructions such as 'winter drear' and 'host on armed host' and of pomposities generally. It was also understood that, in reaction to Victorianism, their verse should avoid all formally religious, philosophic or improving themes; and all sad, wicked, café-table themes in reaction to the 'nineties. Georgian poetry was to be English but not aggressively imperialistic; pantheistic rather than atheistic; and as simple as a child's reading book. These recommendations resulted in a poetry which could be praised rather for what it was not than for what it was. Eventually Georgianism became principally concerned with Nature and love and leisure and old age and childhood and animals and sleep and similar uncontroversial subjects.

Laura Riding and Robert Graves, *A Survey of Modernist Poetry*, 1927, p. 119. Reprinted in Robert Graves, *The Common Asphodel*, 1949, pp. 112–13.

There have been one or two attempts of recent years to anthologise poetry, but the mind of the public had already been predisposed by the appearance of Georgian Poetry and the anthologies which derive from it.

1. Have you ever been on a walking tour?
2. Do you suffer from Elephantiasis of the Soul?
3. Do you make friends easily with dogs, poultry etc?
4. Are you easily exalted by natural objects?
5. Do you live in one place and yearn to be in another place?
6. Can you write in rhyme and metre?

Any one of these conditions, combined of course with the sixth, if conscientiously complied with, is a safe passport to half a dozen anthologies.

Roy Campbell, 'Contemporary Poetry', *Scrutinies*, edited by Edgell Rickword, 1928, p. 172.

And now I've got to quarrel with you about the Ralph Hodgson poem: because I think it's banal in utterance. The feeling is there, right enough – but not in itself, only represented. It's like 'I asked for bread, and he gave me a penny'. Only here and there is the least touch of personality in the poem: it is the currency of poetry, not poetry itself. Every single line of it is poetic currency – and a good deal of emotion handling it about. But it isn't really poetry. I hope to God you won't hate me and think me carping, for this. But look:

> the ruby's and the rainbow's song
> the nightingale's – all three

There's the emotion in the rhythm, but it's loose emotion, inarticulate, common – the words are mere currency. It is exactly like a man who feels very strongly for a beggar, and gives him a sovereign. The feeling is at either end, for the moment, but the sovereign is a dead bit of metal. And this poem is the sovereign.

ibid., p. 236.

To recognize that the dream is a dream, yet refuse to put it away, this is the vital act of comprehension which animates the enduring part of the poetry of the present age . . .

When we say, therefore, that Mr. de la Mare's poetry is characteristic of the age, it is not in the sense that there is much poetry of the same quality to be found in our magazines and bookshops today – there is, alas, very little – but that it makes an appeal to, and in a way satisfies minds which have been tempered by the common experience. The strings have been so tightened that they respond to this touch . . .

John Middleton Murry, 'The Poetry of Walter de la Mare', *Countries of the Mind*, 1931, pp. 89–93.
[An enlarged version of a review printed in *The Athenaeum* in 1920.]

One might say that, in every poet, there dwells an Ariel, who sings, and a Prospero, who comprehends, but in any particular poem, sometimes even in the whole work of a particular poet, one of the partners plays a greater role than the other . . .

Though the role of Prospero in de la Mare's poetry is much greater than one may realize on a first reading, it would not be unfair, I think, to call him an Ariel-dominated poet. Certainly, his most obvious virtues, those which no reader can fail to see immediately, are verbal and formal, the delicacy of his metrical fingering and the graceful architecture of his stanzas. Neither in his technique nor his sensibility, does he show any trace of influences other than English, either continental, like Eliot and Pound, or Classical, like Bridges. The poets from whom he seems to have learned most are the Elizabethan song-writers, Christina Rossetti and, I would rashly guess, Thomas Hardy.

W. H. Auden, Introduction to *A Choice of de la Mare's Verse*, 1963, pp. 14–15.

As the work of some of the Georgian poets bears witness, the danger of the English landscape as a poetic ingredient is that its gentleness can tempt those who love it into writing genteely. De la Mare was protected from this, firstly by his conviction that what our senses perceive of the world about us is not all there is to know, and, secondly, by his sense of the powers of evil. This does not mean that he is a Buddhist who regards the sensory world as illusion, or that he would call what we are normally blind to *super*-natural. His view, I take it, is that our eyes and ears do not lie to us, but do not, perhaps cannot, tell us the whole truth, and that those who deny this, end up actually narrowing their vision.

ibid., p. 21.

Poetry in verse is at one with the tides and the pulse; prose is chaos cut up into beds and borders and fountains and rusticwork like a garden. A merely great intellect can produce great prose, but not poetry, not one line.

Edward Thomas, Letter to Gordon Bottomley, 26 February 1908. John Moore, *The Life and Letters of Edward Thomas*, 1939, p. 308.

[James Elroy Flecker] is one of the 'artificers in verse' that I can't quite get on with, the decorators, like Wilde, who carry Keats' style to its logical extreme without genius. But he did it very well indeed. There are passages reminding me of some of the solid French rhetoricians in verse like Lecompte de Lisle.[37] And if you want brass or even gold why not have it in metal? Words can't be given that character without losing their own, it seems to me.

Edward Thomas, Letter to W. H. Hudson, 9 October 1915, ibid., p. 331.

By the way what I have done so far have been like quintessences of the best parts of my prose books – not much sharper or more intense, but I hope a little: since the first take off they haven't been Frosty very much or so I imagine and I have tried as often as possible to avoid the facilities offered by blank verse and I try not to be long – I even have an ambition to keep under 12 lines (but rarely succeed).

Edward Thomas, Letter to John Freeman, 8 March 1915, ibid., p. 326.

[Sturge] Moore was excellent in principle. But in condemning Frost I think still that he had been misled with supposing that Frost wanted poetry to be colloquial. All he insists on is what he believes he finds in all poets – absolute fidelity to the postures which the voice assumes in the most expressive intimate speech. So long as these tones and postures are there he has not the least objection to any vocabulary whatever or any inversion or variation from any customary grammatical forms of talk. In fact I think he would agree that if these tones and postures survive in a complicated and learned or subtle vocabulary and structure the result is likely to be better than if they survive in the easiest form, that is in the very words and structures of common speech, though

[37] Thomas's spelling.

that is not easy or prose would be better than it is and survive more often . . .

As to my own method I expect it to change if there is anything more than a doting replica of youthful eagerness in this unexpected ebullition. But although it has a plain look, it does so far, I think, represent a culmination as a rule, and does not ask or get much correction on paper.

Edward Thomas, Letter to Gordon Bottomley, 30 June 1915, ibid., pp. 328–9.

You see the central evil is self-consciousness carried as far beyond selfishness as selfishness is beyond self-denial (not very scientific comparison), and now amounting to a disease and all I have got to fight it with is the knowledge that in truth I am not the isolated self-considering brain which I have come to seem – the *knowledge* that I am something more, but not the *belief* that I can reopen the connection between that brain and the rest . . . Please forgive me and try not to give any thought to this flat grey shore which surprises the tide by being inaccessible to it.

Edward Thomas, Letter to Eleanor Farjeon, ? July 1913, ibid., pp. 318–19.

Edward Thomas was like a musician who noted down themes that summon up forgotten expectations. Whether the genius to work them out to the limits of their scope and implication was in him we do not know. The life of literature was a hard master to him; and perhaps the opportunity he would eagerly have grasped was denied him by circumstance. But, if his compositions do not, his themes will never fail – of so much we are sure – to awaken unsuspected echoes even in unsuspecting minds.

John Middleton Murry, review of Edward Thomas, *Last Poems, The Nation*, January 1919. Reprinted, and retitled 'The Poetry of Edward Thomas', in *Aspects of Literature*, 1920, pp. 29–38.

POEMS

RUPERT BROOKE
(1887–1915)

Clouds

Down the blue night the unending columns press
  In noiseless tumult, break and wave and flow,
  Now tread the far South, or lift rounds of snow
Up to the white moon's hidden loveliness.
Some pause in their grave wandering comradeless,
  And turn with profound gesture vague and slow,
  As who would pray good for the world, but know
Their benediction empty as they bless.

They say that the Dead die not, but remain
  Near to the rich heirs of their grief and mirth.
    I think they ride the calm mid-heaven, as these,
In wise majestic melancholy train,
    And watch the moon, and the still-raging seas,
  And men, coming and going on the earth.

W. H. DAVIES
(1871–1940)

The Inquest

I took my oath I would inquire,
  Without affection, hate, or wrath,
Into the death of Ada Wright –
  So help me God! I took that oath.

When I went out to see the corpse,
  The four months' babe that died so young,
I judged it was seven pounds in weight,
  And little more than one foot long.

One eye, that had a yellow lid,
  Was shut – so was the mouth, that smiled;
The left eye open, shining bright –
  It seemed a knowing little child.

For as I looked at that one eye,
  It seemed to laugh, and say with glee:
'What caused my death you'll never know –
  Perhaps my mother murdered me.'

When I went into court again,
  To hear the mother's evidence –
It was a love-child, she explained.
  And smiled, for our intelligence.

'Now, Gentlemen of the Jury,' said
  The coroner – 'this woman's child
By misadventure met its death.'
  'Aye, aye,' said we. The mother smiled.

And I could see that child's one eye
  Which seemed to laugh, and say with glee:
'What caused my death you'll never know –
  Perhaps my mother murdered me.'

The Cat

Within that porch, across the way,
  I see two naked eyes this night;
Two eyes that neither shut nor blink,
  Searching my face with a green light.

But cats to me are strange, so strange –
  I cannot sleep if one is near;
And though I'm sure I see those eyes.
  I'm not so sure a body's there!

A Woman's History

When Mary Price was five years old,
  And had a bird that died,
She laid its body under flowers;
  And called her friends to pray to God,
And sing sad hymns for hours.

When she, before her fifteenth year,
  Was ruined by a man,
The neighbours sought him out, and said –
  'You'll come along and marry her,
Or hang till you are dead.'

When they had found the child he wronged,
  And playing with her doll,
'I'll come along with you,' said she –
  'But I'll not marry anyone
Unless my doll's with me.'

With no more love's heat in her than
  The wax upon her arm;
With no more love-light in her eyes
  Than in the glass eyes of her doll –
Nor wonder, nor surprise.

When Mary Price was thirty-five,
  And he was lying dead,
She wept as though her heart would break:
  But neighbours winked to see the tears
Fall on a lover's neck.

Now, Mary Price is seventy-five,
  And skinning eels alive:
She, active, strong, and full of breath,
  Has caught the cat that stole an eel,
And beaten it to death.

Earth Love

I love the earth through my two eyes,
  Like any butterfly or bee;
The hidden roots escape my thoughts,
  I love but what I see.

A tree has lovely limbs, I know,
  Both large and strong, down under earth;
But all my thoughts are in the boughs,
  That give the green leaves birth.

My friend, his thought goes deeper down,
  Beneath the roots, while mine's above:
He's thinking of a quiet place
  To sleep with his dead Love.

WALTER DE LA MARE
(1873–1956)

Fare Well

When I lie where shades of darkness
Shall no more assail mine eyes,
Nor the rain make lamentation
    When the wind sighs:
How will fare the world whose wonder
Was the very proof of me?
Memory fades, must the remembered
    Perishing be?

Oh, when this my dust surrenders
Hand, foot, lip, to dust again,
May these loved and loving faces
    Please other men!
May the rusting harvest hedgerow
Still the Traveller's Joy entwine,
And as happy children gather
    Posies once mine.

Look thy last on all things lovely,
Every hour. Let no night
Seal thy sense in deathly slumber
    Till to delight
Thou have paid thy utmost blessing;
Since that all things thou wouldst praise
Beauty took from those who loved them
    In other days.

The Ditch

Masked by that brilliant weed's deceitful green,
No glint of the dark waters can be seen
Which, festering, slumbers, with this scum for screen.

It is as though a face, as false as fair,
Dared not, by smiling, show the evil there.

Lost World

Why, inward companion, are you so dark with anguish?
A trickle of rancid water that oozes and veers,
Picking its sluggish course through slag and refuse,
Down at length to the all-oblivious ocean –
What else were apt comparison for your tears?

But no: not of me are you grieving, nor for me either;
Though I, it seems, am the dungeon in which you dwell,
Derelict, drear, with skeleton arms to heaven,
Wheels broken, abandoned, greenless, vacant, silent;
  Nought living that eye can tell.

Blame any man might the world wherein he harbours,
Washing his hands, like Pilate, of all its woes;
And yet in deadly revolt at its evil and horror,
That has brought pure life to this pass, smit through with sorrow,
Since he was its infamous wrecker full well he knows.

Not yours the blame. Why trouble me then with your presence?
Linger no instant, most Beautiful, in this hell.
No touch of time has marred your immutable visage;
Eros himself less radiant was in his dayspring! –
Or nearer draw to your heartsick infidel!

EDWARD THOMAS
(1878–1917)

Rain

Rain, midnight rain, nothing but the wild rain
On this bleak hut, and solitude, and me
Remembering again that I shall die
And neither hear the rain nor give it thanks
For washing me cleaner than I have been
Since I was born into this solitude.
Blessed are the dead that the rain rains upon:
But here I pray that none whom once I loved
Is dying to-night or lying still awake
Solitary, listening to the rain,
Either in pain or thus in sympathy
Helpless among the living and the dead,
Like a cold water among broken reeds,
Myriads of broken reeds all still and stiff,
Like me who have no love which this wild rain
Has not dissolved except the love of death,
If love it be for what is perfect and
Cannot, the tempest tells me, disappoint.

To-Night

Harry, you know at night
The larks in Castle Alley
Sing from the attic's height
As if the electric light
Were the true sun above a summer valley:
Whistle, don't knock, to-night.

I shall come early, Kate:
And we in Castle Alley
Will sit close out of sight
Alone, and ask no light
Of lamp or sun above a summer valley:
To-night I can stay late.

Aspens

All day and night, save winter, every weather,
Above the inn, the smithy, and the shop,
The aspens at the cross-roads talk together
Of rain, until their last leaves fall from the top.

Out of the blacksmith's cavern comes the ringing
Of hammer, shoe, and anvil; out of the inn
The clink, the hum, the roar, the random singing –
The sounds that for these fifty years have been.

The whisper of the aspens is not drowned,
And over lightless pane and footless road,
Empty as sky, with every other sound
Not ceasing, calls their ghosts from their abode,

A silent smithy, a silent inn, nor fails
In the bare moonlight or the thick-furred gloom,
In tempest or the night of nightingales,
To turn the cross-roads to a ghostly room.

And it would be the same were no house near.
Over all sorts of weather, men, and times,
Aspens must shake their leaves and men may hear
But need not listen, more than to my rhymes.

Whatever wind blows, while they and I have leaves
We cannot other than an aspen be
That ceaselessly, unreasonably grieves,
Or so men think who like a different tree.

ANDREW YOUNG
(b. 1885)

Autumn Mist

So thick a mist hung over all,
Rain had no room to fall;
It seemed a sea without a shore;
The cobwebs drooped heavy and hoar
As though with wool they had been knit;
Too obvious mark for fly to hit!

And though the sun was somewhere else
The gloom had brightness of its own
That shone on bracken, grass and stone
And mole-mound with its broken shells
That told where squirrel lately sat,
Cracked hazel-nuts and ate the fat.

And sullen haws in the hedgerows
Burned in the damp with clearer fire;
And brighter still than those
The scarlet hips hung on the briar
Like coffins of the dead dog-rose;
All were as bright as though for earth
Death were a gayer thing than birth.

EDMUND BLUNDEN
(b. 1896)

Malefactors

Nailed to these green laths long ago,
You cramp and shrivel into dross,
Blotched with mildews, gnawed with moss,
And now the eye can scarcely know
The snake among you from the kite,
  So sharp does Death's fang bite.

I guess your stories; you were shot
Hovering above the miller's chicks;
And you, coiled on his threshold bricks –
Hissing you died; and you, sir Stoat,
Dazzled with stableman's lantern stood
  And tasted crabtree wood.

Here then you leered-at luckless churls,
Clutched to your clumsy gibbet, shrink
To shapeless orts; hard by the brink
Of this black scowling pond that swirls
To turn the wheel beneath the mill,
  The wheel so long since still.

There's your revenge, the wheel at tether,
The miller gone, the white planks rotten,
The very name of the mill forgotten,
Dimness and silence met together.
Felons of fur and feather, can
  There lurk some crime in man,

In man your executioner,
Whom here Fate's cudgel battered down?
Did he too filch from squire and clown?
The damp gust makes the ivy whir
Like passing death; the sluices well,
  Dreary as a passing-bell.

SELECT BIBLIOGRAPHY

General

Georgian Poetry, 5 vols., London, 1912–1922. Edited by E.[dward] M.[arsh].

Georgian Poetry, edited by James Reeves, Harmondsworth, 1962.

Ross, Robert H., *The Georgian Revolt: Rise and Fall of a Poetic Ideal 1920–1922*, London, 1967.

Edmund Blunden

Poems of Many Years, London, 1957.
A selection by Rupert Hart-Davis from Blunden's earlier volumes, with twenty hitherto uncollected poems.

A Hongkong House, London, 1962.

Rupert Brooke

Collected Poems, London, 1918.
With a long Memoir by Edward Marsh.

Poetical Works, edited by Geoffrey Keynes, London, 1946.

Hassall, Christopher, *Rupert Brooke*, London, 1964.
A long, authoritative biography, containing valuable material about Brooke and his circle.

W. H. Davies

Complete Poems, London, 1963.

Stonesifer, Richard J., *W. H. Davies: A Critical Biography*, London, 1963.

Walter de la Mare
Collected Poems, London, 1942.
A new edition is being prepared.
A Choice of de la Mare's Verse, edited by W. H. Auden, London, 1963.

Edward Thomas
Collected Poems, London, 1936.
Coombes, H., *Edward Thomas*, London, 1956.
Farjeon, Eleanor, *Memoirs*, Book I: *Edward Thomas*, London, 1958.
Moore, John, *The Life and Letters of Edward Thomas*, London, 1939.
Scannell, Vernon, *Edward Thomas*, London, 1963.
Thomas, Helen, *As It Was*, London, 1926.
—— *World Without End*, London, 1931.

8

POETS OF THE FIRST WORLD WAR

INTRODUCTION

Out of the gutters and slums of Hell –
Disgorged from the vast infernal sewer –
Vomited forth from a world where dwell
Childhood, maidenhood, wifehood pure –
She arose and towered on earth and sea,
Clothed in her green putridity.

These lines about Germany by Sir William Watson are typical of the chauvinistic rubbish spawned at the outbreak of the First World War. Sir Henry Newbolt correctly guessed the prevailing mood and, hastening to gather some of his more resounding patriotic effusions into a new volume, was speedily rewarded with sales of 70,000 copies. Even so wise and gentle a man as Thomas Hardy was infected by the atmosphere of the day. His 'Men Who March Away', though on a different level of achievement from Watson's doggerel, is tinged with a self-righteousness and a religious fervour that he would not normally have admitted into his work:

In our heart of hearts believing
  Victory crowns the just,
  And that braggarts must
  Surely bite the dust.

There were, it is true, poets who disdained the facile appeal to the cruder elements of nationalism and militarism. A. E. Housman, indeed, was widely blamed for showing, in 'Epitaph on an Army of Mercenaries', disrespect towards God and the Regular Army. Ford Madox Ford displayed his customary unworldliness and chivalry. Not only did he refrain from urging his fellow-countrymen to go forward into battle: he actually fought himself, as a volunteer, although well above military age. His poem 'Antwerp' [1] has been almost forgotten, yet T. S. Eliot called it 'the only good poem I have met with on the subject of the war'.[2]

[1] See above, pp. 48–9.

[2] 'Reflections on Contemporary Poetry', *The Egoist*, IV, 10, November 1917, p. 151. 'Antwerp' attempts to portray modern warfare by Imagistic technique. It was written in 1914, and similar attempts were made later by Richard Aldington and Herbert Read.

In fairness to the elderly poets who welcomed the advent of the war with such enthusiasm, we must remember that their emotions were shared by their more youthful contemporaries. Rupert Brooke's sonnet 'Peace' was merely the most famous expression of the mood in which thousands of young men volunteered for military service in the early months of the war. Most of them regarded the conflict, if not as a crusade, at least as a high adventure undertaken for noble ends. It was not until the slaughter on the Somme in 1916 that this sense of pride and exhilaration was replaced by ever-growing doubt and disillusion.

The most eloquent memorial to this vanished faith is Julian Grenfell's poem 'Into Battle', written in Flanders in April 1915 shortly before he was killed. Grenfell, the son and heir of Lord Desborough, was a professional soldier, a man of tremendous courage and daring, who had won the D.S.O. by Christmas 1914, and who rejoiced in living dangerously. Viola Meynell's Memoir, *Julian Grenfell*, which appeared in 1917, quotes a number of Grenfell's letters, and gives a vivid picture of an unusual and disturbing personality. Like so many professional soldiers, Grenfell was endowed with a strong vein of mysticism. At the age of thirteen, during a thunderstorm, he 'suddenly seemed to realize God', and he became devoted to the works of Thomas à Kempis. In the early months of the war Grenfell perfected a technique for stalking and shooting German snipers at point-blank range. There are passages in his letters which suggest that he enjoyed the whole business of killing and of risking his life. He wrote from Flanders in October 1914: 'I *adore* war. It is like a big picnic without the objectlessness of a picnic.' Even more sinister is a letter which introduces a note of perverted mysticism into his simple, bloody-minded song: 'I have never, never felt so well, or so happy, or enjoyed anything so much. It just suits my stolid health, and stolid nerves, and barbaric disposition. The fighting-excitement vitalizes everything, every sight and word and action. One loves one's fellow-man so much more when one is bent on killing him.' Grenfell appears to have lacked the tragic sense, and to have been deficient in the rudiments of social morality. He could offer personal gallantry, animal magnetism, and a vague, pantheistic mysticism: they were anachronistic qualities in the filth and slaughter of trench warfare.

The first poet to grasp the true nature of the conflict was Charles Sorley. His achievement was all the more remarkable in that he died at the age of twenty after spending less than five months in the front line. Within a few days of the outbreak of the war he was expressing his distaste for high-sounding moralizing and emotionalism: 'Our friends and correspondents don't seem to be able to give up physical luxuries without indulging in emotional luxuries as compensation. But I'm thankful to see that Kipling hasn't written a poem yet.'[3] While defending many of the poems in Hardy's *Satires of Circumstance* against his parents' criticisms, he expressed his distaste for 'Men Who March Away', which he called 'the most arid poem in the book, besides being untrue of the sentiments of the ranksman going to war: "Victory crowns the just" is the worst line he ever wrote – filched from a leading article in *The Morning Post*'.[4]

Having spent several months in Germany before the declaration of war, Sorley had learned to respect and admire the Germans. He detested everything that seemed hypocritical, tawdry and false in British propaganda and sentiment: the humbug preached by churchmen and journalists,[5] and the emotionalism that followed the death of Rupert Brooke.[6] As early as August 1914 he had reached the point which Sassoon, Owen and Rosenberg did not attain until 1916 or 1917 – the realization that the war was a hideous fratricidal massacre:

> And in each other's dearest ways we stand,
> And hiss and hate. And the blind fight the blind.[7]

A month later we find him displaying an intuitive perception of what modern warfare was really like:

> A hundred thousand million mites we go
> Wheeling and tacking o'er the eternal plain.

This was written eight months before his first experience of combat.

His attitude to the war was complex, even ambiguous. He never abandoned the ideals of self-sacrifice, courage, and devotion to duty which he had learned at Marlborough, nor could the war diminish what his housemaster called 'an extraordinary thrust of life'. He discovered that 'in that no-man's land and long graveyard there is a freedom and a spur'. Yet this passage is followed by a description of the terror and the moral degradation engendered by war.[8] In a letter dated 5 October 1915, eight days before his death, he writes movingly of the complex of emotions which were agitating him, on what he called 'the eve of our crowning hour': 'I dread my own censorious self in the coming conflict – I also have great physical dread of pain . . . Pray that I ride my frisky nerves with a cool and steady hand when the time

[3] Letter to A. E. Hutchinson, ? 10 August 1914. *The Letters of Charles Sorley*, 1919, p. 222. Sorley's rejoicing was premature: Kipling's 'For All We Have And Are' warned his countrymen that 'The Hun is at the gate' and called for 'iron sacrifice Of body, will, and soul'.

[4] Letter to his parents, 30 November 1914. Ibid., p. 246.

[5] Letter to A. E. Hutchinson, 14 November 1914. Ibid., pp. 240–1.

[6] See below, p. 142.

[7] 'To Germany'.

[8] Letter to Arthur Watts, 26 August 1915. See below, pp. 142–3.

arrives.'[9] One or two of the poems written in the last three months of his life reiterate the commonplaces of public-school morality. An epistle in verse, 'I have not brought my Odyssey', dated 12 July 1915, contains such lines as:

> And now the fight begins again,
> The old war-joy, the old war-pain.
> Sons of one school across the sea
> We have no fear to fight.

Yet there were deeper elements in Sorley's nature which were far stronger than his conventional responses to the daily routine of war. The sensitivity to the poetry of the earth, the awareness of mystery and of mortality, the feeling of communion with the dead, which had been part of his inner life even as a schoolboy, pervade the best of his later poems – 'Lost', written in December 1914, two sonnets on death, dated 12 June 1915, and the sonnet, 'When you see millions of the mouthless dead'.[10] This poem, found among his possessions, was probably his last, and it marks his final acceptance of death as the great leveller, the means of union between friend and foe, the prelude to a richer life: 'Great death has made all his for evermore.'

Sorley was almost alone in his vision of the war as a fratricidal tragedy of which both the Germans and the British were victims. Not until the physical horror of the fighting had grown almost unendurable did the combatants, still less the civilians, begin to apprehend the significance of the carnage. Even as late as 1916 Arthur Waugh referred to 'the cleansing fire'[11] of the war, and Newbolt's high-minded obtuseness betrayed him into writing this kind of rhapsodic nonsense: 'Ah! It's a Great Age to live in – the High Dream of England . . . Think of the fleet going up the Dardanelles. Think of the Centuries – think of Chivalry victorious.'[12]

It was, perhaps, the common soldiers who first apprehended the horror and suffering of the war in their full intensity. The British army kept its class-structure largely unimpaired throughout the war, and the officers, thanks partly to their privileged and responsible positions, saw the conflict in a more heroic light than the other ranks. Almost from the start the 'Tommies' improvised verses which are likely to be remembered as the last authentic folk-poetry to be composed by Englishmen. A. J. P. Taylor, in his magnificent historical narrative, has described the nature of these songs: 'The tunes were usually adapted from contemporary music-hall "hits". The words were self-depreciatory

[9] *The Letters of Charles Sorley*, 1919, pp. 311–13.
[10] See below, p. 148. [11] See above, p. 114.
[12] Letter to Lady Hylton, 31 October 1918. *The Later Life and Letters of Sir Henry Newbolt*, edited by Margaret Newbolt, 1942, p. 258.

and often obscene. No other army has ever gone to war, proclaiming its own incompetence and reluctance to fight, and no army has fought better. The humble Englishman found his voice, and these songs preserve him for posterity.'[13] But precisely because they were the rough, genuine, obscene songs of the trenches they did not reach the ears of the literate men and women living snug at home.

It was Siegfried Sassoon who first revealed to the civilian population the real lineaments of Newbolt's Chivalry. Like Julian Grenfell (and like those other poets who were to portray the truth about the war, Blunden, Read, and Owen), Sassoon was a man of great physical courage who was decorated for gallantry. He earned the nickname of 'Mad Jack' for his reckless exploits, and an early poem 'The Kiss', inspired by his disgust at 'the barbarities of the famous bayonet-fighting lecture', is, despite Sassoon's conscious intention, energized by what Grenfell exultingly described as 'joy of battle'.[14] Early in 1916 he began to write realistic poems about trench warfare, and in the summer of 1917 decided to protest to his superiors about the prolongation of the slaughter. Robert Graves asked Marsh to intervene on Sassoon's behalf with the authorities, and persuaded Sassoon to appear before a Medical Board. The Under-Secretary of State for War informed the House of Commons that Sassoon had succumbed to a nervous breakdown, and he was in fact sent to hospital at Craiglockhart for neurasthenics. There, in August 1917, he met Wilfred Owen, who left Craiglockhart in November. A few weeks later, having volunteered for service overseas, Sassoon was posted to Egypt, where he arrived in February 1918, and was transferred to France in May 1918. A head wound in May 1918 ended his active service, and his final meeting with Owen took place in Britain in July.

Compared with the richest and most tragic work of Owen and Rosenberg, Sassoon's poems of protest may seem a little thin and over-simplified. Yet the best of his poems have the passion, intensity, and unswerving honesty that are likely to preserve them from oblivion even when the First World War is a distant memory of a remote past.

Sassoon's gradual realization of the war's futility and horror was experienced by other poets at about the same period. Arthur Graeme West suffered a total revulsion from the war in August 1916 but returned to France, and was killed by a sniper's bullet in April 1917. His *Diary of a Dead Officer* (1918), though mainly in prose, contains a few powerful passages of verse, which convey the horror and bitterness inspired in him by the carnage:

[13] A. J. P. Taylor, *English History 1914–1945*, 1965, p. 62.
[14] See I. M. Parsons, *Men Who March Away*, 1965, p. 17.

> . . . and everywhere the dead.
> Only the dead were always present – present
> As a vile sickly smell of rottenness.
> The rustling stubble and the early grass,
> The slimy pools – the dead men stank through all,
> Pungent and sharp . . .
>
> Next was a bunch of half a dozen men
> All blown to bits, an archipelago
> Of corrupt fragments.

Sassoon reproduces in some of his poems the thoughtless blasphemy of the common soldier: West foreshadows Owen's agonized speculations about the love of God and the meaning of human suffering:

> Ah how good God is
> To suffer us be born just now, when youth
> That else would rust, can slake his blade in gore
> Where very God Himself does seem to walk
> The bloody fields of Flanders He so loves.

There were even one or two civilian poets who began to face the truth about the war. Strangely enough it was Rudyard Kipling who, more than any other poet of his generation, understood and shared the bitter contempt of the fighting soldier for men in high places, war profiteers, politicians, and civilians in cushy jobs, all of whom seemed indifferent to the agony of their countrymen in the trenches. Kipling's talent for hatred, which had always been formidable, was sharpened by grief at the death of his only son in action in 1915, and his poems inspired by the war contain some of his most savage invective.

Kipling, however, did not experience at first hand 'the hell where youth and laughter go'.[15] Wilfred Owen, who lived in that hell, recorded his experiences there in poems unrivalled in majesty and weight by any other war poetry of the time. His major poems were all written during 1917 and 1918, although he had begun to practise his craft before the outbreak of the war. The transformation of Owen from a sensuous, immature poet to a major writer recalls the equally sudden flowering of Keats's genius a hundred years earlier.

After his harrowing experiences of warfare in the winter of 1916–17, Owen suffered a breakdown, and was sent to Craiglockhart hospital where, in August 1917, he summoned up the courage to knock on Sassoon's door and to introduce himself. Although Sassoon disclaims any direct influence on Owen, he has described with modesty and perception the indirect influence which he may have exercised on his younger

[15] Siegfried Sassoon, 'Suicide in the Trenches'.

contemporary.[16] Owen's tribute to Sassoon is generous and unequivocal: 'And you have *fixed* my life – however short. You did not light me: I was always a mad comet; but you have fixed me. I spun round you a satellite for a month, but I shall swing out soon, a dark star in the orbit where you will blaze.'[17] Writing to his mother on the last day of 1917, Owen revealed his conviction that he was a poet, and, incidentally, proudly claimed kinship with the Georgians: 'I am held peer by the Georgians; I am a poet's poet. I am started. The tugs have left me; I feel the great swelling of the open sea taking my galleon.'[18]

In the ten months of life that were left him he grew continually in stature and in imaginative power. His hatred was directed not against the Germans but against the most thoughtless and callous of his countrymen. He wished that 'the Boche would have the pluck to come right in and make a clean sweep of the pleasure boats, and the promenaders on the Spa, and all the stinking Leeds and Bradford war-profiteers now reading *John Bull* on Scarborough Sands'.[19] When on leave in England, he carried in his pockets photographs of the mutilated and the wounded so that he might show them to anybody who spoke about the glory of war.

Yet, much as he loathed the war and believed that participation in it was anti-Christian, Owen returned to the Front on 31 August 1918, having in all probability drawn up the Preface and the table of contents for his projected volume of war poems. When, in July 1918, he learned that he was posted back to France he wrote: 'I am glad. That is I am much gladder to be going out again than afraid. I shall be better able to cry my outcry, playing my part.'[20] His letter to his mother written in October 1918 is even more explicit: 'I came out in order to help these boys – directly by leading them as well as an officer can, indirectly by watching their sufferings that I may speak of them as well as a pleader can. I have done the first.'[21] Like Charles Sorley in the early days of the war, Owen performed his military duties with resolute courage. The phrase, 'My nerves are in perfect order' occurs in letters written to his mother and to Sassoon in October 1918, the month in which he was awarded the Military Cross. He was killed in action a week before the Armistice.

W. B. Yeats's criticism of Owen's attitude of passive suffering is legitimate and dignified;[22] but there is no excuse for the intemperate outburst to Dorothy Wellesley whereby he attempted to justify his exclusion of Owen from *The Oxford Book of Modern Verse*.[23] New-

[16] *Siegfried's Journey 1916–1920*, 1945, pp. 59–61.

[17] Letter to Siegfried Sassoon, November 1917. *The Collected Poems of Wilfred Owen*, edited by C. Day Lewis, 1963, p. 171.

[18] ibid., p. 172.

[19] ibid., pp. 174–5.

[20] ibid., p. 174.

[21] ibid., p. 178.

[22] See below, p. 147.

[23] See below, pp. 147–8.

bolt's dismissal of Owen as 'limited' and 'hardly normal'[24] is what one might expect from a poet who, after seeing films of the war, could shroud the ghastly reality in a pious commonplace:

> O fellowship whose phantom tread
> Hallows a phantom ground –
> How in a gleam have these revealed
> The faith we had not found.[25]

One of the most profound judgments ever passed on war is contained in Frederic Manning's Prefatory Note to *Her Privates We* (1930): 'War is waged by men; not by beasts, or by gods. It is a peculiarly human activity. To call it a crime against mankind is to miss at least half its significance; it is also the punishment of a crime.' Owen apprehended this truth more deeply and intimately than any other poet of the war, and his poems enact, with matchless precision and grandeur, the crime and the punishment.

Isaac Rosenberg struggled throughout his life against poverty and neglect, nor has he received since his death the recognition that he deserves. Born at Bristol in 1890, the son of a Lithuanian Jew and a Latvian Jewess, he was brought up in the slums of Whitechapel. Three rich Jewish ladies paid for him to complete his training as a painter at the Slade School, and he was encouraged to pursue his double vocation as painter and poet by Marsh and by four leading Georgian poets, Abercrombie, Binyon, Bottomley, and R. C. Trevelyan. He was a friend of Ezra Pound, admired F. S. Flint, and may have read many of T. E. Hulme's writings.

Unlike almost every other war-poet of any merit, Rosenberg served not as a commissioned officer but as a private soldier. Deprived of those amenities which Sassoon and Owen enjoyed at intervals, cut off from intercourse with men who shared his interests, Rosenberg probably endured a more dispiriting life in the trenches than any of his fellow-poets. It is no disparagement of Sassoon's courage to remark that if Rosenberg had ventured a similar protest against the war he would have been imprisoned or ignominiously shot. When in 1937 Marsh opened an exhibition of Rosenberg's paintings in Whitechapel he still thought of him as 'poor little Rosenberg'.[26] Yet Rosenberg's imagination was on a grand scale, his vision of the war was Apocalyptic, his spirit moved in regions beyond the confines of human life. Characteristically, he believed that his strange, ecstatic 'Daughters of War' was his best poem: 'It has taken me about a year to write; for I have changed and re-changed it and thought hard over that poem and striven to get that

[24] See below, p. 147. [25] 'The War Films'.
[26] *Ambrosia and Small Beer*, arranged by Christopher Harsall, 1964, p. 53.

sense of inexorableness the human (or inhuman) side of this war has. It even penetrates behind human life.'[27]

He did not live long enough to bring to fruition the major works which he had planned, and the most ambitious poems which are printed in his *Collected Works* lack the artistic perfection of Owen's finest achievements. But his visionary power and the intensity of his spiritual life communicate themselves to us in poem after poem. The last letter he wrote was dated 28 March 1918, three days before his death. It was to Edward Marsh, and it was completed by the light of an inch of candle, so that Rosenberg was telling the literal truth when he wrote: 'I must measure my letter by the light.'[28] The phrase, however, may serve as epitaph on a potentially major poet who was granted only a brief candle.

Almost all the good war poetry written during the two final years of the conflict echoed the same tragic rage and compassion that pervade the verse of Rosenberg and of Owen. One of the volumes published at this period was Herbert Read's *Naked Warriors* (1919), which was much admired by T. S. Eliot: 'Mr. Read's book is on a very high level of war poetry. It is the best war poetry that I can remember having seen.'[29] The best of Read's poems, and verse in a similar vein of anger, pity, and disillusion by Robert Graves, Richard Aldington, W. W. Gibson, and Osbert Sitwell (to name a few poets), can be found in many anthologies. There were, moreover, two poets who made a distinctive contribution to the poetry of the war, and whose work is inspired by an attitude of mind and spirit unlike that of Owen, Rosenberg and the lesser poets of revulsion and despair. One of these poets – Edmund Blunden – is well known; the other – Ivor Gurney – has been almost totally forgotten.

The poems of Owen and Rosenberg explore in depth the spiritual hell that war brings into being. They portray unsparingly the physical and emotional lineaments of modern war, the pain, weariness, madness and degradation of human beings under intolerable strain. We forget, in reading these tragic documents, that most soldiers enjoyed a few moments of respite from the horror of trench warfare, moments that were all the more poignant and sweet because they were so brief and precarious. Blunden's achievement was to crystallize these moments into poetry, to make us aware of the contrast between the evil destructiveness of war, and the human warmth and happiness which some-

[27] Letter to Edward Marsh. *Collected Works*, edited by Gordon Bottomley and Denys Harding, 1937, p. 319.

[28] ibid., p. 322.

[29] 'Reflections on Contemporary Poetry', *The Egoist*, VI, 3, July 1919, p. 39. I have omitted from this chapter any consideration of Read's long poem *The End of a War* and of David Jones's *In Parenthesis*, since both were written some years after the Armistice of 1918.

how managed to survive even in the trenches. Yet Blunden's poetry comprehends the hideous terror of war. Nobody has depicted with greater skill the sinister landscape of France and Flanders corrupted, it seems, by the malignancy of the elements and the very heavens:

Sharp-fanged searches the frost, and shackles
The sleeping water in broken cellars,
And calm and fierce the witch-moon watches,
Curious of evil.[30]

And in 'Concert Party: Busseboom', Blunden takes us from this evil landscape into the shelter of a concert hall where laughter and gaiety charm away the memory of war – but only until the sunset, when

We heard another matinée,
  We heard the maniac blast

Of barrage south by Saint Eloi,
  And the red lights flaming there
Called madness: Come, my bonny boy,
  And dance to the latest air.

To this new concept, white we stood;
  Cold certainty held our breath;
While men in the tunnels below Larch Wood
  Were kicking men to death.

Whereas the work of Owen and Rosenberg is tinged with the terrifying impersonality that seems to be inseparable from all major art, Blunden's poems never shed their gentle humanity. Nor, strangely enough, do the poems of Ivor Gurney, despite the long periods during which he lay in the exile of asylums.

Gurney, who was a musician as well as a poet, served in the ranks from 1916 until the end of the war. His mind gave way under the stress of battle, and after 1922 he was permanently confined in mental hospitals until his death in 1937. He loved Tudor church music; and his poetry bears traces of that love, in its austere, intricate melody, its mingled harshness and aspiring purity, its sharp, earthy flavour. He was influenced by Campion, Housman, Edward Thomas, and Gerard Manley Hopkins, learning from them a fastidiousness of diction, a piercing simplicity, a fidelity to experience and a lyrical intensity. Few of his poems are free from the wildness and confusion that are symptoms of his mental condition, yet in one or two poems about the war he achieves a rare poise and certainty, in which a cool irony helps him to exert control over his complex material. Edmund Blunden's tribute to this tragic composer and poet is both a beautiful commemoration of

30 'January Full Moon, Ypres'.

a gifted man destroyed by war, and a reminder that there were very close affinities of spirit beween the best Georgian verse and the most valuable poetry of the First World War:

> Whatever was attractive and poetically moving to the generation of writers called Georgian was so to him also, and he was content to be of that generation; but neither easy sentiment nor an indifferent 'eye on the object' can be imputed to him, nor yet languor nor studied homeliness of expression. He perished, one may say, from the merciless intensity of his spirit both in watching the forms of things moving apace in the stream of change and in hammering out the poetic forms for their just representation and acclamation.[31]

CRITICISM

The voice of our poets and men of letters is finely trained and sweet to hear; it teems with sharp saws and rich sentiment: it is a marvel of delicate technique: it pleases, it flatters, it charms, it soothes: it is a living lie.

Charles Sorley, paper on John Masefield read to the Literary Society, Marlborough, on 3 November 1912, *The Letters of Charles Sorley*, 1919, pp. 37–8.

[Brooke] is far too obsessed with his own sacrifice, regarding the going to war of himself (and others) as a highly intense, remarkable and sacrificial exploit, whereas it is merely the conduct demanded of him (and others) by the turn of circumstances, where non-compliance with this demand would have made life intolerable. It was not that 'they' gave up anything of that list he gives in one sonnet: but that the essence of these things had been endangered by circumstances over which he had no control, and he must fight to recapture them. He has clothed his attitude in fine words; but he has taken the sentimental attitude.

Charles Sorley, letter to Mrs. Sorley, 28 November 1915, ibid., p. 263.

Looking into the future one sees a holocaust somewhere: and at present there is – thank God – enough of 'experience' to keep the wits edged (a callous way of putting it, perhaps). But out in front at night in that no-man's land and long graveyard there is a freedom and a spur. Rustling of the grasses and grave tap-tapping of distant workers: the tension and silence of encounter, when one struggles in the dark for moral victory over the enemy patrol: the wail of the exploded bomb and the animal cries of wounded men. Then death and the horrible thankfulness when one sees that the next man is dead: 'We won't have to *carry* him in under fire, thank God; dragging will do': hauling in of the great resistless body in the dark, the smashed head rattling: the

[31] Edmund Blunden, 'Concerning Ivor Gurney', *Poems by Ivor Gurney*, 1954, p. 19.

relief, the relief that the thing has ceased to groan: that the bullet or bomb that made the man an animal has now made the animal a corpse. One is hardened by now: purged of all false pity: perhaps more selfish than before. The spiritual and the animal get so much more sharply divided in hours of encounter, taking possession of the body by swift turns.

Charles Sorley, letter to Arthur Watts, 26 August 1915, ibid., pp. 305–6.

Brooke's early poems exhibit a youthful exuberance of passion, and an occasional coarseness of utterance, which offended finer tastes; but these were but dross which, as his last sonnets show, was purged away (if I may be permitted this word) in the fire of the Great Ordeal which is proving the well-spring of a Renaissance of English poetry.

Helen B. Trundlett, letter printed in *The Egoist*, IV, 11, December, 1917, p. 165.

[This letter, and the letters attributed to J. A. D. Spence, Charles James Grimble, Charles Augustus Conybeare, and Muriel A. Schwarz, were all written by T. S. Eliot, who was Assistant Editor of *The Egoist*. When writing this parody of jingoistic criticism, Eliot may have had in mind Arthur Waugh's review entitled 'The New Poetry'. See above, p. 114.]

The Poetry Review you sent is good – the articles are too breathless, and want more packing, I think. The poems by the soldier are vigorous but, I feel a bit commonplace. I did not like Rupert Brookes begloried sonnets for the same reason. What I mean is second hand phrases 'lambent fires' etc takes from its reality and strength. It should be approached in a colder way, more abstract, with less of the million feelings everybody feels; or all these should be concentrated in one distinguished emotion. Walt Whitman in 'Beat, drums, beat,' has said the noblest thing on war.

Isaac Rosenberg, letter to Mrs. Herbert Cohen, early June 1916, *Collected Works*, edited by Gordon Bottomley and Denys Harding, 1937, p. 348.

[Rosenberg's spelling, grammar, and punctuation have been left uncorrected in this passage and in the other extracts from his letters.]

I liked your criticism of 'Dead mans dump'. Mr. Binyon has often sermonised lengthily over my working on two different principles in the same thing and I know how it spoils the unity of a poem. But if I couldn't before, I can now, I am sure plead the absolute necessity of fixing an idea before it is lost, because of the situation its conceived in. Regular rhythms I do not like much, but of course it depends on where the stress and accent are laid. I think there is nothing finer than the vigorous opening of Lycydas for music; yet it is regular. Now I think if

Andrew Marvell had broken up his rhythms more he would have been considered a terrific poet.

Isaac Rosenberg, letter to Edward Marsh, postmarked 27 May 1917, ibid., p. 317.

I think with you that poetry should be definite thought and clear expression, however subtle; I don't think there should be any vagueness at all; but a sense of something hidden and felt to be there. Now when my things fail to be clear I am sure it is because of the luckless choice of a word or the failure to introduce a word that would flash my idea plain as it is to my own mind.

Isaac Rosenberg, letter to Edward Marsh, postmarked 30 July 1917, ibid., p. 319.

In reading and re-reading these poems I have been strongly impressed by their depth and integrity. I have found a sensitive and vigorous mind energetically interested in experimenting with language, and I have recognized in Rosenberg a fruitful fusion between English and Hebrew culture. Behind all his poetry there is a racial quality – biblical and prophetic. Scriptural and sculptural are the epithets I would apply to him. His experiments were a strenuous effort for impassioned expression; his imagination had a sinewy and muscular aliveness; often he saw things in terms of sculpture, but he did not carve or chisel; he *modelled* words with fierce energy and aspiration, finding ecstasy in form, dreaming in grandeurs of superb light and deep shadow; his poetic visions are mostly in sombre colours and looming sculptural masses, molten and amply wrought. Watching him working with words, I find him a poet of movement; words which express movement are often used by him and are essential to his natural utterance.

Rosenberg was not consciously a 'war poet'. But the war destroyed him, and his few but impressive 'Trench Poems' are a central point in this book.

Siegfried Sassoon, Foreword to Rosenberg's *Collected Works,* edited by Gordon Bottomley and Denys Harding, 1937, p. ix. Reprinted in his *Collected Poems,* 1949, p. vii.

Yet, in spite of my hatred of war and 'Empery's insatiate lust of power', there was an awful attraction in its hold over my mind, which since childhood had shown a tendency towards tragic emotions about human existence. While at Lancaster Gate I was disquieted by a craving to be back on the Western Front as an independent contemplator. No longer feeling any impulse to write bitterly, I imagined myself describing it in a comprehensive way, seeing it like a painter and imbuing my poetry with Whitmanesque humanity and amplitude . . .

I was developing a more controlled and objective attitude towards the War. To remind people of its realities was still my main purpose, but I now preferred to depict it impersonally, and to be as much 'above the battle' as I could. Unconsciously, I was getting nearer to Wilfred Owen's method of approach. (For it was not until two years later, when I edited his poems, that I clearly apprehended the essentially compassionate significance of what he had been communicating.)

Siegfried Sassoon, *Siegfried's Journey, 1916–1920*, 1945, pp. 69–71.

It has been loosely assumed and stated that Wilfred [Owen] modelled his war poetry on mine. My only claimable influence was that I stimulated him towards writing with compassionate and challenging realism. His printed letters are evidence that the impulse was already strong in him before he had met me. The manuscript of one of his most dynamically descriptive war poems, *Exposure*, is dated February 1917, and proves that he had already found an authentic utterance of his own.

Siegfried Sassoon, ibid., p. 60.

They want to call No Man's Land 'England' because we keep supremacy there. It is like the eternal place of gnashing of teeth; the Slough of Despond could be contained in one of its crater-holes; the fires of Sodom and Gomorrah could not light a candle to it – to find the way to Babylon the Fallen. It is pockmarked like a body of foulest disease, and its odour is the breath of cancer. I have not seen any dead. I have done worse. In the dank air I have *perceived* it, and in the darkness, *felt*. Those 'Somme Pictures' are the laughing-stock of the army – like the trenches on exhibition in Kensington. No Man's Land under snow is like the face of the moon, chaotic, crater-ridden, uninhabitable, awful, the abode of madness.

Wilfred Owen, letter to his mother, 19 January 1917, *The Collected Poems of Wilfred Owen*, edited by C. Day Lewis, 1963, p. 160.

I can quite believe [Tennyson] never knew happiness for one moment such as I have – for one or two moments. But as for misery, was he ever frozen alive, with dead men for comforters? Did he hear the moaning at the Bar, not at twilight and the evening bell only, but at dawn, noon, and night, eating and sleeping, walking and working, always the close moaning of the Bar; the thunder, the hissing, and the whining of the Bar? – Tennyson, it seems, was always a great child. So should I have been, but for Beaumont Hamel. (Not before January 1917 did I write the *only* lines of mine that carry the stamp of maturity – these:

But the old happiness is unreturning,
Boys have no grief as grievous as youth's yearning;
Boys have no sadness sadder than our hope.)

Wilfred Owen, letter to his mother, 8 August 1917, ibid., p. 168.

Catalogue? Photograph? Can you photograph the crimson-hot iron as it cools from the smelting? That is what Jones's blood looked like, and felt like. My senses are charred.

I shall feel again as soon as I dare, but now I must not. I don't take the cigarette out of my mouth when I write Deceased over their letters.

But one day I will write Deceased over many books.

Wilfred Owen, letter to Siegfried Sassoon, 10 October 1918, ibid., p. 176.

This book is not about heroes. English poetry is not yet fit to speak of them.

Nor is it about deeds, or lands, nor anything about glory, honour, might, majesty, dominion, or power, except War.

Above all I am not concerned with Poetry.

My subject is War, and the pity of War.

The Poetry is in the pity.

Yet these elegies are to this generation in no sense consolatory. They may be to the next. All a poet can do today is warn. That is why the true Poets must be truthful.

(If I thought the letter of this book would last, I might have used proper names; but if the spirit of it survives – survives Prussia – my ambition and those names will have achieved themselves fresher fields than Flanders . . .)

Wilfred Owen, Preface to his projected volume of war poems found among his papers, ibid., p. 31.

Read *Georgian Poetry* and read 'Strange Meeting'. Compare Wilfred Owen's poem with the very finest things in the Georgian book – Mr. Davies's 'Lovely Dames', or Mr. de la Mare's 'The Tryst', or 'Fare Well', or the twenty opening lines of Mr. Abercrombie's disappointing poem. You will not find those beautiful poems less beautiful than they are; but you will find in 'Strange Meeting' an awe, an immensity, an adequacy to that which has been most profound in the experience of a generation. You will, finally, have the standard that has been lost, and the losing of which makes the confusion of a book like *Georgian Poetry* possible, restored to you. You will remember those forgotten things – that poetry is rooted in emotion, and that it grows by the mastery of emotion, and that its significance finally depends upon the quality and comprehensiveness of the emotion. You will recognize that the tricks of the trade have never been and never will be discovered by which ability can conjure emptiness into meaning.

J[ohn]. M[iddleton]. M[urry]., 'The Condition of English Poetry', *The Athanaeum*, 4675, 5 December 1919, pp. 1283–5. Reprinted in *Aspects of Literature*, 1920, pp. 139–49.

[A review by Murry of *Georgian Poetry 1918–1919* and *Wheels. Fourth Cycle.*]

[Sassoon] has sent me Wilfred Owen's Poems, with an Introduction by himself. The best of them I knew already – they are terribly good, but of course limited, almost all on one note. I like better Sassoon's two-sided collection – there are more than two sides to this business of war, and a man is hardly normal any longer if he comes down to one. Owen and the rest of the broken men rail at the old men who sent the young to die: they have suffered cruelly, but in the nerves and not the heart – they haven't the experience or the imagination to know the extreme human agony – 'Who giveth me to die for thee, Absalom my son, my son.' . . . I don't think these shell-shocked war poems will move our grandchildren greatly – there's nothing fundamental or final about them – at least they only put one figure into a very big equation, and that's not one of the unknown but one of the best known quantities.

Sir Henry Newbolt, letter to Lady Hylton, 2 August 1924, *The Later Life and Letters of Sir Henry Newbolt*, edited by Margaret Newbolt, 1942, pp. 314–15.

I have a distaste for certain poems written in the midst of the great war; they are in all anthologies, but I have substituted Herbert Read's *End of a War* written long after. The writers of these poems were invariably officers of exceptional courage and capacity, one a man constantly selected for dangerous work, all, I think, had the Military Cross; their letters are vivid and humorous, they were not without joy – for all skill is joyful – but felt bound, in the words of the best known, to plead the suffering of their men. In poems that had for a time considerable fame, written in the first person, they made that suffering their own. I have rejected these poems for the same reason that made Arnold withdraw his *Empedocles on Etna* from circulation; passive suffering is not a theme for poetry. In all the great tragedies, tragedy is a joy to the man who dies; in Greece the tragic chorus danced. When man has withdrawn into the quicksilver at the back of the mirror no great event becomes luminous in his mind; it is no longer possible to write *The Persians, Agincourt, Chevy Chase*: some blunderer has driven his car on to the wrong side of the road – that is all.

W. B. Yeats, Introduction to *The Oxford Book of Modern Verse*, 1936, p. xxxiv.

When I excluded Wilfred Owen, whom I consider unworthy of the poet's corner of a country newspaper, I did not know I was excluding a revered sandwich-board Man of the revolution and that somebody has put his worst and most famous poem in a glass-case in the British Museum – however if I had known it I would have excluded him just the same. He is all blood, dirt and sucked sugar stick (look at the selection in *Faber's Anthology* – he calls poets 'bards', a girl a 'maid' and talks about 'Titanic wars'). There is every excuse for him but none for those who like him.

W. B. Yeats, letter to Dorothy Wellesley, 21 December [1936], *The Letters of W. B. Yeats*, edited by Allan Wade, 1954, p. 874.

POEMS

CHARLES HAMILTON SORLEY
(1895–1915)

When you see millions of the mouthless dead

When you see millions of the mouthless dead
Across your dreams in pale battalions go,
Say not soft things as other men have said,
That you'll remember. For you need not so.
Give them not praise. For, deaf, how should they know
It is not curses heaped on each gashed head?
Nor tears. Their blind eyes see not your tears flow.
Nor honour. It is easy to be dead.
Say only this, 'They are dead.' Then add thereto,
'Yet many a better one has died before.'
Then, scanning all the o'ercrowded mass, should you
Perceive one face that you loved heretofore,
It is a spook. None wears the face you knew.
Great death has made all his for evermore.

WILFRID WILSON GIBSON
(1878–1962)

Mark Anderson

On the low table by the bed
Where it was set aside last night,
Beyond the bandaged lifeless head,
It glitters in the morning light –

And as the hours of morning pass
I cannot sleep, I cannot think,
But only gaze upon the glass
Of water that he could not drink.

SIEGFRIED SASSOON
(1886–1967)

Attack

At dawn the ridge emerges massed and dun
In the wild purple of the glow'ring sun,
Smouldering through spouts of drifting smoke that shroud
The menacing scarred slope; and, one by one,
Tanks creep and topple forward to the wire.
The barrage roars and lifts. Then, clumsily bowed
With bombs and guns and shovels and battle-gear,
Men jostle and climb to meet the bristling fire.
Lines of grey, muttering faces, masked with fear,
They leave their trenches, going over the top,
While time ticks blank and busy on their wrists,
And hope, with furtive eyes and grappling fists,
Flounders in mud. O Jesus, make it stop!

ISAAC ROSENBERG
(1890–1918)

August 1914

What in our lives is burnt
In the fire of this?
The heart's dear granary?
The much we shall miss?

Three lives hath one life –
Iron, honey, gold.
The gold, the honey gone –
Left is the hard and cold.

Iron are our lives
Molten right through our youth.
A burnt space through ripe fields
A fair mouth's broken tooth.

Break of Day in the Trenches

The darkness crumbles away –
It is the same old druid Time as ever.
Only a live thing leaps my hand –
A queer sardonic rat –
As I pull the parapet's poppy
To stick behind my ear.

Droll rat, they would shoot you if they knew
Your cosmopolitan sympathies
(And God knows what antipathies).
Now you have touched this English hand
You will do the same to a German –
Soon, no doubt, if it be your pleasure
To cross the sleeping green between.
It seems you inwardly grin as you pass
Strong eyes, fine limbs, haughty athletes
Less chanced than you for life,
Bonds to the whims of murder,
Sprawled in the bowels of the earth,
The torn fields of France.
What do you see in our eyes
At the shrieking iron and flame
Hurled through still heavens?
What quaver – what heart aghast?
Poppies whose roots are in man's veins
Drop, and are ever dropping;
But mine in my ear is safe,
Just a little white with the dust.

Returning, We Hear the Larks

Sombre the night is:
And, though we have our lives, we know
What sinister threat lurks there.

Dragging these anguished limbs, we only know
This poison-blasted track opens on our camp –
On a little safe sleep.

But hark! Joy – joy – strange joy
Lo! Heights of night ringing with unseen larks:
Music showering on our upturned listening faces.

Death could drop from the dark
As easily as song –
But song only dropped,
Like a blind man's dreams on the sand
By dangerous tides;
Like a girl's dark hair, for she dreams no ruin lies there,
Or her kisses where a serpent hides.

WILFRED OWEN
(1893–1918)

Exposure

Our brains ache, in the merciless iced east winds that knive us . . .
Wearied we keep awake because the night is silent . . .
Low, drooping flares confuse our memory of the salient . . .
Worried by silence, sentries whisper, curious, nervous,
        But nothing happens.

Watching, we hear the mad gusts tugging on the wire,
Like twitching agonies of men among its brambles.
Northward, incessantly, the flickering gunnery rumbles,
Far off, like a dull rumour of some other war.
        What are we doing here?

The poignant misery of dawn begins to grow . . .
We only know war lasts, rain soaks, and clouds sag stormy.
Dawn massing in the east her melancholy army
Attacks once more in ranks on shivering ranks of gray,
        But nothing happens.

Sudden successive flights of bullets streak the silence.
Less deathly than the air that shudders black with snow,
With sidelong flowing flakes that flock, pause, and renew;
We watch them wandering up and down the wind's nonchalance,
        But nothing happens.

Pale flakes with fingering stealth come feeling for our faces –
We cringe in holes, back on forgotten dreams, and stare, snow-dazed,
Deep into grassier ditches. So we drowse, sun-dozed,
Littered with blossoms trickling where the blackbird fusses.
        Is it that we are dying?

Slowly our ghosts drag home: glimpsing the sunk fires, glozed
With crusted dark-red jewels; crickets jingle there;
For hours the innocent mice rejoice: the house is theirs;
Shutters and doors, all closed: on us the doors are closed, –
        We turn back to our dying.

Since we believe not otherwise can kind fires burn;
Nor ever suns smile true on child, or field, or fruit.
For God's invincible spring our love is made afraid;
Therefore, not loath, we lie out here; therefore were born,
        For love of God seems dying.

To-night, His frost will fasten on this mud and us,
Shrivelling many hands, puckering foreheads crisp.
The burying-party, picks and shovels in their shaking grasp,
Pause over half-known faces. All their eyes are ice,
    But nothing happens.

Futility

Move him into the sun –
Gently its touch awoke him once,
At home, whispering of fields unsown.
Always it woke him, even in France,
Until this morning and this snow.
If anything might rouse him now
The kind old sun will know.

Think how it wakes the seeds, –
Woke, once, the clays of a cold star.
Are limbs, so dear-achieved, are sides,
Full-nerved – still warm – too hard to stir?
Was it for this the clay grew tall?
– O what made fatuous sunbeams toil
To break earth's sleep at all?

The Chances

I mind as 'ow the night afore that show
Us five got talkin', – we was in the know.
'Over the top to-morrer; boys, we're for it.
First wave we are, first ruddy wave; that's tore it!'
'Ah well,' says Jimmy, – an' 'e's seen some scrappin' –
'There ain't no more nor five things as can 'appen:
Ye get knocked out; else wounded – bad or cushy;
Scuppered; or nowt except yer feelin' mushy.'

One of us got the knock-out, blown to chops.
T'other was 'urt, like, losin' both 'is props.
An' one, to use the word of 'ypocrites,
'Ad the misfortoon to be took be Fritz.
Now me, I wasn't scratched, praise God Almighty,
(Though next time please I'll thank 'im for a blighty).
But poor young Jim, 'e's livin' an' 'e's not;
'E reckoned 'e'd five chances, an' 'e 'ad;
'E's wounded, killed, and pris'ner, all the lot,
The bloody lot all rolled in one. Jim's mad.

At a Calvary near the Ancre

One ever hangs where shelled roads part.
  In this war He too lost a limb,
But His disciples hide apart;
  And now the Soldiers bear with Him.

Near Golgotha strolls many a priest,
  And in their faces there is pride
That they were flesh-marked by the Beast
  By whom the gentle Christ's denied.

The scribes on all the people shove
  And brawl allegiance to the state,
But they who love the greater love
  Lay down their life; they do not hate.

IVOR GURNEY
(1890–1937)

The Bohemians

Certain people would not clean their buttons,
Nor polish buckles after latest fashions,
Preferred their hair long, putties comfortable,
Barely escaping hanging, indeed hardly able,
In Bridge and smoking without army cautions
Spending hours that sped like evil for quickness,
(While others burnished brasses, earned promotions).
These were those ones who jested in the trench,
While others argued of army ways, and wrenched
What little soul they had still further from shape,
And died off one by one, or became officers
Without the first of dream, the ghost of notions
Of ever becoming soldiers, or smart and neat,
Surprised as ever to find the army capable
Of sounding 'Lights out' to break a game of Bridge,
As to fear candles would set a barn alight.
In Artois or Picardy they lie – free of useless fashions.

EDMUND BLUNDEN
(b. 1896)

Festubert: The Old German Line

Sparse mists of moonlight hurt our eyes
With gouged and scourged uncertainties
Of soul and soil in agonies.

One derelict grim skeleton
That drench and dry had battened on
Still seemed to wish us malison;

Still zipped across the gouts of lead
Or cracked like whipcracks overhead;
The gray rags fluttered on the dead.

Their Very Memory

Hear, O hear,
They were as the welling waters,
Sound, swift, clear,
They were all the runnings waters'
Music down the greenest valley.

Might words tell
What an echo sung within me?
What proud bell
Clangs a note of what within me
Pealed to be with those enlisted?

When they smiled,
Earth's inferno changed and melted
Greenwood mild;
Every village where they halted
Shone with them through square and alley.

Now my mind
Faint and few records their showings,
Brave, strong, kind –
I'd unlock you all their doings
But the keys are lost and twisted.

This still grows,
Through my land or dull or dazzling
Their spring flows;
But to think of them's a fountain,
Tears of joy and music's rally.

SELECT BIBLIOGRAPHY

General

Anthology of War Poetry 1914–1918, edited by Robert Nichols, London, 1943.
With a long Introduction in the form of a dialogue between Nichols and Julian Tennyson.

Up the Line to Death, edited by Brian Gardner, London, 1964.

Men who March Away, edited by I. M. Parsons, London, 1965.
Two good anthologies, which cover most of the field.

The Long Trail, edited by John Brophy and Eric Partridge, 2nd. ed., London, 1965.
A collection of songs sung in the trenches.

Bergonzi, Bernard, *Heroes' Twilight*, London, 1965.

Blunden, Edmund, *War Poets 1914–1918*, London, 1958; 2nd ed., 1964.

Johnston, John H., *English Poetry of the First World War*, Princeton and London, 1964.
An extremely valuable study. Devotes a chapter apiece to Herbert Read and David Jones as poets who wrote long, quasi-epic poems about the war some years after the Armistice of 1918.

Wilfred Owen

The Collected Poems of Wilfred Owen, edited by C. Day Lewis, London, 1963.
Incorporates Edmund Blunden's *Memoir* (1931).

Collected Letters, edited by Harold Owen and John Bell, London, 1967.

Owen, Harold, *Journey from Obscurity: Wilfred Owen 1893–1918*, 3 vols., London, 1963–5.

Welland, D. S. R., *Wilfred Owen: A Critical Study*, London, 1960.

Isaac Rosenberg

Collected Works, edited by Gordon Bottomley and Denys Harding, London, 1937.

Collected Poems, 1949, is an abbreviated version of *Collected Works*.

Siegfried Sassoon

Collected Poems 1908–1956, London, 1961.

Thorpe, Michael, *Siegfried Sassoon*, London, 1966.

Charles Sorley

Marlborough and Other Poems, Cambridge, 1916; 4th. ed., enlarged and rearranged, 1919.

The Letters of Charles Sorley, Cambridge, 1919.

Press, John, 'Charles Sorley', *A Review of English Literature*, VII, 2, April 1966, pp. 43–60.

9

WHEELS AND EDITH SITWELL

INTRODUCTION

Wheels, an anthology of poems edited by Edith Sitwell, appeared in six annual cycles from 1916 to 1921. Apart from Edith, Osbert, and Sacheverell Sitwell, the contributors included Nancy Cunard, Aldous Huxley, Alan Porter, Iris Tree, and Sherard Vines. All the contributors were young, and some of them were members of families well known in society and in the fashionable artistic world. *Wheels* was intended to be an act of defiance, a deliberate rebellion against the stuffy canons of respectable, conservative society. It mocked explicitly or implicitly the standards of poetic decorum and middle-class romanticism associated with Marsh and his Georgians; it undermined the dignified postures of academic men of letters; its tone was anti-militaristic, sophisticated and cynical. Not surprisingly, it evoked abusive hostility and delighted applause. Some of those who greeted it with a measure of approval were fully conscious of its defects, but welcomed it as a useful weapon with which to assail the Georgians and the older generation entrenched in positions of literary authority. T. S. Eliot's review in *The Egoist* is a notable example of this strategic approach.[1]

Reading the six cycles fifty years after the inception of *Wheels*, one is struck by the poor quality of the verse. Most of the poems are thin and trivial, technically inferior to the work of the despised Georgians, their smartness long faded, their febrility and hollowness cruelly exposed by the passage of time:

> I sometimes think that all our thoughts are wheels
> Rolling forever through the painted world,
> Moved by the cunning of a thousand clowns
> Dressed paper-wise with blatant rounded masks.

These opening lines of Nancy Cunard's poem, 'Wheels', which was the first poem in the 1916 cycle, conjure up the atmosphere of the entire series – the world of the opulent Edwardian nursery into which have been smuggled the ballet designs of Bakst and the drawings of Aubrey Beardsley.

The virtues and vices of *Wheels* were brilliantly dissected in a review in *The Athenaeum*.[2] Yet, apart from its intrinsic merits, *Wheels* may

[1] See below, p. 159. [2] See below, pp. 160–1.

claim some attention as a document in the history of modern verse. In its pages, one hears, for the first time, the voices of some very young poets seeking to express the moral discontent and the aesthetic aims of a generation in revolt against the tyranny of pre-1914 values. Secondly, in the 1919 cycle, *Wheels* printed a number of poems by Wilfred Owen, then almost completely unknown. Edith Sitwell, who at this time was helping Siegfried Sassoon to prepare Owen's poems for publication, deserves the credit of being one of the very first readers to recognize his quality. Finally, *Wheels* was the gaudy vessel in which the Sitwells launched themselves on their long disputatious voyage.

This particular function of *Wheels* led to some lively exchanges of mockery and abuse. An almost totally forgotten publication, entitled *Cranks* (1921), supposedly compiled by Obert, Sebert and Ethelberta Standstill, contains some caustic parodies of the Sitwells' verse and prose, including 'Idyll' by Ethelberta Standstill, which is uncomfortably near the mark:

> Walnut larks in the cotton-wool air
> Choke the ear. On the hill-sides bare
> Wooden sheep with hearthrug backs
> Follow clay shepherds with creaking slacks.

The Sitwells were not slow to respond; and the skirmishes over *Wheels* turned out to be the opening engagements in the long campaign undertaken by the family against its adversaries. The polemical technique of the Sitwells, perfected in later years, was first practised in the pages of *Wheels*. Their tireless self-advertisement drew from F. R. Leavis one of his most acerb remarks when, after tracing the history of the Georgian movement, he observed: 'The opposition to the Georgians was already at the time in question (just after the war) Sitwellism. But the Sitwells belong to the history of publicity rather than of poetry.'[3]

The work of Osbert and of Sacheverell Sitwell lies beyond the scope of this section, which is primarily concerned with the poetry of their sister, from the early experiments printed in *Wheels* to the final achievements of her old age. Even now, critical opinion is sharply divided about her significance, nor is it likely that the disputants will be reconciled. Few if any judgments about literature are purely literary; the divergences over Edith Sitwell are inseparable from the personal, cultural, social and educational principles and prejudices which have inspired them. Given the background from which a critic has emerged, and the circles in which he moves, one can make a pretty fair guess at his attitude towards Edith Sitwell.

It would be tedious to explore in detail the quarrel between the two

[3] F. R. Leavis, *New Bearings in English Poetry*, 1932, p. 73.

camps, which is epitomized in John Lehmann's editorial comment in the October 1954 issue of the *London Magazine*, in which he awards 'the booby prize for the most inept remark of 1954 to Messrs. Davie and Cruttwell who have solemnly announced that they consider the author of *Facade, Gold Coast Customs* and *Street Songs* to be "no poet at all".' All one can do in a brief space is to outline the conflicting views, advance a tentative opinion and leave the reader to form his own conclusions.

The best account of Edith Sitwell's poetic development can be found in her introductory essay to her *Collected Poems* (1959).[4] Indeed, the eulogies pronounced on her work by her admirers add little to her own exegeses and asseverations. From a very early age she was sharply aware of the qualities which distinguished her from the common herd. When asked by a family friend, 'What are you going to be when you grow up little E?', she replied, 'A genius'. She referred to Rimbaud as 'in some ways my closest spiritual relation'.

In the eyes of herself and her admirers she progressed with the inexorable certainty of genius from the dazzling verbal experiments of her early verse, through the spiritual agony of *Gold Coast Customs* and the tragic grandeur of the war poems, to the majestic assurance of her post-war verse, which crowns her achievement of fifty years and concludes her long hymn to life. She is, on this view, a major poet whose visionary power is sustained by her technical resourcefulness.

Such claims are rejected by a large body of readers who can discern little in her work but fraudulent glitter and pretentiousness. The early poems seem to them amusing exercises in verbal juggling; and they argue that, throughout her career, Edith Sitwell made scarcely any advance in true poetic achievement. According to their view, she remained essentially the poet of *Wheels*. She picked up various modern tricks; she aped the discoveries of Eliot, Pound, and Yeats; she de-developed an inflated vocabulary and a repertoire of emotional gestures and rhetorical effects: but the resulting poems are grandiloquent shams. Her pride in her Plantagenet ancestry, the Byzantine weirdness of her costume and jewellery, her fondness for oracular pronouncements were all gimmicks designed to conceal the hollowness of her vatic utterances. Her verse has what Burke once called 'all the contortions of the Sybil without the inspiration'.

I find it impossible to accept either of these extreme views. Compared with Yeats, Eliot, Pound, Lawrence, Muir, Graves, and Auden, she appears to be a minor figure, whose manipulation of language and deployment of a few obsessive symbols soon became monotonous and unsatisfying. Without questioning the sincerity of her religious convictions or the ardour of her mystical faith, one may still feel that her

[4] See below, pp. 161–3.

vision is strained, her imagination overwrought, and that her poems represent a working out of private fantasies rather than a liberating celebration of common human passions, or a profound exploration of imaginative truth,

Yet to deny her any portion of merit is no less unjustified. The early poems are ingenious and entertaining, the first-fruits of a genuine devotion to poetry which gave her the strength to endure a life that was often lonely and unhappy. She insisted that even the most artificial of her early poems were grounded in observation of the natural world: 'Speaking of my earliest poems, it was suggested by some critics that I was greatly influenced by Diaghilev's Russian Ballet. This was not so . . . I was influenced, rather, by the outer surroundings of my childhood.'[5] And not only by the outer surroundings. Her preoccupation with images of cold indifference, isolation, betrayal, corruption, and suffering probably stems from her own terror and loneliness as a young child.

Nor is it fair to say that her work exhibits no genuine development. *Gold Coast Customs* and the poems inspired by the war reflect with a strange intensity her perception of spiritual evil and her horrified revulsion at the bestial cruelties of man to man. And there are passages in the later poems which achieve a fine harmony of language, a controlled splendour of imagery and rhythm.

Edith Sitwell was the chronicler of the English Eccentrics; and she may be dismissed by the more uncompromising of her opponents as an eccentric who projected herself into the sphere of literature rather than the hunting field, the *salon*, or the political arena. But when all the personal loyalties and animosities which she evoked have faded, and her arrogance in controversy has been forgotten, a later generation may accord her a small but distinctive place in the history of poetry as well as of publicity.

CRITICISM

Wheels is a more serious book [than *Georgian Poetry 1916–1917*]. It is not Mr. S. P. B. Mais's sort of poetry at all; these are not the good boys of the Sixth Form. The book as a whole has a dilettante effect, refreshing after the schoolroom. The authors are certainly conscious of the fact that literature exists in other languages than their own. While the Georgians have the appearance of ignorance, the Cyclists have a little the air of smattering. Instead of rainbows, cuckoos, daffodils, and timid hares, they give us garden-gods, guitars and mandolins, Lancret rather than Watteau, though they seem to have thrown Pierrot overboard. They need Catullus, Homer, Heine, Gautier; they have extracted the juice from Verlaine and Laforgue . . .

[5] *Taken Care Of*, 1965, p. 47.

SACHEVERELL SITWELL. The most important and most difficult poet in the volume. In fact, the best that has appeared for several years . . . He has an idiom which looks at first sight like rhetoric, and one finds with a shock that the words have values. He tends in his weaker moments to fly off like a beautiful but ineffectual aeroplane, beating its propeller vainly in a tree, but when he has a definite concrete sensation, as in 'The Feathered Hat', he is all right.

'Apteryx', 'Verse Pleasant and Unpleasant', review of *Wheels, A Second Cycle, The Egoist,* V, 3, March 1918, p. 44.
['Apteryx' was a pseudonym of T. S. Eliot's.]

As for the verse of the present time, the lack of curiosity in technical matters, of the academic poets of today (Georgian et caetera) is only an indication of their lack of curiosity in moral matters. On the other hand, the poets who consider themselves most opposed to Georgianism, and who know a little French, are mostly such as could imagine the Last Judgment only as a lavish display of Bengal lights, Roman candles, catherine-wheels, and inflammable fire-balloons. *Vous, hypocrite lecteur....*

T. S. Eliot, 'The Lesson of Baudelaire', *The Tyro,* I, 1921, p. 4.

The new fashion was not in all respects so very new, but the most unexpected, and therefore the newest mode is to take the last but one and remake it. So the daffodil and the rainbow and the cuckoo were to be put away, and the Harlequinades of the harlotry players and the Columbines of Verlaine and Symons to be had out again. We are all relieved from a certain tension, as at the accession of Charles II. 'Wheels' affected us as the painted furniture at Messrs Heal's affected those who were weary of the furniture of William Morris, and as the furniture of Morris must have affected people coeval with Morris. 'Wheels' marked a change in fashion. *Vers libre* and Cubism already existed, but 'Wheels' at least acknowledged the fact; it showed a willingness to experiment, a tolerance of various emotions, and a complete indifference to simplicity. This last item is most important: for the previous literary mode had been wholly corrupted by simplicity.

Great simplicity is only won by an intense moment or by years of intelligent effort, or by both. It represents one of the most arduous conquests of the human spirit: the triumph of feeling and thought over the natural sin of language . . . Simplicity was not hard won by the Georgians, it was given them by the fairy, and so, securely simple in their hearts, they neglected the more pharisaical virtue of simplicity in expression. 'Wheels', by contrast, has stood on the side of intelligence . . .

In a smaller way, Miss Edith Sitwell has arrived at more nearly perfect accomplishment than her brother [Sacheverell]. She is the only writer on whom the cyclical garments look well. She has, of course, her own vices. She has looked too long on modern painting; her colours are crude and exaggerated. The sun is very bright; the grass is very green, and dotted with red parasols and negroes. Her bird is the parrot, or perhaps macaw. There are weaknesses of technique: 'twixt', 'I fain', 'did kill'; in two successive poems faces are in cubes; more than once the light is 'sequined'. Yet her coloured furniture is so cleverly done, at times, that we wonder whether she is not fully justified in doing nothing else . . . She is unusual among contemporaries in that she cannot fall into vulgarity or cheapness.

'The Post Georgians', anonymous review of *Wheels. A Third Cycle*, *The Athenaeum*, 4641, 11 April 1919, pp. 171–2.

The fact is that anything in the world may be made to assume [a frightful, nightmarish] significance if you isolate it from its context, dwell upon it as a thing-in-itself, a solitary, unique existence. By thinking about it hard enough, you can make the sunshine dance and sing, you can cause the whole landscape to crepitate and twitch galvanically as it does in the poetry of Miss Sitwell. Brilliantly accomplished and exquisite as the poetry of this talented writer often is, one is always painfully conscious of its limitations. It is difficult to see how it can advance. Obviously, you cannot carry the process of dissociation beyond a certain point. Great poetry is surely created by the opposite method, by something analogous to the mystical discipline, by a passing outwards from the immediacies of consciousness towards the universal.

Aldous Huxley, 'The Subject-Matter of Poetry', *The Chapbook*, II, 9, March 1920, p. 15.

Rhythm is one of the principal translators between dream and reality. Rhythm might be described as, to the world of sound, what light is to the world of sight. It shapes and gives new meaning. Rhythm was described by Schopenhauer as melody deprived of its pitch.

The great architect, Monsieur Le Corbusier, said that, as the result of the Machine Age, 'new organs awake in us, another diapason, a new vision'. He said of persons listening to the sound of certain machinery that 'the noise was so round that one believed a change in the acoustic functions was taking place'. It was therefore necessary to find rhythmical expressions for the heightened speed of our time . . .

The poems in *Facade* are *abstract* poems – that is, they are, too, in many cases, virtuoso exercises in technique of an extreme difficulty, in the same sense as that in which certain studies by Liszt are studies in transcendental technique in music.

My experiments in *Facade* consist of inquiries into the effect on rhythm and on speed of the use of rhymes, assonances, and dissonances, placed at the beginning and in the middle of lines, as well as at the end, and in most elaborate patterns. I experimented, too, with the effect upon speed of the use of equivalent syllables – a system that produces great variation.

Edith Sitwell, 'Some Notes on My Own Poetry', *Collected Poems*, 1957, pp. xv–xvi.

My actual experiments led eventually to the poem 'Gold Coast Customs'. It is a poem about the state that led up to the second World War. It is a definite prophecy of what would arise from such a state – what *has* arisen. (It was written in 1929.)

. . . Do we smell and see

The sick thick smoke from London burning . . .?

The organization of the poem, speaking of this world that has broken down, but where a feverish, intertwining, seething movement, a vain seeking for excitement, still existed, presented considerable difficulty. I tried to give a concentrated essence of that world through a movement which at times interweaves like worms intertwining, which at times has a jaunty wire-jerked sound, or rears itself up like a tidal wave rushing forward, or swells like a black sea-swell by means of violently stretching vowels, then . . . sinks into a deliberate pulselessness.

ibid., pp. xxxv–xxxvi.

After 'Gold Coast Customs' I wrote no poetry for several years, with the exception of a long poem called 'Romance', and one poem in which I was finding my way.

Then, after a year of war, I began to write again – of the state of the world, of the terrible rain

Dark as the world of man, black as our loss –
Blind as the nineteen hundred and forty nails
Upon the Cross –

falling alike upon guilty and guiltless, upon Dives and Lazarus. I wrote of the sufferings of Christ, the Starved Man hung upon the Cross, the God of the Poor Man, who bears in His Heart all wounds.

In one poem I wrote of the world reduced to the Ape as mother, teacher, protector.

But, too, with poor Christopher Smart, I blessed Jesus Christ with the Rose and his people, which is a nation of living sweetness.

My time of experiments was done.

Now, for the most part, I use lines of great length – these need considerable technical control – sometimes unrhymed, but with occasional rhymes, assonances, and half-assonances, used, outwardly and inwardly in the lines, to act as a ground rhythm.

ibid., p. xli.

To what ideals would I reach in my poetry? (How far I am from these no one could see more clearly than I.)

Technically, I would come to a vital language – each word possessing an infinite power of germination – I would attain to the 'hard and bounding line' that Blake said was necessary to all art, as to all virtue. Spiritually, to give holiness to each common day. To 'speak for a moment with all men of their other lives'.[6] To produce a poetry that is the light of the Great Morning, wherein all beings whom we see passing in the common street are transformed into the epitome of all beauty, or of all joy, or of all sorrow.

'Who were those went by?'
'Queen Hecuba and Helen.'

My poems are hymns of praise to the glory of life.

ibid., pp. xlv–xlvi.

I shall be content... with saying again just what I believe about these three versifying oddmedods [the Sitwells]: They have as writers a talent for perching head into wind, for appropriating, like bower-birds, shining oddments of culture, and for mimicking, like starlings, the product of more harmonious throats. Ignorance, deficiency in ideas and insensibility they are able to defeat within themselves by tireless advertisement and by confiding in the ignorance, deficiency in ideas and insensitivity of reviewers, their gullibility and their day to day memory. They are everybody's highbrow artists, cartooning themselves for the mob as the 'queer men' of poetry.

G[eoffrey]. E. G[rigson]., 'New Books on Poetry – and Miss Sitwell', *New Verse*, 12, December 1934, pp. 16–17.

Among her fawns, cats, columbines, clowns, wicked faries, into that phantasmagoria which reminds me of a ballet called *The Sleeping Beauty*, loved by the last of the Tsars, she interjects a nightmare horror of death and decay. I commend to you *The Hambone and the Heart*, and *The Lament of Edward Blastock*, as among the most tragic poems of our time. Her language is the traditional language of literature, but twisted, torn, complicated, jerked here and there by strained

[6] Arthur Rimbaud, *Une Saison en enfer*.

resemblances, unnatural contacts, forced upon it by terror or by some violence beating in her blood, some primitive obsession that civilization can no longer exorcise. I find her obscure, exasperating, delightful.

W. B. Yeats, 'Modern Poetry: A Broadcast', 1936, *Essays and Introductions*, 1961, pp. 500–1.

Edith Sitwell has a temperament of a strangeness so high-pitched that only through this artifice could it find expression. One cannot think of her in any other age or country. She has transformed with her metrical virtuosity traditional metres reborn not to be read but spoken, exaggerated metaphors into mythology, carrying them from poem to poem, compelling us to go back to some first usage for the birth of the myth; if the storm suggests the bellowing of elephants, some later poem will display 'The elephant trunks of the sea'. Nature appears before us in a hashish-eater's dream. This dream is double; in its first half, through separated metaphor, through mythology, she creates, amid crowds and scenery that suggest the Russian Ballet and Aubrey Beardsley's final phase, a perpetual metamorphosis that seems an elegant, artificial childhood; in the other half, driven by a necessity of contrast, a nightmare vision, like that of Webster, of the emblems of mortality.

W. B. Yeats, Introduction to *The Oxford Book of Modern Verse*, 1936, pp. xviii–xix.

Nobody could have used symbols more wilfully than Yeats, yet he shows us that any symbols may be used to make powerful and beautiful poems. This does not happen in Edith Sitwell's work because there is no reference through the symbols to reality as there is in Yeats, there are few memorable and exact images, there is nothing but an endless Swinburnian flow of would-be evocative words . . .

Yeats's terrible figure [in 'The Second Coming'] is real because it is something that the poet conceived, understood, *saw*, and put down with the finest and tightest control. Edith Sitwell's rhetoric is the product merely of words ringing like bells in her head. Those who thought otherwise for a few years were deceived by the experience of war, war the most powerful blurrer of the intelligence, the arch-nurse of empty phrases. At no other time than during the war could poems which reverted in their language to Victorian archaism and rhetoric, poems so lacking in coherent thought and so determined to ignore the world of objects in which we live, have deceived so many intellectual critics.

Julian Symons, 'Miss Edith Sitwell have and had and heard', *The London Magazine*, IV, 8, November 1964, p. 63.

[The title of the article is a quotation from Gertrude Stein.]

POEMS

Sir Beelzebub

When
Sir
Beelzebub called for his syllabub in the hotel in Hell
            Where Proserpine first fell,
Blue as the gendarmerie were the waves of the sea,
            (Rocking and shocking the bar-maid).

Nobody comes to give him his rum but the
Rim of the sky hippopotamus-glum
Enhances the chances to bless with a benison
Alfred Lord Tennyson crossing the bar laid
With cold vegetation from pale deputations
Of temperance workers (all signed In Memoriam)
Hoping with glory to trip up the Laureate's feet,
            (Moving in classical metres) . . .

Like Balaclava, the lava came down from the
Roof, and the sea's blue wooden gendarmerie
Took them in charge while Beelzebub roared for his rum.
            . . . None of them come!

Still Falls the Rain

The Raids, 1940.   *Night and Dawn*

Still falls the rain –
Dark as the world of man, black as our loss –
Blind as the nineteen hundred and forty nails
Upon the Cross.

Still falls the Rain
With a sound like the pulse of the heart that is changed to the hammer-
    beat
In the Potter's Field, and the sound of the impious feet

On the Tomb:
Still falls the Rain
In the Field of Blood where the small hopes breed and the human brain
Nurtures its greed, that worm with the brow of Cain.

Still falls the Rain
At the feet of the Starved Man hung upon the Cross.
Christ that each day, each night, nails there, have mercy on us –
On Dives and on Lazarus:
Under the Rain the sore and the gold are as one.

Still falls the Rain –
Still falls the Blood from the Starved Man's wounded Side:
He bears in His Heart all wounds, – those of the light that died,
The last faint spark
In the self-murdered heart, the wounds of the sad uncomprehending dark,
The wounds of the baited bear, –
The blind and weeping bear whom the keepers beat
On his helpless flesh . . . the tears of the hunted hare.

Still falls the Rain –
Then – O Ile leape up to my God: who pulles me doune –
See, see where Christ's blood streames in the firmament:
It flows from the Brow we nailed upon the tree
Deep to the dying, to the thirsting heart
That holds the fires of the world, – dark-smirched with pain
As Caesar's laurel crown.

Then sounds the voice of One who likes the heart of man
Was once a child who among beasts has lain –
'Still do I love, still shed my innocent light, my Blood, for thee.'

A Girl's Song in Winter

for Cyril Connolly

That lovely dying white swan the singing sun
Will soon be gone. But seeing the snow falling, who could tell one
From the other? The snow, that swan-plumaged circling creature, said,
'Young girl, soon the tracing of Time's bird-feet and the bird-feet of snow
Will be seen upon your smooth cheek. Oh, soon you will be
Colder, my sweet, than me!'

SELECT BIBLIOGRAPHY

Wheels

Wheels, edited by Edith Sitwell, 6 cycles, 1916–21.

Edith Sitwell's name does not appear as editor of the first two cycles. The first four cycles were published by Blackwell, Oxford; the fifth by Leonard Parsons, London; the sixth by C. W. Daniel, London.

Edith Sitwell

Collected Poems, London, 1957.

Contains a long Introduction by the author, entitled 'Some notes on My Own Poetry'.

The Outcasts, London, 1962.

Music and Ceremonies, New York, 1963.

The American edition of *The Outcasts*, with a few additional poems.

Taken Care Of, London, 1965.

Edith Sitwell did not live to correct the proofs of this autobiography.

10

EDWIN MUIR AND ROBERT GRAVES

INTRODUCTION

The rise and fall of poetic reputations, the influence of fashion on poetic taste, the means whereby poets lever themselves into prominence – these and kindred matters, though not of the first importance, should not be ignored by the student of poetry. Apart from the intrinsic merits of their work, Edwin Muir and Robert Graves are worth studying as examples of writers who, after years of neglect, became widely accepted as poets of the front rank.

Admittedly both Muir and Graves achieved some measure of recognition between the wars. Graves indeed had been hailed as a youthful soldier-poet, and he continued to produce volumes of poems and of literary criticism during the twenties and the thirties. Yet his verse and his criticism were not of a kind to commend him to conservative opinion, nor did he provide a rallying-point for the young and the revolutionary, who gave their allegiance first to T. S. Eliot and later to W. H. Auden. Until the late 1940s Graves was generally known as the author of a remarkable autobiography and of brilliantly unconventional historical novels rather than as a poet.

Muir, like Graves, was respected by his fellow-writers as a poet of integrity and as a good critic, but his verse was not greatly admired. Louis MacNeice's review of Muir's *Variations on a Time Theme* is typical of intelligent critical opinion at this time:

> I have such a respect for sincerity that I should like to say more in praise of Mr. Muir, but he reminds me too much of a type of Royal Academy picture of a decade or so back – stilted allegorical nudes walking through a grey landscape. But he is not bogus. This book should give a pleasant afternoon to those who like a decorous defeatism.[1]

It is not easy to determine exactly when and for what reasons Muir and Graves began to acquire their current reputations. The process was gradual, nor was it fostered by any spectacular critical campaign. I was given a little selection of Graves's poems called *No More Ghosts* (1940) in the autum of that year, and immediately became aware of a highly individual voice speaking about things that mattered to me. A few years later on an East African farm I read Muir's *The Narrow*

[1] *New Verse*, 9, June 1934, p. 20.

Place (1943) and again experienced a feeling of delight and gratitude. It is probable that at about this time other individuals, scattered all over the world, recognized in Graves and in Muir certain qualities that were particularly valuable in the middle of a war: a vision which was personal without being impenetrably private; a total absence of political clap-trap; an honesty and generosity of mind and heart which faced evil yet retained hope in goodness and love; a technical skill which never degenerated into barren virtuosity.

On the surface no two poets could have appeared more dissimilar. Graves, a man of upper-middle-class stock, had been educated at Charterhouse and commissioned during the First World War. Muir, the son of a crofter in the Orkneys, left school at fourteen and lived on the fringe of the proletariat until he escaped to a wider life. Unlike Muir, who was always subject to long bouts of sickness, Graves was a man of robust physique, a good boxer, a man of considerable strength and daring. It is clear from Graves's writings that his relationships with women have been passionate and stormy, while Muir's long, happy marriage with Willa Anderson gave him an inner stability which sustained him in all his misfortunes. Finally, whatever view we take of Muir's Christian orthodoxy, he was a religious man, whose innocence and unquestioning acceptance of spiritual truths contrasts markedly with Graves's restless ingenuity and scepticism.

Yet the resemblances between them are at least as striking as the divergences. Both spent the major part of their working lives abroad and, partly for this reason, stayed indifferent to the shifts of literary fashion. Paradoxically, both remained deeply conscious of their roots and proud of their native lands. Some of Muir's most powerful and haunting poems are on Scottish themes, particularly those derived from her history and her theological traditions, while he gave much thought to the linguistic problems of a Scottish poet born into an English-speaking environment. Although Graves seldom writes about Ireland he declares in the Foreword to his *Collected Poems* (1959) that 'these poems have never adopted a foreign accent or colouring; they remain true to the Anglo-Irish poetic tradition into which I was born'.

This strong consciousness of nationality should not be mistaken for parochialism or chauvinism. Graves has a good knowledge of the Classics and of Spanish literature, while Edwin and Willa Muir's translations of Kafka would alone be enough to secure them a place in our literature. The Muirs knew many writers and intellectuals of Central Europe between the wars, though not the fashionable cosmopolitan figures whose names adorn dozens of memoirs by hangers on. Like Graves, Muir seems to have been largely unaffected by French literature, and to have totally ignored the doctrines of French Symbolism which have shaped the course of Anglo-American modernism.

Another link between these two poets is their use of myth. In Muir's work the Fall of Troy, the wanderings of Odysseus, the image of the Labyrinth, Eden, the Fall of Man, and the entire range of Christian myth and symbol furnish the material for many, though by no means all, of his best poems. Graves's employment of myth is far more sophisticated, and at times it is hard to decide whether his constant invocation of the Mother Goddess and the Muse is more than an elaborate game. But although it is impossible to pin Graves down into declaring what precisely he means by the White Goddess (still less her successor, the Black Goddess) we need not doubt that he has devoted many years to her service.[2]

There are two final points of similarity between Graves and Muir. Both men at various periods suffered severe nervous breakdowns and were greatly helped by psychoanalysis, learning in the process how the images in their poems were related to their nightmares and fears. Both have written excellent autobiographies, which reflect with remarkable fidelity the distinctive character of their authors. Their fondness for self-scrutiny appears also in two poems, Muir's 'The Face' and Graves's 'The Face in the Mirror'. One could learn a good deal about these poets by comparing the two poems, noting how Muir is primarily concerned with the exploration of psychological depths:

> See me with all the terrors on my roads,
> The crusted shipwrecks rotting in my seas.

Graves begins by turning a disenchanted eye on his physical appearance:

> Crookedly broken nose – low tackling caused it,
> Cheeks, furrowed; coarse grey hair, flying frenetic;
> Forehead, wrinkled and high;
> Jowls, prominent; ears, large; jaw, pugilistic;
> Teeth, few; lips, full and ruddy; mouth, ascetic.

Only after establishing his physical identity does he attempt to convey the nature of his inner life, interrogating the mirrored man,

> And once more ask him why
> He still stands ready, with a boy's presumption,
> To court the queen in her high silk pavilion.

The decisive event in Muir's life was the enforced removal of his family from the Orkneys to Glasgow, the prelude to the death of his father and one of his brothers. To a sensitive adolescent such as Muir the shock of these events must have been overwhelming. Life in the Orkneys, though harsh and frugal, retained a traditional dignity and ceremony, whereas the existence in Glasgow endured by Muir was

[2] See below, pp. 177–9.

degrading and meaningless. It was like passing at one bound from pre-Industrial rural England into the jungle of late-nineteenth-century capitalism. Much that is loosely called archetypal in Muir's imagery takes its colouring from the shock of being wrenched away from his childhood Eden into a hell of poverty and squalor. Troy was spiritually not very far from the Orkneys, and the preoccupation in Muir's poems with the fall of cities and castles, betrayal, wanderings, labyrinths, pilgrimages, and journeyings home springs from his own loss of Troy as much as from his experiences of Europe after 1918.

Muir is not commonly thought of as a political poet, yet he suffered at first hand the pangs of social misery which the poets of the thirties studied in the pages of text-books or on the platforms of public meetings. He worked in a bone-factory; his brother-in-law was on the dole; his friends were murdered or tortured or exiled by the Nazis. His breakdown in the late 1940s was caused by the Communist coup in Prague and by the agony of witnessing for a second time the obliteration of the innocent and the gifted by a new brand of totalitarian cruelty.

He reacted to his early poverty by embracing a form of Nietzschean socialism, which he abandoned because of its arrogance, although his verse never lost certain elements of Nietzschean metaphysics. As John Holloway has pointed out in his essay on Muir,[3] his poetry has some affinities with Kafka and with the art of the German Expressionists, but what differentiates Muir from them is his sense of joy and serenity. In his sonnet, 'Milton', he imagines the poet's despair as he heard, though he could not see, the devilish din of hell. But the poem ends:

> A footstep more, and his unblinded eyes
> Saw far and near the fields of Paradise.

In 1939, before the outbreak of war, he found himself saying the Lord's Prayer aloud and discovered that he had been a Christian for years without knowing it. After his breakdown he worked for the British Council in Rome where he rejoiced to find everywhere the symbols of the Incarnation. He combined an unworldly wisdom and innocence with a shrewd gaiety, and although his eyes and hopes were fixed on a region beyond time he never lost his relish for the small pleasures of human life. To the end of his days he was delighted if he heard on the radio that his favourite football team, Hamilton Academicals, had won their match.

His philosophy became more explicitly Christian in his final years, although he excluded from his *Collected Poems* four poems printed in *One Foot in Eden* which were burdened with ecclesiastical dogma, and, as he lay dying, said with great urgency to Willa Muir 'There are no absolutes, no absolutes'. He chose nonetheless to be buried in the

3 'The Modernity of Edwin Muir', *The Colours of Clarity*, 1964, pp. 95–112.

Anglican graveyard of Swaffham Prior, and if he was not an orthodox Christian it remains true that his vision of the Divine Imagination was illuminated by the light of the Gospels.

If for Muir the decisive moment of his life was his exile from the Orkneys, for Graves the traumatic experience was the First World War. In his foreword to *Collected Poems* (1959), Graves tells us that the first poem, 'In the Wilderness', 'shows where I stood at the age of nineteen before getting caught up by the First World War, which permanently changed my outlook on life'. In *Whipperginny* (1923) Graves speaks in the Author's Note of certain feeble bucolic poems as 'bankrupt stock' and refers to 'the desire to escape from a painful war neurosis into an Arcadia of amatory fancy'. Looking back on his collection of verse and prose published in the mid 1920s, he observes: 'My hope was to help the recovery of public health of mind as well as my own by the writing of "therapeutic" poems'.[4] The key to his poetic development in the inter-war years is to be found in his Foreword to *Collected Poems* (1938), especially the passage where he explains why he has felt obliged 'to manifest poetic faith by a close and energetic study of the disgusting, the contemptible, and the evil'.[5]

The most fruitful episode of his career was the partnership with Laura Riding, which lasted from 1926 until 1939, during which time his genius flowered and gave us many of his finest, most deeply felt poems. His cult of the White Goddess has not fundamentally changed his concept of poetry, although it has provided him with fresh themes and a new critical vocabulary. Douglas Day has pointed out that, in his early books, Graves's 'defence of romanticism and his dislike of classicism were dressed in semi-Freudian attire; and that, in *The White Goddess*, the same points of view are expressed in a mythological, religious, framework'.[6] Moreover, Graves himself confirms in the Foreword to *Collected Poems* (1965) that he has steadily explored one major theme: 'My main theme was always the practical impossibility, transcended only by a belief in miracle, of absolute love continuing between man and woman.'

This is not to suggest that Graves is a poet of limited scope. Indeed, one of the main delights which he affords is the variety of his subject-matter, tone, mood, texture, stanzaic patterns and rhythmical movement. He is a master of love poetry, poems celebrating the White Goddess and the Orphic Mysteries, metaphysical riddles, embittered meditations on human life, quirky satires, and what one may call emblematic poems.[7]

[4] Robert Graves, *The Common Asphodel*, 1949, p. 7.
[5] See below, p. 176.
[6] Douglas Day, *Swifter Than Reason*, 1963, p. 167.
[7] See Donald Davie's essay, 'Impersonal and Emblematic', *Listen*, III, 3 and 4, Spring 1960, pp. 31–6.

The verse which he has published during the past few years, for all its professional cunning, seems to me inferior to his finest achievements of the three previous decades. Graves once spoke of the difficulty in writing true poetry when one is constricted by didacticism of any kind. Only when the teacher 'breaks his main argument in digressions after loveliness and terror, only then does Poetry appear. It flashes out with the surprise and shock of a broken electric circuit'.[8] In this later verse one seldom experiences this unmistakable shock. Yet even if there has been a weakening, not of Apollonian craftsmanship but of poetic magic, we should be grateful for all that he has given us.

The work of certain poets is of value mainly because it reveals to us a pattern of imaginative order. Other poets construct poems which move us less through what they show than through what they are – a dance of words imbued with sensuous energy. Insofar as this distinction is valid, Muir belongs to the first and Graves to the second category. Almost every poem of Graves is, verbally, extremely dextrous and elegant, sparkling with vitality. Muir, on the contrary, is often flat and monotonous; in his weaker poems the rhythms are leaden, the imagery is conventional, the diction unremarkable. What gives his verse its peculiar grace is the translucence of the writing which permits us to see undimmed the spiritual truth that he has perceived. The apparent lack of technical skill, like the poet's self-effacement, is a precondition of the poem's success.

In spite of all their differences, Muir and Graves are alike in their lifelong indifference to poetic fashion and in their steadfast dedication to their art. They do not rank among the great revolutionary poets such as Donne, Milton, Pope, Wordsworth, Eliot, and Pound, who have permanently altered our concept of what poetry is and what it can perform. Their place is rather with George Herbert, Marvell, Crabbe, Arnold, Hardy, and other masters great and small who, working within a recognized tradition, have left it richer and more varied by the exercise of their skill and integrity.

CRITICISM

Human beings are understandable only as immortal spirits; they become natural then, as natural as young horses; they are absolutely unnatural if we try to think of them as a mere part of the natural world . . . I do not have the power to prove that man is immortal and that the soul exists; but I know that there must be such a proof, and that compared with it every other demonstration is idle. It is true that human life without immortality would be inconceivable to me, though that is not the ground for my belief. It would be inconceivable because

[8] Robert Graves, *On Modern Poetry*, 1922, p. 99.

if man is an animal by direct descent I can see human life only as a nightmare populated by animals wearing top-hats and kid gloves, painting their lips and touching up their cheeks and talking in heated rooms, rubbing their muzzles together in the moment of lust, going through innumerable clever tricks, learning to make and listen to music, to gaze sentimentally at sunsets, to count, to acquire a sense of humour, to give their lives for some cause, or to pray . . .

But I believe that man has a soul and that it is immortal, not merely because on any other supposition life would be inconceivable and monstrous . . . My belief in immortality, so far as I can divine its origin, and that is not far, seems to be connected with the same impulse which urges me to know myself. I can never know myself; but the closer I come to knowledge of myself the more certain I must feel that I am immortal, and, conversely, the more certain I am of my immortality the more intimately I must come to know myself. For I shall attend and listen to a class of experiences which the disbeliever in immortality ignores or dismisses as irrelevant to temporal life. The experiences I mean are of little practical use and have no particular economic or political interest. They come when I am least aware of myself as a personality moulded by my will and time: in moments of contemplation when I am unconscious of my body, or indeed that I have a body with separate members; in moments of grief or prostration; in happy hours with friends; and, because self-forgetfulness is most complete then, in dreams and day-dreams and in that floating, half-discarnate state which precedes and follows sleep. In these hours there seems to be knowledge of my real self and simultaneously knowledge of immortality.

Edwin Muir, *An Autobiography*, 1954, pp. 51–4.
[*An Autobiography* is a revised and enlarged version of
The Story and the Fable, 1940.]

I remember stopping for a long time one day to look at a little plaque on the wall of a house in the Via degli Artisti, representing the Annunciation. An angel and a young girl, their bodies inclined towards each other, their knees bent as if they were overcome by love, 'tutto tremente', gazed upon each other like Dante's pair; and that representation of a human love so intense that it could not reach farther seemed the perfect earthly symbol of the love that passes understanding. A religion that dared to show forth such a mystery for everyone to see would have shocked the congregations of the north, would have seemed a sort of blasphemy, perhaps even an indecency. But here it was publicly shown, as Christ showed himself on the earth.

That these images should appear everywhere, reminding everyone of the Incarnation, seemed to me natural and right, just as it was right that my Italian friends should step out frankly into life. This open declaration was to me the very mark of Christianity, distinguishing it from the older religions.

ibid., p. 278.

I think that if any of us examines his life, he will find that most good has come to him from a few loyalties, and a few discoveries made many generations before he was born, which must always be made anew. These too may sometimes appear to come by chance, but in the infinite web of things and events chance must be something different from what we think it to be. To comprehend that is not given to us, and to think of it is to recognize a mystery, and to acknowledge the necessity of faith. As I look back on the part of the mystery which is my own life, my own fable, what I am most aware of is that we receive more than we can ever give; we receive it from the past, on which we draw with every breath, but also – and this is a point of faith – from the Source of the mystery itself, by the means which religious people call Grace.

ibid., p. 281.

The idea of the 'eternal recurrence' remained essential to Muir's vision, however modified by Platonic and Christian elements. Nietzsche's cosmology, Plato's metaphysics, and Christ's ethic of love are at first opposed, then blended, and finally fused in Muir's poetry.

Michael Hamburger, 'Edwin Muir', *Encounter*, XV, 6, December 1960, p. 49.

I am not competent to discuss the theological implications of Muir's treatment of Eden and the Fall as archetypes of human experience, or to decide how far it would satisfy the requirements of any sectarian orthodoxy. However, since more than one recent writer on Muir has in fact claimed such orthodoxy for him, or claimed him for such orthodoxy, and since this misunderstanding is likely to be perpetuated despite the evidence of the definitive *Collected Poems*, it is necessary to state once more that neither Muir's Italian illumination, nor his earlier awakening to the significance of the Lord's Prayer was a religious conversion in any accepted sense of the word.

At one period when he was writing the poems in *One Foot in Eden*, Muir himself drew attention to the imaginative aspect of the conciliatory and transfiguring power, akin to divine grace, that dominates the book. 'Perhaps in the imagination of mankind the transfiguration has become a powerful symbol, standing for many things, among them those transformations of reality which the imagination itself creates', he said in 1952 . . .[9]

The new volume omits all those poems from *One Foot in Eden*

[9] From a broadcast in the Scottish Home Service. Quoted from J. C. Hall's monograph, *Edwin Muir*, London, 1956. [Michael Hamburger's footnote.]

which could possibly qualify as Christian devotional or apologist verse . . . Clearly Muir was anxious to remain uncommitted to the last; a visionary poet, deeply concerned with the example of Christ, not a Christian poet.

ibid., pp. 51–2.

The great central fact about Muir's work is that although in his vision the powers of evil were great, ultimately the powers of good and goodness were greater; and they were greater because they were also humbler, more primaeval, nearer to life in its archaic simplicity; which Muir was able to see not far below life's surface distractions. This, in the end, is the inner vision of joy which the iconic quality of his verse predominantly serves; and it is this sense of the simple but spacious powers of goodness held by life in reserve, that is ultimately what demands, and what justifies, Muir's simple but often monumental imagery; and his grave and lucid rhythms; and the honesty and spareness of his diction.

John Holloway, 'The Poetry of Edwin Muir', *The Hudson Review*, XIII, 1960–61, pp. 565–6.
Reprinted, and retitled 'The Modernity of Edwin Muir', in *The Colours of Clarity*, 1964, pp. 95–112. The passage above occurs on pp. 110–11.

That the proportion of what would be called 'unpleasant poems' is so high in this twenty-three year sequence surprised me on first looking it over. But I see this now not as a furious reaction against the anodynic tradition of poetry in which I was educated but as the blurted confession of a naturally sanguine temperament: that the age into which I was born, in spite of its enjoyable lavishness of entertainment, has been intellectually and morally in perfect confusion. To manifest poetic faith by a close and energetic study of the disgusting, the contemptible, and the evil is not very far in the direction of poetic serenity, but it has been the behaviour most natural to a man of my physical and literary inheritances. Other steps remain, and a few have already been taken. I should say that my health as a poet lies in my mistrust of the comfortable point-of-rest. Certainly, this suspicious habit, this dwelling upon discomfort and terror, has brought me good luck: for in the midst of my obstinate stumblings there have some sudden flashes of grace and knowledge –

As to the common brute it falls
To see real miracles
And howl with irksome joy.

Robert Graves, Foreword to *Collected Poems*, 1938, pp. xxiii–xxiv.
[The verse quotation is by Laura Riding.]

The nucleus of every poem worthy of the name is rhythmically formed in the poet's mind, during a trance-like suspension of his normal habits of thought, by the supra-logical reconciliation of conflicting emotional ideas. The poet learns to induce the trance in self-protection whenever he feels unable to resolve an emotional conflict by simple logic. If interrupted during this preliminary process of composition he will experience the disagreeable sensations of a sleep-walker disturbed; and if able to continue until the draft is completed will presently come to himself and wonder: was the writer really he?

Robert Graves, *The Common Asphodel*, 1949, p. 1.

[The first section of this book, pp. 1–25, is called 'Observations on Poetry 1922–25', and reprints passages from four short books about poetry published between these dates.]

Prose is the art of manifest statement: the periods and diction may vary with the emotional mood, but the latent meanings of the words that compose it are largely disregarded. In poetry a supplementary statement is framed by a precise marshalling of these latent meanings; yet the reader would not be aware of more than the manifest statement were it not for the heightened sensibility induced in him by the rhythmic intoxication of verse.

ibid., p. 3.

'What is the use or function of poetry nowadays?' is a question not the less poignant for being defiantly asked by so many stupid people or apologetically answered by so many silly people. The function of poetry is religious invocation of the Muse; its use is the experience of mixed exaltation and horror that her presence excites.

Robert Graves, *The White Goddess*, 1948, pp. 11–12.

The test of a poet's vision, one might say, is the accuracy of his portrayal of the White Goddess and of the island over which she rules. The reason why the hairs stand on end, the skin crawls and a shiver runs down the spine when one writes or reads a true poem is that a true poem is necessarily an invocation of the White Goddess, or Muse, the Mother of All Living, the ancient power of fright and lust – the female spider or the queen-bee whose embrace is death.

ibid., p. 20.

Poetry began in the matriarchal age, and derives its magic from the moon, not from the sun. No poet can hope to understand the nature of poetry unless he has had a vision of the Naked King crucified to the lopped oak, and watched the dancers, red-eyed from the acrid smoke of the sacrificial fires, stamping out the measure of the dance, their bodies bent uncouthly forward, with a monotonous chant of: 'Kill! Kill! Kill!' and 'Blood! blood! blood!'

ibid., p. 393.

When I say that a poet writes his poems for the Muse, I mean simply that he treats poetry with a single-minded devotion which may be called religious, and that he allows no other activity in which he takes part, whether concerned with his livelihood or with his social duties, to interfere with it.

Robert Graves, 'The Poet and his Public', *The Crowning Privilege*, 1955, p. 187.

The main theme of poetry is, properly, the relations of man and woman, rather than those of man and man, as the Apollonian Classicals would have it.

Robert Graves, *The White Goddess*, 1948, p. 392.

Since the source of creative intelligence in poetry is not scientific intelligence, but inspiration – however this may be scientifically accounted for – why not attribute inspiration to the Lunar Muse, the oldest and most convenient European term for the source in question?

Robert Graves, 'The White Goddess', *Steps*, 1958, p. 96.

Whether God is a metaphor or a fact cannot be reasonably argued; let us likewise be discreet on the subject of the Goddess ...

No Muse-poet can grow conscious of the Muse except by experience of some woman in whom the Muse-power is to some degree or other resident . . . the real, perpetually obsessed Muse-poet makes a distinction between the Goddess as revealed in the supreme power, glory, wisdom and love of woman, and the individual woman in whom the Goddess may take up residence for a month, a year, some years, or even longer.

ibid., pp. 101–2.

Nearly all magic poems in English are the work of young people ... The poet, as he grows old and reasonable, tends to lose his power of falling in love, or even of remaining in love ... The Literary Establishment has a bright label for what he then produces, if he follows the right models energetically enough. It is 'Major Poetry' – which casually consigns the magical poems of his early manhood to the category of 'Minor Poems'. Having by this time graduated as a solid member of society, the new major poet transfers his allegiance from the White Goddess of Inspiration to Apollo, the god of musical and artistic achievement . . . For Apollo is invoked by major poets for his harmonious architectural concepts, his scientific exactness, his musical masonary – Apollo's lyre had made Troy rise, the Greeks claimed.

Robert Graves, 'Sweeney Among the Blackbirds', ibid., p. 113.

At Hierapolis, Jerusalem and Rome [Ishtar] acknowledged a mysterious sister, the Goddess of Wisdom, whose temple was small and unthronged. Call her the Black Goddess; Provencal and Sicilian 'Black Virgins' are so named because they derive from an ancient tradition of Wisdom as Blackness. This Black Goddess, who represents a miraculous certitude in love, ordained that the poet who seeks her must pass uncomplaining through all the passionate ordeals to which the White Goddess may subject him.

Robert Graves, 'Intimations of the Black Goddess', *Mammon and the Black Goddess*, 1965, p. 162.

In his poetry Mr. Graves . . . has remembered what he has suffered, and, in remembering, has transformed pain into the excellence of art. He is a very fine poet, and a poet whose vision of some things, of love, of suffering, of pain, of honour, is much deeper, stronger and calmer than the vision that most of us can claim. His temperament may estrange intimacy; his chief preoccupations may be irrelevant to our most urgent contemporary problems. And when he deals with the theme of the body in a prison he may be dealing with a theme rather excessively private (in the sense that readers, like myself, who have not a parallel feeling about their own bodies, have to make a rather conscious effort of sympathy.) Nevertheless, in his later work in verse – as, indeed, in his better work in prose – he is a model for young writers of a strong and pure style. His journeys may lie rather aside from what we think of as our main roads; but his is a very pure and individual talent, which, if we do care at all for good and honest writing, we ought not to ignore or decry.

G. S. Fraser, 'The Poetry of Robert Graves', *Vision and Rhetoric*, 1959, p. 148.
[Fraser's essay was first published in *The Changing World*, II, autumn 1947, pp. 51–63.]

The Goddess was awesome, mysterious, alternately loving and cruel – altogether a figure that commanded the utmost in respect, devotion, and fear. Moreover, the lore connected with her worship was arcane enough to satisfy Graves's fondness for the dark alleys of erudition. The poet who aspired to attract her favours needed a vast reservoir of learning, ingenuity, tact, and – most of all – independence of imagination and unconventionality, and Graves knew himself to possess all these qualities. As Graves conceived of her, she was scornful of science and the more logically oriented philosophies, as the barren products of a patriarchal society; and Graves had long been opposed to both of these. Furthermore, the dark and bloody rites that were so integral a part of Goddess-worship provided an ideal outlet for Graves's attraction to the horrible, the grotesque, and the supernatural. She was, in short, the perfect Muse for a poet with a taste for the idiosyncratic and bizarre; and she caught, held, and enriched Graves's imagination as nothing before had been able to do. Whether she manifested herself as Mother, Nymph, or Crone, the White Goddess stood for the feminine principle as superior to the masculine; and Graves was prepared to pay her – or her representatives – all the homage due from a loyal and humble subject.

Douglas Day, *Swifter than Reason*, 1963, pp. 187–8.

POEMS

EDWIN MUIR
(1887–1959)

The Child Dying

Unfriendly friendly universe,
I pack your stars into my purse,
And bid you, bid you so farewell.
That I can leave you, quite go out,
Go out, go out beyond all doubt,
My father says, is the miracle.

You are so great, and I so small:
I am nothing, you are all:
Being nothing, I can take this way.
Oh I need neither rise nor fall,
For when I do not move at all
I shall be out of all your day.

It's said some memory will remain
In the other place, grass in the rain,
Light on the land, sun on the sea,
A flitting grace, a phantom face,
But the world is out. There is no place
Where it and its ghost can ever be.

Father, father, I dread this air
Blow from the far side of despair,
The cold cold corner. What house, what hold,
What hand is there? I look and see
Nothing-filled eternity,
And the great round world grows weak and old.

Hold my hand, oh hold it fast –
I am changing! – until at last
My hand in yours no more will change,
Though yours change on. You here, I there,
So hand in hand, twin-leafed despair –
I did not know death was so strange.

Orpheus' Dream

And she was there. The little boat
Coasting the perilous isles of sleep,
Zones of oblivion and despair,
Stopped, for Eurydice was there.
The foundering skiff could scarcely keep
All that felicity afloat.

As if we had left earth's frontier wood
Long since and from this sea had won
The lost orginal of the soul,
The moment gave us pure and whole
Each back to each, and swept us on
Past every choice to boundless good.

Forgiveness, truth, atonement, all
Our love at once – till we could dare
At last to turn our heads and see
The poor ghost of Eurydice
Still sitting in her silver chair,
Alone in Hades' empty hall.

One Foot in Eden

One foot in Eden still, I stand
And look across the other land.
The world's great day is growing late,
Yet strange these fields that we have planted
So long with crops of love and hate.

Time's handiworks by time are haunted,
And nothing now can separate
The corn and tares compactly grown.
The armorial weed in stillness bound
About the stalk; these are our own.
Evil and good stand thick around
In the fields of charity and sin
Where we shall lead our harvest in.

Yet still from Eden springs the root
As clean as on the starting day.
Time takes the foliage and the fruit
And burns the archetypal leaf
To shapes of terror and of grief
Scattered along the winter way.
But famished field and blackened tree
Bear flowers in Eden never known.
Blossoms of grief and charity
Bloom in these darkened fields alone.
What had Eden ever to say
Of hope and faith and pity and love
Until was buried all its day
And memory found its treasure trove?
Strange blessings never in Paradise
Fall from these beclouded skies.

ROBERT GRAVES
(b. 1893)

The Cool Web

Children are dumb to say how hot the day is,
How hot the scent is of the summer rose,
How dreadful the black wastes of evening sky,
How dreadful the tall soldiers drumming by.

But we have speech, to chill the angry day,
And speech, to dull the rose's cruel scent.
We spell away the overhanging night,
We spell away the soldiers and the fright.

There's a cool web of language winds us in,
Retreat from too much joy or too much fear:
We grow sea-green at last and coldly die
In brininess and volubility.

But if we let our tongues lose self-possession,
Throwing off language and its watery clasp.
Before our death, instead of when death comes,
Facing the wide glare of the children's day,
Facing the rose, the dark sky and the drums
We shall go mad no doubt and die that way.

Pure Death

We looked, we loved, and therewith instantly
Death became terrible to you and me.
By love we disenthralled our natural terror
From every comfortable philosopher
Or tall, grey doctor of divinity:
Death stood at last in his true rank and order.

It happened soon, so wild of heart were we,
Exchange of gifts grew to a malady:
Their worth rose always higher on each side
Till there seemed nothing but ungivable pride
That yet remained ungiven, and this degree
Called a conclusion not to be denied.

Then we at last bethought ourselves, made shift
And simultaneously this final gift
Gave: each with shaking hands unlocks
The sinister, long, brass-bound coffin-box,
Unwraps pure death, with such bewilderment
As greeted our first love's acknowledgement.

Certain Mercies

Now must all satisfaction
Appear mere mitigation
Of an accepted curse?

Must we henceforth be grateful
That the guards, though spiteful,
Are slow of foot and wit?

That by night we may spread
Over the plank bed
A thin coverlet?

That the rusty water
In the unclean pitcher
Our thirst quenches?

That the rotten, detestable
Food is yet eatable
By us ravenous?

That the prison censor
Permits a weekly letter?
(We may write: 'we are well.')

That, with patience and deference,
We do not experience
The punishment cell?

That each new indignity
Defeats only the body,
Pampering the spirit
With obscure, proud merit?

Mid-winter Waking

Stirring suddenly from long hibernation,
I knew myself once more a poet
Guarded by timeless principalities
Against the worm of death, this hillside haunting;
And presently dared open both my eyes.

O gracious, lofty, shone against from under,
Back-of-the-mind-far clouds like towers;
And you, sudden warm airs that blow
Before the expected season of new blossom,
While sheep still gnaw at roots and lambless go –

Be witness that on waking, this mid-winter,
I found her hand in mine laid closely
Who shall watch out the Spring with me.
We stared in silence all around us
But found no winter anywhere to see.

SELECT BIBLIOGRAPHY

Edwin Muir

Collected Poems 1921–1958, London, 1960.

The Story and the Fable: An Autobiography, London, 1940.

An Autobiography, London, 1964.
A revised and enlarged version of *The Story and the Fable*, which had carried Muir's story only as far as 1922.

Essays on Literature and Society, London, 1949; revised and enlarged edition, 1965.

The Estate of Poetry, London, 1962.

Butter, P. H., *Edwin Muir*, Edinburgh, 1962.

—— *Edwin Muir: Man and Poet*, Edinburgh, 1966.

Hall, J. C., *Edwin Muir*, London, 1956.

Hamburger, Michael, 'Edwin Muir', *Encounter*, XV, 6, December 1960, pp. 46–53.

Holloway, John, *The Colours of Clarity*, London, 1964.
Contains a valuable essay on Muir.

Muir, Willa, *Belonging: a Memoir*, London, 1968.

Raine, Kathleen, *Defending Ancient Springs*, London, 1967.
Contains a valuable essay on Muir.

Robert Graves

Collected Poems 1965, London, 1965.
In every successive edition of his *Collected Poems* Graves has suppressed poems that no longer pass muster with him, but has restored some of them in later editions. The bibliography of his poems is extremely complicated.

The White Goddess, London, 1948; revised and enlarged edition, 1952.

The Common Asphodel: Collected Essays on Poetry 1922–1949, London, 1949.
A brilliant collection, greatly superior to his later criticism.

Goodbye to All That, London, 1929.
A superb autobiography.

Cohen, J. M., *Robert Graves*, Edinburgh, 1960.

Day, Douglas, *Swifter Than Reason: The Poetry and Criticism of Robert Graves*, Chapel Hill and London, 1963.

Fraser, G. S., *Vision and Design*, London, 1959.
Contains a first-rate essay on Graves first published in 1947, before the publication of *The White Goddess*, and before Graves had become widely admired.

Seymour-Smith, Martin, *Robert Graves*, London, 1956; 2nd. ed., 1965.

11

W. H. AUDEN

INTRODUCTION

During the 1930s W. H. Auden was universally recognized as the dominant figure among the poets of his generation. Even those who ironically dubbed him the Kipling or the Rupert Brooke of the Left were testifying to his pre-eminence, and to his power of attracting fervent admiration. Some of the awe-struck tributes lavished on him by his coevals now seem a trifle ridiculous:

> Look west, Wystan, lone flyer, birdman, my bully boy!
> Plague of locusts, creeping barrage, has left earth bare;
> Suckling and centenarian are up in air,
> No wing-room for Wystan, no joke for kestrel joy.[1]

> But there waited for me in the summer morning
> Auden, fiercely. I read, shuddered and knew . . .[2]

One can understand why, after paying homage to Auden in the *New Verse* double number devoted to his work in November 1937, Dylan Thomas should have added an irreverent postscript: 'Congratulations on Auden's seventieth birthday'. It is arguable that no poet since Byron has won so high a reputation at so early an age. In addressing a letter in verse to Byron, Auden was saluting both a kindred spirit and a poet who had enjoyed a similar renown and adulation. One wonders whether, in 1937, Auden anticipated that, like Byron, he would choose to exile himself from the country where his roots grew so deep.

Auden has always displayed an omnivorous appetite for information of every kind, and a delight in classifying the facts which he acquires or observes:

> My first remark at school did all it could
> To shake a matron's monumental poise;
> 'I like to see the various types of boys.'[3]

Even his nursery library provides some fascinating clues to his later development,[4] while he seems to have been possessed at an early age by that love of words which he regards as the hall-mark of a poet: '"Why

[1] C. Day Lewis, *The Magnetic Mountain.*

[2] Charles Madge, 'Letter to the Intelligentsia'.

[3] 'Letter to Lord Byron', Part IV, *Letters from Iceland*, 1937, p. 205.

[4] Monroe K. Spears, *The Poetry of W. H. Auden*, 1963, p. 61.

do you want to write poetry?" If the young man answers: "I have important things I want to say", then he is not a poet. If he answers: "I like hanging around words, listening to what they say", then maybe he is going to be a poet.'[5]

Auden is an insatiable reader, a mere list of his favourite authors testifying to the bewildering diversity of his tastes and interests: Groddeck, Homer Lane, John Layard, Freud, D. H. Lawrence, Lewis Carroll, Hans Andersen, the brothers Grimm, Kafka, Beatrix Potter, Jules Verne, George Macdonald, Firbank, Tolkien, Jane Austen, Proust, Colette, Henry James, Kierkegaard, and a number of modern theologians – these are some of the authors who have captured his imagination at various stages of his career. His love of poetry was strongly fostered by Walter de la Mare's anthology, *Come Hither* (1923). In the summer of 1923 he discovered his first great master, Thomas Hardy, and the next year became a devotee of Edward Thomas. There followed spells of passionate absorption in T. S. Eliot, Edwin Arlington Robinson, Emily Dickinson, Bridges, Hopkins, Skelton, Anglo-Saxon poetry and Rilke. In 1941 he declared that the three greatest influences on his work were Dante, Langland, and Pope.[6]

During his stay in Berlin in 1928–9, Auden was greatly impressed by Brecht, whom he describes as a remarkable writer but a 'most unpleasant man'.[7] The influence of Brecht is apparent in Auden's work for the theatre and in his ballads; he also helped to give Auden's thought a distinctive Marxist tinge. The role of Marxism and of psychoanalytical theory in Auden's poetry of the 1930s has been discussed so often and so exhaustively that it would be wearisome to rake over the old ground yet once again. It is enough to say that, despite Christopher Caudwell's strictures on bourgeois Marxists,[8] Auden's idiosyncratic use of Marxist dialectics and psychoanalytical terms gave his early poems a remarkable sharpness and heady excitement. The highly compressed dramatic power of a poem such as 'Our Hunting Fathers',[9] first printed in 1934, owes much to Auden's synoptic view of history and to the clinching force of the final two lines, which are a concealed quotation from Lenin:

To hunger, work illegally,
And be anonymous.

Auden's departure for the United States seemed like a betrayal to many of his followers. An anonymous reviewer descended to the level of remarking that Auden's love of Henry James was understandable,

[5] 'Squares and Oblongs', *Poets at Work*, edited by Charles D. Abbott, 1948, p. 171.
[6] 'Criticism in a Mass Society', *The Intent of the Critic*, edited by D. A. Stauffer, 1941, p. 132.
[7] Monroe K. Spears, *The Poetry of W. H. Auden*, 1963, p. 91.
[8] See below, pp. 206–7. [9] See below, pp. 193–4.

since both had changed nationality for the same reason – that England was at war. In fact, Auden and Isherwood left for the States on 18 January 1939, at a time when Government spokesmen were asserting that the prospects for peace had never been brighter. Auden did not become an American citizen until April 1946. Moreover, it is unlikely that physical cowardice played any part in his decision to leave England: he had voluntarily gone to Spain during the Civil War and to China during the Japanese invasion. Auden has consistently refused to discuss his motives for emigrating, and speculation on the subject is pointless.

Most readers feel, nonetheless, that Auden's departure from England marks a dramatic break in his career, and that his poetry underwent a decisive change after he had settled in the States. Some of his critics, including men who honoured him in the 1930s, believe that his emigration has damaged his genius beyond repair, and that all his distinctive virtues were drained away after 1939 by this act of emotional surrender.[10] This process has, it is alleged, been hastened by an even more disastrous failure of nerve, his conversion to Christianity and his abandonment of the humanist values of the 1930s. He has even been accused of tampering with the texts of his early poems in order to disguise the nature of his youthful convictions.[11]

The most vital question is whether Auden's poetic powers have deteriorated in the past quarter of a century. It is easy but scarcely convincing to compare the most striking of his early poems with the feeblest productions of his later years, and then to exclaim in pious horror at this Christian rake's progress. Many of Auden's more recent poems are slack, trivial and coy, and John Bayley has forcibly reminded us that technical virtuosity may coexist with emotional nullity.[12] But it is equally true that many of his early poems are silly, pretentious, slapdash, and needlessly obscure. In preparing for publication in the United States his *Collected Poems* (1945), Auden discarded various poems, including 'A Communist to Others'. He wrote against this poem the comment 'O God, what rubbish'.[13] The truth is that Auden has always been an unusually prolific and uneven poet, capable of turning out a masterpiece at a time when his gifts seem to have deserted him. The proper scale of comparison is between his finest work before 1939 and his finest work since then.

Apart from his reversion to the Christian faith, the most decisive single factor in Auden's later development has been his ever-growing devotion to the art of music. He has acknowledged his debt to Walter

[10] Randall Jarrell wrote some damaging reviews of Auden's later work. For an extract from his review of *The Age of Anxiety*, see below, pp. 192–3.

[11] J. W. Beach, *The Making of the Auden Canon*, 1957. Some of Beach's contentions are disputed in Monroe K. Spears, *The Poetry of W. H. Auden*, 1963.

[12] See below, p. 193.

[13] Monroe K. Spears, *The Poetry of W. H. Auden*, 1963, p. 154.

Greatorex, the music master at Gresham's,[14] and from an early age he loved various forms of vocal music. Many of his pre-war poems were songs and other musical pieces. It was not, however, until after 1937 that he began to appreciate the world of Italian opera, a 'world so beautiful and so challenging to my own cultural heritage'.[15] Ever since then, as his love of music has grown deeper and more intense, his poetry has become correspondingly more and more elaborate, baroque and operatic. Eliot believed that the poet was more likely to find the germ of a poem in the concert room rather than in the opera house.[16] It is not fanciful to suppose that just as Eliot's later verse owes much to the structure and mood of Beethoven's and of Bartok's string quartets, so Auden's later poems draw sustenance from the operas of Mozart and of Verdi. Even though Auden may have lost or sacrificed that disturbing sharpness and intellectual daring which characterized his poetry in the 1930s, the most beautiful of his later poems are endowed with a richness and a haunting solemnity that lay beyond the range of his early work.

To read his literary criticism, the best of which is collected in *The Dyer's Hand* (1963), is to become aware of the extraordinary range and vitality of his intelligence. His emotional power is no less remarkable: anybody who believes that Auden died as a poet in 1939 should turn to the title poem of *The Shield of Achilles* (1955).[17] Unpredictable, erratic, marvellously gifted, a maddening virtuoso, a dedicated poet who nevertheless believes that to the religious man art and science are small beer, Auden will doubtless continue to delight and to dazzle us with the brilliance of his genius.

CRITICISM

There on the old historic battlefield,
  The cold ferocity of human wills,
The scars of struggle are as yet unhealed;
  Slattern the tenements on sombre hills,
  And gaunt in valleys the square-windowed mills
That, since the Georgian house, in my conjecture
Remain our finest native architecture . . .

Clearer than Scafell Pike, my heart has stamped on
The view from Birmingham to Wolverhampton . . .
Tramlines and slagheaps, pieces of machinery,
That was, and still is, my ideal scenery.

W. H. Auden, 'Letter to Lord Byron', Part II,
Letters from Iceland, 1937, pp. 50–1.

[14] ibid., p. 340. [15] W. H. Auden, *The Dyer's Hand*, 1963, p. 40.
[16] T. S. Eliot, *The Music of Poetry*, 1942, p. 28. [17] See below, pp. 196–7.

With northern myths my little brain was laden,
  With deeds of Thor and Loki and such scenes;
My favourite tale was Andersen's *Ice Maiden*;
  But better far than any kings or queens
  I liked to see and know about machines:
And from my sixth until my sixteenth year
I thought myself a mining engineer.

'Letter to Lord Byron', Part IV, ibid., p. 205.

All youth's intolerant certainty was mine as
  I faced life in a double-breasted suit;
I bought and praised but did not read Aquinas,
  At the *Criterion*'s verdict I was mute,
  Though Arnold's I was ready to refute;
And through the quads dogmatic words rang clear,
'Good poetry is classic and austere.'

ibid., p. 209.

My first Master was Thomas Hardy, and I think I was very lucky in my choice. He was a good poet, perhaps a great one, but not *too* good. Much as I loved him, even I could see that his diction was often clumsy and forced and that a lot of his poems were plain bad. This gave me hope where a flawless poet might have made me despair. He was modern without being too modern. His world and sensibility were close enough to mine – curiously enough his face bore a striking resemblance to my father's – so that, in imitating him, I was being led towards not away from myself, but they were not so close as to obliterate my identity. If I looked through his spectacles, at least I was conscious of a certain eyestrain. Lastly, his metrical variety, his fondness for complicated stanza forms, were an invaluable training in the craft of making. I am also thankful that my first Master did not write in free verse or I might then have been tempted to believe that free verse is easier to write than stricter forms, whereas I now know it is infinitely more difficult.

W. H. Auden, *Making, Knowing and Judging*, 1956, p. 10.
Reprinted in *The Dyer's Hand*, 1963, p. 38.

Auden's surest triumphs represent a recovery of the archaic imagery – fells, scarps . . . the becks with their pot-holes left by the receding glaciers of the age of ice. His dominant contrast is the contrast between this scene and the modern age of ice: foundries with their fires cold, flooded coal-mines, silted harbors – the debris of the new ice age. The advent of the new age of ice, a 'polar peril', supplies the background for his finest poetry.

Cleanth Brooks, *Modern Poetry and the Tradition*, 1939, p. 126.

When we collaborate, I have to keep a sharp eye on him – or down flop the characters on their knees . . . If Auden had his way, he would turn every play into a cross between grand opera and high mass.

Christopher Isherwood, 'Some Notes on Auden's Early Poetry', *New Verse*, 26–27, November 1937, p. 4. Reprinted in *Exhumations*, 1966, p. 17.

The various 'kerygmas' of Blake, of Lawrence, of Freud, of Marx, to which, along with most middle-class intellectuals of my generation, I paid attention between twenty and thirty, had one thing in common. They were all Christian heresies; that is to say, one cannot imagine their coming into existence except in a civilization which claimed to be based, religiously, on the belief that the Word was made flesh and dwelt among us, and that, in consequence, matter, the natural order, is real and redeemable, not a shadowy appearance or the cause of evil, and historical time is real and significant, not meaningless or an endless series of cycles . . .

I have come to realize that what is true in what they say is implicit in the Christian doctrine of the nature of man, and that what is not Christian is not true; but each of them brought to some particular aspect of life that intensity of attention that is characteristic of one-sided geniuses (needless to say, they all contradicted each other), and such comprehension of Christian wisdom as I have, little though it be, would be very much less without them.

W. H. Auden, untitled essay in *Modern Canterbury Pilgrims*, edited by James A. Pike, 1956. Quoted by Monroe K. Spears, *The Poetry of W. H. Auden*, 1963, p. 174.

Many of the books which have been most important to him have not been works of poetry or criticism but books which have altered his way of looking at the world and himself, and a lot of these, probably, are what an expert in their field would call 'unsound'. The expert, no doubt, is right, but it is not for a poet to judge; his duty is to be grateful.

And among the experiences which have influenced his writing, a number may have been experiences of other arts. I know, for example, that through listening to music I have learned much about how to organize a poem, how to obtain variety and contrast through change of tone, tempo and rhythm, though I could not say just how. Man is an analogy-drawing animal; that is his great good fortune. His danger is of treating analogies as identities, of saying, for instance, 'Poetry should be as much like music as possible'. I suspect that the people who are most likely to say this are the tone-deaf. The more one loves another art, the less likely it is that one will wish to trespass upon its domain.

W. H. Auden, *Making, Knowing and Judging*, 1956, pp. 23–4.

The impulse to create a work of art is felt when, in certain persons, the passive awe provoked by sacred beings or events is transformed into a desire to express that awe in a rite of worship or homage, and to be fit homage, this rite must be beautiful. This rite has no magical or idolatrous intention; nothing is expected in return. Nor is it, in a Christian sense, an act of devotion. If it praises the Creator, it does so indirectly by praising His creatures – among which may be human notions of the Divine Nature. With God as Redeemer, it has, so far as I can see, little if anything to do.

ibid., p. 30.

Whatever its actual content and overt interest, every poem is rooted in imaginative awe. Poetry can do a hundred and one things, delight, sadden, disturb, amuse, instruct – it may express every possible shade of emotion, and describe every conceivable kind of event, but there is only one thing that all poetry must do; it must praise all it can for being and for happening.

ibid., p. 33.

[*Making, Knowing and Judging* was delivered before the University of Oxford on 11 June 1956 as Auden's Inaugural Lecture as Professor of Poetry. It is reprinted in *The Dyer's Hand* (1963), pp. 31–60, except for a short concluding paragraph about Hardy's 'Afterwards', followed by the text of that poem. The three passages quoted above occur respectively on pp. 51–2, p. 57, and p. 60.]

Poetry is not magic. In so far as poetry, or any other of the arts, can be said to have an ulterior purpose, it is, by telling the truth, to disenchant and disintoxicate.

W. H. Auden, 'Writing', *The Dyer's Hand*, 1963, p. 27.

The characteristic style of 'Modern' poetry is an intimate tone of voice, the speech of one person addressing one person, not a large audience; whenever a modern poet raises his voice he sounds phony. And its characteristic hero is neither the 'Great Man' nor the romantic rebel, both doers of extraordinary deeds, but the man or woman in any walk of life who, despite all the impersonal pressures of modern society, manages to acquire and preserve a face of his own.

W. H. Auden, 'The Poet and the City', *The Massachusetts Review*, Spring 1962.
Reprinted in *The Dyer's Hand*, 1963, p. 84.

The Age of Anxiety is the worst thing Auden has written since 'The Dance of Death'; it is the equivalent of Wordsworth's 'Ecclesiastical Sonnets'. The man who, during the thirties, was one of the five or six best poets in the world has gradually turned into a rhetoric mill grinding away at the bottom of Limbo, into an automaton that keeps making little jokes, little plays on words, little rhetorical engines, as compulsively and unendingly and uneasily as a neurotic washes his hands.

Randall Jarrell, *The Nation*, 18 October 1947.
Quoted by Monroe K. Spears, *The Poetry of W. H. Auden*, 1963, p. 239.

Auden is no longer slapdash. But such regularity [the employment of Scaldic metres and of verbal tricks of late Norse poetry] has its own dangers – it may come to produce a poetry that 'does the poet's thinking and writing for him', as Goethe put it, a substitute for any deeper movement and expansion of the poet's mind.

John Bayley, *The Romantic Survival*, 1957, p. 178.

Thou shalt not be on friendly terms
With guys in advertising firms,
  Nor speak with such
As read the Bible for its prose,
Nor, above all, make love to those
  Who wash too much.

Thou shalt not live within thy means
Nor on plain water and raw greens.
  If thou must choose
Between the chances, choose the odd;
Read *The New Yorker*, trust in God;
  And take short views.

W. H. Auden, from 'Under Which Lyre'.

POEMS

Our Hunting Fathers

Our hunting fathers told the story
  Of the sadness of the creatures,
Pitied the limits and the lack
  Set in their finished features;
Saw in the lion's intolerant look,
Behind the quarry's dying glare,
Love raging for the personal glory
  That reason's gift would add,
The liberal appetite and power,
  The rightness of a god.

Who, nurtured in that fine tradition,
  Predicted the result,
Guessed Love by nature suited to
  The intricate ways of guilt,
That human ligaments could so
His southern gestures modify
And make it his mature ambition
  To think no thought but ours,
To hunger, work illegally,
  And be anonymous?

Twelve Songs

I

Say this city has ten million souls,
Some are living in mansions, some are living in holes:
Yet there's no place for us, my dear, yet there's no place for us.

Once we had a country and we thought it fair,
Look in the atlas and you'll find it there:
We cannot go there now, my dear, we cannot go there now.

In the village churchyard there grows an old yew,
Every spring it blossoms anew:
Old passports can't do that, my dear, old passports can't do that.

The consul banged the table and said:
'If you've got no passport you're officially dead':
But we are still alive, my dear, but we are still alive.

Went to a committee; they offered me a chair;
Asked me politely to return next year:
But where shall we go to-day, my dear, but where shall we go to-day?

Came to a public meeting; the speaker got up and said:
'If we let them in, they will steal our daily bread';
He was talking of you and me, my dear, he was talking of you and me.

Thought I heard the thunder rumbling in the sky;
It was Hitler over Europe, saying: 'They must die';
We were in his mind, my dear, we were in his mind.

Saw a poodle in a jacket fastened with a pin,
Saw a door opened and a cat let in:
But they weren't German Jews, my dear, but they weren't German Jews.

Went down the harbour and stood upon the quay,
Saw the fish swimming as if they were free:
Only ten feet away, my dear, only ten feet away.

Walked through a wood, saw the birds in the trees;
They had no politicians and sang at their ease:
They weren't the human race, my dear, they weren't the human race.

Dreamed I saw a building with a thousand floors,
A thousand windows and a thousand doors;
Not one of them was ours, my dear, not one of them was ours.

Stood on a great plain in the falling snow;
Ten thousand soldiers marched to and fro:
Looking for you and me, my dear, looking for you and me.

Master and Boatswain

At Dirty Dick's and Sloppy Joe's
  We drank our liquor straight,
Some went upstairs with Margery,
  And some, alas, with Kate;
And two by two like cat and mouse
The homeless played at keeping house.

There Wealthy Meg, the Sailor's Friend,
  And Marion, cow-eyed,
Opened their arms to me but I
  Refused to step inside;
I was not looking for a cage
In which to mope in my old age.

The nightingales are sobbing in
  The orchards of our mothers,
And hearts that we broke long ago
  Have long been breaking others;
Tears are round, the sea is deep:
Roll them overboard and sleep.

The Shield of Achilles

She looked over his shoulder
  For vines and olive trees,
Marble well-governed cities
  And ships upon untamed seas,
But there on the shining metal
  His hands had put instead
An artificial wilderness
  And a sky like lead.

A plain without a feature, bare and brown,
  No blade of grass, no sign of neighbourhood,
Nothing to eat and nowhere to sit down,
  Yet, congregated on its blankness, stood
  An unintelligible multitude,
A million eyes, a million boots in line,
Without expression, waiting for a sign.

Out of the air a voice without a face
  Proved by statistics that some cause was just
In tones as dry and level as the place:
  No one was cheered and nothing was discussed;
  Column by column in a cloud of dust
They marched away enduring a belief
Whose logic brought them, somewhere else, to grief

She looked over his shoulder
  For ritual pieties,
White flower-garlanded heifers,
  Libation and sacrifice,
But there on the shining metal
  Where the altar should have been,
She saw by his flickering forge-light
  Quite another scene.

Barbed wire enclosed an arbitrary spot
  Where bored officials lounged (one cracked a joke)
And sentries sweated for the day was hot:
  A crowd of ordinary decent folk
  Watched from without and neither moved nor spoke
As three pale figures were led forth and bound
To three posts driven upright in the ground.

The mass and majesty of this world, all
 That carries weight and always weighs the same
Lay in the hands of others; they were small
 And could not hope for help and no help came:
 What their foes liked to do was done, their shame
Was all the worst could wish; they lost their pride
And died as men before their bodies died.

She looked over his shoulder
 For athletes at their games,
Men and women in a dance
 Moving their sweet limbs
Quick, quick, to music,
 But there on the shining shield
His hands had set no dancing-floor
 But a weed-choked field.

A ragged urchin, aimless and alone,
 Loitered about that vacancy, a bird
Flew up to safety from his well-aimed stone:
 That girls are raped, that two boys knife a third,
 Were axioms to him, who'd never heard
Of any world where promises were kept,
Or one could weep because another wept.

The thin-lipped armourer,
 Hephaestos hobbled away,
Thetis of the shining breasts
 Cried out in dismay
At what the god had wrought
 To please her son, the strong
Iron-hearted man-slaying Achilles
 Who would not live long.

SELECT BIBLIOGRAPHY

Works by W. H. Auden
Collected Shorter Poems 1930–1944, London, 1950.
Collected Shorter Poems 1927–1957, London, 1956.
Collected Longer Poems, London, 1968.
Homage to Clio, London, 1960.
About the House, London, 1966.
The Dyer's Hand, New York, 1962; London, 1963.
 A collection of Auden's critical essays.

Some Biographical and Critical Studies

Bayley, John, *The Romantic Survival*, London, 1957.
Contains a brilliant essay on Auden.

Beach, Joseph Warren, *The Making of the Auden Canon*, Minneapolis, 1957.

Blair, John G., *The Poetic Art of W. H. Auden*, Princeton and London, 1965.

Everett, Barbara, *Auden*, Edinburgh, 1964.

Hoggart, Richard, *Auden: An Introductory Essay*, London, 1951.

Scarfe, Francis, *Auden and After*, London, 1942.

Spears, Monroe K., *The Poetry of W. H. Auden*, New York and London, 1963.

—— *Auden*, edited by Monroe K. Spears, Englewood Cliffs (New Jersey), 1964.
A symposium.

12

POETS OF THE 1930s

INTRODUCTION

W. H. Auden once referred to the deplorable habit of classifying poets by decades, and it would be ridiculous to suppose that the course of poetry alters punctually every ten years. Yet it so happens that one can trace three distinct phases in the development of English verse between 1930 and 1960 which correspond very roughly to the divisions of the decades. The first runs from the publication of Auden's *Poems* in 1930 to his *Another Time* in 1940. The second, lasting from 1940 until the early 1950s, covers the publication of a mass of verse inspired by the Second World War and the emergence of poets a few years younger than Auden. The third marks the appearance of poets who were in their teens, or even younger, when the war began and who are sharply differentiated in many ways from the two previous generations of poets.

This is, of course, an extremely crude division, and it is impossible to place certain poets firmly in any one of these categories. For example, Bernard Spencer's first collection of poems came out in 1946, and the bulk of his verse was written after that date, yet he seems essentially a poet of the thirties; while Kathleen Raine, who, like Spencer, regularly contributed to the little magazines of the 1930s, belongs in spirit to the forties, as does David Gascoyne, although his first volume of poems, *Roman Balcony*, was published as early as 1932. As for George Barker, Roy Fuller, and F. T. Prince, one could with equal justification number them among the poets of the thirties or the forties. The placing of poets in decades is useful only so long as one remembers that it is a rough and ready arrangement.

The legend still persists that the poets of the thirties banded themselves together as undergraduates at Oxford and planned to devote themselves to left-wing propaganda. The four most famous names of the period, Auden, Day Lewis, Spender, and MacNeice, were indeed up at Oxford in the late 1920s, and they all for a time held left-wing views of varying degrees of intensity. Yet Day Lewis had gone down from Oxford before Spender arrived; the other three were up at the same time only during the academic year 1926–7; they did not all know one another until after the publication of *New Signatures* in 1932; and it was not until 1947 in Venice that Auden, Day Lewis, and Spender found themselves together in one room. Nor is it true that most of their early poems were on political themes.[1]

They did, however, concern themselves more directly than either the Georgians or T. S. Eliot had done with the social and political aspects of human life. This was partly because the brutal facts of the day, such as unemployment, Communism, Nazism and Fascism, were inescapable, and partly because they belonged to a generation which had been encouraged by its teachers to develop a social conscience. There were, moreover, certain poetic reasons which drove them to look for their material in the world of politics, national and international. In their eyes the greatest weakness of the Georgians was their preoccupation with individual hopes and fears, their reluctance to tackle the kind of large-scale, impersonal problems which shaped the daily lives of most human beings. Much as they admired Eliot, they deliberately turned away from his complexity and allusiveness in order that they might communicate with their fellow-men and urge them to follow certain right courses of action.

They were greatly influenced by the poems of Gerard Manley Hopkins which, though published by Robert Bridges in 1918, did not have any appreciable effect on English poetry until the early 1930s. Many young writers from Auden and Rex Warner down to Ted Hughes have imitated Hopkins's sprung verse, though never very happily, but his true importance as an example lies elsewhere. First, he showed that it was possible to break with the normal metrical and stanzaic patterns which had governed English poetry since the time of Elizabeth I, and yet still to employ powerful and elaborate formal devices that give language poetic intensity and memorability. Secondly, he demonstrated that one could make dogmatic statements about religion and politics without lapsing into Tennysonian moralizing. Paradoxical as it may seem, the young poets of the thirties who wanted to incorporate the doctrines of Marx and of Freud into their verse found a precedent and a justification for their poetic methods in the work as an ascetic Victorian Jesuit.

One must not exaggerate the attachment of these poets to any specific cause. Auden was always more deeply concerned with the nature of man than with political solutions to current problems; MacNeice was too sceptical and ironical to swallow left-wing panaceas; Day Lewis, the only one of them to embrace Communism formally, was perpetually uneasy travelling on the Party line even though he held a valid ticket; and Spender was guilty of quoting approvingly Thomas Mann's dictum that Karl Marx must read Frederick Hölderlin, an injunction which no dedicated Communist would endorse. Indeed such wholehearted Marx-

[1] See Louis MacNeice, 'Lost Generations?' *The London Magazine*, IV, 4, April 1957, pp. 53–4.

ists as Christopher Caudwell [2] and John Cornford, who died in Spain fighting for their beliefs, castigated the wobbly, frivolous attitudes of those who wanted to be in the vanguard of the struggle for social justice while clinging to the emotional luxury of being liberals, humanists and bourgeois poets. Cornford's polemical 'Keep Culture out of Cambridge' dismisses with equal contempt Eliot, Auden, D. H. Lawrence, and the Surrealists:

> Wind from the dead land, hollow men,
> Webster's skull and Eliot's pen . . .
> All the tricks we once thought smart,
> The Kestrel joy and the change of heart,
> The dark, mysterious urge of the blood,
> The donkey's shitting on Dali's food,
> There's none of these fashions have come to stay,
> And there's nobody here got time to play.
> All we've brought are our party cards
> Which are no bloody good for your bloody charades.

Unfortunately they were no bloody good for poetry. The story unfolded by Hugh D. Ford in *A Poets' War* (1965) makes depressing reading: the cynical lies, the shallow rhetoric, the turgid slogans which flourished so abundantly were sufficiently persuasive to lure to their death in Spain some of the most talented and honourable young writers of the day. But the verse written by the British combatants is almost entirely devoid of poetic merit. Even Cornford's verse is raised to the intensity of good poetry only when the orthodoxy of a political *credo* is quickened by the poignant fear and self-questioning of the lonely individual. His best-known poem, 'To Margot Heinemann', is almost a reversion to the mood of 1914 and to a type of poem which could have been written by his mother's friend, Rupert Brooke. Almost, but not quite – the romantic, plangent opening line, 'Heart of the heartless world', conceals a quotation from Marx, for whom the heart of the heartless world was the disinterested struggle for social justice. In the thirties, Rupert Brooke must read Karl Marx.

To speculate about Cornford's development had he survived the Spanish Civil War is pointless. It is, however, relevant to observe that the most valuable poetry by the poets of the thirties was written after that decade and its problems had vanished. This is particularly true of Louis MacNeice, who, after going through a bad patch in the late 1940s and early 1950s, revealed himself in his three final volumes as a poet of disturbingly sardonic power. He carried over into the post-war world the kind of concern for man-in-society which had given the best poetry of the thirties its urgency and vitality; and in his last poems he

[2] See below, pp. 206–7.

surveyed with a terrifying, unsmiling gaiety the fears and neuroses that lurk within us.

We may perceive in Bernard Spencer also a fruitful mingling of the political and the personal so characteristic of the thirties. Spencer's Mediterranean landscapes are permeated not only by reveries of sexual love but by the memory of injustice and cruelty inflicted on the slaves and the proletariat of the Ancient World, spiritual ancestors of the men who made the hunger march from Jarrow to London and who died for the Spanish Republic. Spencer never played at being a public-school Communist, nor did he lard his verse with political tags; but, like the most intelligent and humane of his coevals, he felt a personal responsibility for the victims of an unjust social order. In 'Greek Excavations', he discovers among the pottery and the coins

> The minimum wish
> For the permanence of the basic things of a life,
> For children and friends and having enough to eat
> And the great key of a skill;
> The life the generals and the bankers cheat.

The voice of the thirties speaks in these lines with eloquence and dignity.

Yet we may be doing an injustice to the decade by suggesting that it had only one voice. A young New Zealand critic, casting a cold eye on English verse since 1909, has argued that the Georgians so much despised by the poets of the thirties were in fact revolutionaries who made a genuine attempt to break down the wall of Edwardian literary conservatism: 'The wall of conservatism was broken finally by war and depression (though the same bricks were to be stacked in a new formation by some of the socialist writers of the thirties).'[3] This controversial assessment of Auden's generation is a reminder that the innovators of the period were by no means all committed to the advancement of left-wing opinions. There was, for example, the attempt to transplant French surrealism into the unreceptive soil of English verse. Although it produced no more than a handful of tolerable poems, it left its mark upon the poetry of men who found the doctrines of surrealism pretentious and absurd: '"Who but Donne," wrote Dr. Johnson, "would have thought that a good man is a telescope?" Any of us here, since the climate has changed, might think it. For two great taboos have been lifted off the modern poet – the taboo on using his brains and the taboo on so-called free association.'[4]

William Empson, one of the most original poets of the decade, never submitted to the dictates of Auden and his followers. 'Just a smack at

[3] C. K. Stead, *The New Poetic*, 1964, p. 125.

[4] Louis MacNeice, 'Experience with Images', *Orpheus*, II, 1949, pp. 126–7.

Auden' is a rude gesture towards the Master himself, while 'Autumn on Nan-Yueh' smartly deflates a whole gang of poetasters.

> Besides, I do not really like,
>   The verses about 'Up the Boys',
> The revolutionary romp.

Yet the very title of his second book of poems, *The Gathering Storm*, suggests how conscious he was, even in China, of the coming war. The most obvious characteristic of his verse is its extreme difficulty, but at his best one forgets the ingenuity and the intellectual strain, and is both moved by the laconic stoicism and ravished by the musical precision of the poetry. His own account of 'The Teasers' explains why some of his verse is impenetrably obscure, and suggests the essential nature of his art:

> No, I'm afraid that the business of guessing what it means when there isn't enough evidence to tell the answer is one we've all trained ourselves in. I just cut out the bits I thought were in bad taste and it didn't leave enough to make any sense really. That's what happened to 'The Teasers'. But a beautiful metrical invention, I do say. I wish I'd been able to go on with it because it sings so; but that was what happened. I could only give this cut version.[5]

Roy Campbell was, in many ways, the mirror-image of his detested MacSpaunday. His tough South African upbringing, his polemical brand of Roman Catholicism, his itch to pummel his opponents and his hatred of cliques in power all drove him to fight in Spain on Franco's side, and to waste his talent on vulgarly monotonous diatribes against Communist degenerates. What survives of his copious verse is a handful of lyrics and translations unblemished by the musty quarrels of the decade.

Finally, we should not ignore a writer whose enormous popularity in the 1950s among people who seldom read verse tends to conceal the fact that he belongs to the poets of the 1930s. John Betjeman, apart from being an extremely cunning deviser of intricate tunes and a word-painter of Tennysonian landscapes, is a sharp-eyed social historian whose verse is packed with the sort of detail painstakingly gathered by the Mass-Observation teams. Edmund Wilson saluted him as the best English poet of his generation; Auden dedicated to him *The Age of Anxiety*, and chose him as the only representative of contemporary English poets in *The Oxford Book of Light Verse*; Philip Larkin,

[5] *The Review*, 6 and 7, June 1963, p. 28.

correctly designated by Donald Davie as our unofficial Poet Laureate, has recognized in Betjeman a kindred spirit of an earlier decade. Whereas Auden's favourite view of society is that of the hawk or the airman, Betjeman perambulates on foot among the buildings, the individuals, and the social classes which he chronicles as minutely as Trollope or Mayhew. The nostalgia for Edwardian cosiness, the Gothic revivalism and other Betjemanesque foibles cloak the fact that he is an unsparing observer of society who is all the more conscious of its frailties and absurdities because he sees us moving towards death, sustained by no faith, determined to ignore our destination, pathetic as Lupin Pooter.

What links all the good poets of the 1930s is their consciousness of belonging to a society drifting towards a large-scale catastrophe. Their courage and vitality in continuing to work and to hope deserve to be commemorated when we are remembering the thirties.[6]

CRITICISM

Poetry is but a means of achieving that which I have called tragic integrity, and whenever new problems arise which cannot be directly solved by action, or old problems take new forms, new tragic poems will be necessary and will be written. But at all times, even in times of stable tradition, a lyric poetry is possible. Such a time will come toward the end of the lives of some of us now living, but meanwhile there will be upheaval, destruction of tradition, and urgent need for action. Therefore, in the poems of Day Lewis, Wystan Auden, and Stephen Spender there is new life and energy.

Michael Roberts, *Critique of Poetry*, 1934, pp. 248–9.

Nearly all my friends who during this period became active in left-Wing movements, or at least sympathetic to Left-Wing ideas, had had the same kind of upbringing. Rex Warner, MacNeice and myself were sons of clergymen; Auden had a devout Anglo-Catholic mother: Spender came from an 'old-fashioned Liberal' family. We had all been to public schools, with their traditions both of authoritarianism and of service to the community. We had all, I think, lapsed from the Christian faith, and tended to despair of Liberalism as an effective instrument for dealing with the problems of our day, if not to despise it as an outworn creed.

C. Day Lewis, *The Buried Day*, 1960, p. 209.

[6] See Donald Davie, 'Remembering the Thirties', below, p. 208.

If my faith was shaky – I was and remained sceptical about a good deal in Communist theory and practice – at least I had hope: no-one who did not go through this political experience during the Thirties can quite realize how much hope there was in the air then, how radiant for some of us was the illusion that man could, under Communism, put the world to rights . . .

Nevertheless, this living in two worlds was dangerously near sitting on the fence. It certainly must have encouraged my own chronic malady, the divided mind. I never ceased to be aware of the forces in myself which kept pulling me towards the past, the status quo, the traditions and assumptions in which I had been brought up; and it is significant that the only two political poems of any value which I wrote – 'The Conflict' and 'In Me Two Worlds' – though they end with a confident statement of the choice made, are poems of the divided mind, while the shrill, schoolboyish decisiveness which served for satire in other political verse of mine demonstrates the unnatural effort I had to make in order to avoid seeing both sides.

ibid., pp. 211–13.

I remembered how under the Roman Empire intellectuals spent their time practising rhetoric although they would never use it for any practical purpose; they swam gracefully around in rhetoric like fish in an aquarium tank. And our intellectuals also seemed to be living in tanks . . .

But there was an important exception – the group of poets who had appeared in *New Signatures*, published in 1931.[7] They were all politically Left, but it was not the jogtrot, compromising Left of my landlady's garden parties. The English Labour Party is notoriously lacking in glamour; these young poets had turned to the tomb of Lenin, the great flirtation had begun with the Third International. The strongest appeal of the Communist Party was that it demanded sacrifice; you had to sink your ego. At the moment there seemed to be a confusion between the state and the community, and I myself was repelled by the idolization of the state; but that was all right, it is written: 'The state shall wither away.' Young men were swallowing Marx with the same naïve enthusiasm that made Shelley swallow Rousseau.

I had a certain hankering to sink my ego, but was repelled by the priggishness of the Comrades and suspected that their positive programme was vitiated by wishful thinking and over-simplification. I joined them however in their hatred of the *status quo*, I wanted to smash the aquarium. During Christmas of 1933 . . . I sat down deliberately and wrote a long poem called *Eclogue for Christmas*. I wrote it with a kind of cold-blooded passion and when it was done it surprised me. Was I really as concerned as all that with the Decline of the West?

[7] *New Signatures*, edited by Michael Roberts, was in fact published in 1932.

Did I really feel so desperate? Apparently I did. Part of me must have been feeling like that for years.

Louis MacNeice, *The Strings Are False*, 1965, pp. 145–6.

[This unfinished autobiography, edited by E. R. Dodds, was written in 1940–1941.]

I consider that the poet is a blend of the entertainer and the critic or informer; he is not a legislator, however unacknowledged, nor yet essentially a prophet . . . I would have a poet able-bodied, fond of talking, a reader of the newspapers, capable of pity and laughter, informed in economics, appreciative of women, involved in personal relationships, actively interested in politics, susceptible to physical impressions.

Louis MacNeice, *Modern Poetry*, 1938, pp. 198–9.

Every poet knows that poetic sense is not the same thing as common sense or logical sense. And every poet knows that poetic shape is not a mere matter of mechanical symmetry. But does the reader know this? He does – when he himself is poeticising, i.e., talking; he will then use all sorts of hidden allusions, double meanings, irony, hyperboles and fancy variations from baby-talk to 'meaningless' swear-words; he will also play many tricks with rhythm. But once he starts reading, he wants to be spoon-fed; he demands that poetry should be simpler than talk . . .

There is therefore some relation between words as used by a poet and words as used by the public, which includes the critic. There is also a relation between verse rhythm and speech rhythm. The poet introduces new subtleties into both rhythm and meaning (the two interact on each other), but he is still only using with a new precision tools which lie ready to everyone's hand. And he is using them for an end which is as much social as personal; as Christopher Caudwell wrote, 'the instinctive ego of art is the common man into which we retire to establish contact with our fellows'.

Louis MacNeice, 'Poetry, The Public and The Critic', *The New Statesman and Nation*, 8 October 1949, pp. 380–1.

[Certain bourgeois artists] announce themselves as prepared to merge with the proletariat, to accept its theory and its organization, in every field of concrete living except that of art. Now this reservation – unimportant to an ordinary man – is absolutely disastrous for an artist, precisely because his most important function is to be an artist. It leads to a gradual separation between his living and his art – his living as a proletarian diverging increasingly from his art as a bourgeois. All his proletarian aspirations gather at one pole, all his bourgeois art at the other. Of course this separation cannot take place without a mutual distortion. His proletarian living bursts into his art in the form of crude and grotesque scraps of Marxist phraseology and the mechanical application of the living proletarian theory – this is very clearly seen in the three English poets most closely associated with the revolutionary movement. His bourgeois art bursts into his proletarian living in the form of extraordinary and quite unnecessary outbursts of bourgeois 'independence' and indiscipline or quite apparent bourgeois distortions of the party's revolutionary theory.

Christopher Caudwell, *Illusions and Reality*, 1937, pp. 284–5.

The year 1936 was not only the middle of a decade but also the heart of the Thirties dream . . .

The political and aesthetic dreams somehow blended together, so that the sectarian Communist was to lie down with the unpolitical aesthete (at no other time in this century could such an artist as Virginia Woolf have written in the *Daily Worker*), the working class Socialist to bed with the middle class Surrealist, and all were to join together in a European movement whose triumph was historically inevitable. It is easy now to see that most of those involved were unprepared to do more than attend a meeting or two and wait for that historically inevitable success to come about, easy to see that they were deceived: yet behind the movement at this time were the most generous impulses of humanity, impulses more valuable by far than the barren knowingness of the Fifties. It is better to be waiting for Lefty than to be waiting for Godot.

Julian Symons, *The Thirties*, 1960, pp. 51–2.

RICKS: *What do you feel about the influence you're supposed to have had on the poets of the fifties?*

EMPSON: Well, honestly, I don't like much of it. But it's largely because I'm an old buffer: the point has been reached where it is unusual for new poetry to seem very good to me. I haven't liked it very much; but I haven't liked any poetry whether it's supposed to be imitating me or not. This seems a fairly irrelevant angle, but the fact is that I don't react very readily to any modern poetry. I was hearing a young poet give a reading of his work, and he was explaining afterwards how much he hated all the other ones his age. He was talking about one of these and I said 'He has a singing line, hasn't he?' Meaning, as I thought, that he had the root of the matter in him. This chap pounced and said 'That's it, you've got it! Just a writer of lyrics!' He thought that if it sounds pretty that means you're bad.

Christopher Ricks and William Empson, 'William Empson in Conversation with Christopher Ricks', *The Review*, 6 and 7, June 1963, p. 32.

Hearing one saga, we enact the next.
We please our elders when we sit enthralled;
But then they're puzzled; and at last they're vexed
To have their youth so avidly recalled.

It dawns upon the veterans after all
That what for them were agonies, to us
Are high-brow thrillers, though historical;
And all their feats quite strictly fabulous.

This novel written fifteen years ago,
Set in my boyhood and my boyhood home,
These poems about 'abandoned workings', show
Worlds more remote than Ithaca or Rome.

The Anschluss, Guernica – all the names
At which those poets thrilled, or were afraid,
For me mean schools and schoolmasters and games;
And in the process someone is betrayed.

Ourselves perhaps. The Devil for a joke
Might carve his own initials on our desk,
And still we'd miss the point, because he spoke
An idiom too dated, Audenesque . . .

Even to them the tales were not so true
As not to be ridiculous as well:
The ironmaster met his Waterloo,
But Rider Haggard rode along the Fell.

'Leave for Cape Wrath to-night!' They lounged away
On Fleming's trek or Isherwood's ascent.
England expected every man that day
To show his motives were ambivalent . . .

A neutral tone is nowadays preferred.
And yet it may be better, if we must,
To find the stance impressive and absurd
Than not to see the hero for the dust.

For courage is the vegetable king,
The sprig of all ontologies, the weed
That beards the slag-heap with its hectoring,
Whose green adventure is to run to seed.

Donald Davie, from 'Remembering the Thirties'.

POEMS

C. DAY LEWIS
(b. 1904)

The Conflict

I sang as one
Who on a tilting deck sings
To keep men's courage up, though the wave hangs
That shall cut off their sun.

As storm-cocks sing,
Flinging their natural answer in the wind's teeth,
And care not if it is waste of breath
Or birth-carol of spring.

As ocean-flyer clings
To height, to the last drop of spirit driving on
While yet ahead is land to be won
And work for wings.

Singing I was at peace,
Above the clouds, outside the ring:
For sorrow finds a swift release in song
And pride its poise.

Yet living here,
As one between two massing powers I live
Whom neutrality cannot save
Nor occupation cheer.

None such shall be left alive:
The innocent wing is soon shot down,
And private stars fade in the blood-red dawn
Where two worlds strive.

The red advance of life
Contracts pride, calls out the common blood,
Beats song into a single blade,
Makes a depth-charge of grief.

Move then with new desires,
For where we used to build and love
Is no man's land, and only ghosts can live
Between two fires.

LOUIS MACNEICE
(1907–63)

The Sunlight on the Garden

The sunlight on the garden
Hardens and grows cold,
We cannot cage the minute
Within its nets of gold,
When all is told
We cannot beg for pardon.

Our freedom as free lances
Advances towards its end;
The earth compels, upon it
Sonnets and birds descend;
And soon, my friend,
We shall have no time for dances.

The sky was good for flying
Defying the church bells
And every evil iron
Siren and what it tells:
The earth compels,
We are dying, Egypt, dying

And not expecting pardon,
Hardened in heart anew,
But glad to have sat under
Thunder and rain with you,
And grateful too
For sunlight on the garden.

Beni Hasan

It came to me on the Nile my passport lied
Calling me dark who am grey. In the brown cliff
A row of tombs, of portholes, stared and stared as if
They were the long-dead eyes of beasts inside
Time's cage, black eyes on eyes that stared away
Lion-like focused on some different day
On which, on a long-term view, it was I, not they, had died.

The Taxis

In the first taxi he was alone tra-la,
No extras on the clock. He tipped ninepence
But the cabby, while he thanked him, looked askance
As though to suggest someone had bummed a ride.

In the second taxi he was alone tra-la
But the clock showed sixpence extra; he tipped according
And the cabby from out his muffler said: 'Make sure
You have left nothing behind tra-la between you.'

In the third taxi he was alone tra-la
But the tip-up seats were down and there was an extra
Charge of one-and-sixpence and an odd
Scent that reminded him of a trip to Cannes.

As for the fourth taxi, he was alone
Tra-la when he hailed it but the cabby looked
Through him and said: 'I can't tra-la well take
So many people, not to speak of the dog.'

After the crash

When he came to he knew
Time must have passed because
The asphalt was high with hemlock
Through which he crawled to his crash
Helmet and found it no more
Than his wrinkled hand what it was.

Yet life seemed still going on:
He could hear the signals bounce
Back from the moon and the hens
Fire themselves black in the batteries
And the silence of small blind cats
Debating whether to pounce.

Then he looked up and marked
The gigantic scales in the sky,
The pan on the left dead empty
And the pan on the right dead empty,
And knew in the dead, dead calm
It was too late to die.

STEPHEN SPENDER
(b. 1909)

The Pylons

The secret of these hills was stone, and cottages
Of that stone made,
And crumbling roads
That turned on sudden hidden villages.

Now over these small hills, they have built the concrete
That trails black wire;
Pylons, those pillars
Bare like nude giant girls that have no secret.

The valley with its gilt and evening look
And the green chestnut
Of customary root,
Are mocked dry like the parched bed of a brook.

But far above and far as sight endures
Like whips of anger
With lightning's danger
There runs the quick perspective of the future.

This dwarfs our emerald country by its trek
So tall with prophecy:
Dreaming of cities
Where often clouds shall lean their swan-white neck.

BERNARD SPENCER
(1909–63)

The Rendezvous

I take the twist-about, empty street
– balconies and drapes of shadow
– and glimpse chalk slogans on each wall,
(now governments have done their work)
that the fanatic or the duped,
even children are taught to scrawl:
the patriotic, 'Tyrants', 'Vengeance',
'Death to', etc.

Hooped
the barbed wire lies to left and right
since glass crashing, cars on fire,
since the mob howled loose that night,
gawky, rusty, useful wire
with little dirty fangs each way,
(what craftsman makes this fright?).
Black on that chemist's lighted window
steel helmets, rifle tops. I sense
the full moon wild upon my back
and count the weeks. Not long from this
the time we named comes round.

And true
to loves love never thought of, here
with bayonet and with tearing fence,
with cry of crowds and doors slammed to,
waits the once known and dear, once chosen
city of our rendezvous.

WILLIAM EMPSON
(b. 1906))

Missing Dates

Slowly the poison the whole blood stream fills.
It is not the effort nor the failure tires.
The waste remains, the waste remains and kills.

It is not your system or clear sight that mills
Down small to the consequence a life requires;
Slowly the poison the whole blood stream fills.

They bled an old dog dry yet the exchange rills
Of young dog blood gave but a month's desires;
The waste remains, the waste remains and kills.

It is the Chinese tombs and the slag hills
Usurp the soil, and not the soil retires.
Slowly the poison the whole blood stream fills.

Not to have fire is to be a skin that shrills.
The complete fire is death. From partial fires
The waste remains, the waste remains and kills.

It is the poems you have lost, the ills
From missing dates, at which the heart expires.
Slowly the poison the whole blood stream fills.
The waste remains, the waste remains and kills.

NORMAN CAMERON
(1905–53)

The Thespians at Thermopylae

The honours that the people give always
Pass to those use-besotted gentlemen
Whose numskull courage is a kind of fear,
A fear of thought and of the oafish mothers
('Or with your shield or on it') in their rear.
Spartans cannot retreat. Why, then, their praise
For going forward should be less than others'.
But we, actors and critics of one play,
Of sober-witted judgment, who could see
So many roads, and chose the Spartan way,
What has the popular report to say
Of us, the Thespians at Thermopylae?

ROY CAMPBELL
(1902–57)

Autumn

I love to see, when leaves depart,
The clear anatomy arrive,
Winter, the paragon of art,
That kills all forms of life and feeling
Save what is pure and will survive.

Already now the clanging chains
Of geese are harnessed to the moon:
Stripped are the great sun-clouding planes.
And the dark pines, their own revealing,
Let in the needles of the noon.

Strained by the gale the olives whiten
Like hoary wrestlers bent with toil
And, with the vines, their branches lighten
To brim our vats where summer lingers
In the red froth and sun-gold oil.

Soon on our hearth's reviving pyre
Their rotted stems will crumble up:
And like a ruby, panting fire,
The grape will redden on your fingers
Through the lit crystal of the cup.

JOHN BETJEMAN
(b. 1906)

Middlesex

Gaily into Ruislip Gardens
  Runs the red electric train,
With a thousand Ta's and Pardon's
  Daintily alights Elaine;
Hurries down the concrete station
With a frown of concentration,
Out into the outskirt's edges
Where a few surviving hedges
Keep alive our lost Elysium – rural Middlesex again.

Well cut Windsmoor flapping lightly,
  Jacqmar scarf of mauve and green
Hiding hair which, Friday nightly,
  Delicately drowns in Drene;
Fair Elaine the bobby-soxer,
Fresh-complexioned with Innoxa,
Gains the garden – father's hobby –
Hangs her Windsmoor in the lobby,
Settles down to sandwich supper and the television screen.

Gentle Brent, I used to know you
  Wandering Wembley-wards at will,
Now what change your waters show you
  In the meadowlands you fill!
Recollect the elm-trees misty
And the footpaths climbing twisty
Under cedar-shaded palings,
Low laburnum-leaned-on railings,
Out of Northolt on and upward to the heights of Harrow hill

Parish of enormous hayfields
  Perivale stood all alone,
And from Greenford scent of mayfields
  Most enticingly was blown
Over market gardens tidy,
Taverns for the *bona fide*,
Cockney anglers, cockney shooters,
Murray Poshes, Lupin Pooters
Long in Kensal Green and Highgate silent under soot and stone.

SELECT BIBLIOGRAPHY

General

New Signatures, edited by Michael Roberts, London, 1932.

New Country, edited by Michael Roberts, London, 1933.

The Faber Book of Modern Verse, edited by Michael Roberts, London, 1936; 2nd. ed., with supplement by Ann Ridler, 1951; 3rd. ed., 1965.
Three anthologies which are important documents in the history of poetic taste in the 1930s.

New Verse, edited by Geoffrey Grigson, London, 1939.
A selection of poems from the first thirty numbers (1933–1938) of Grigson's periodical *New Verse*.

Poems for Spain, edited by Stephen Spender and John Lehmann, London, 1939.

Poetry of the Thirties, edited by Robin Skelton, Harmondsworth, 1964.
An anthology of poems first printed in the thirties.

Caudwell, Christopher, *Illusion and Reality*, London, 1937.

Ford, Hugh D., *A Poets' War*, Pennsylvania and London, 1965.
A study of English poets and the Spanish Civil War.

Fraser, G. S., *Vision and Rhetoric*, London, 1959.
Contains essays on Empson, MacNeice and Spender.

Lewis, C. Day., *A Hope for Poetry*, Oxford, 1934; 2nd. ed., 1936.

MacNeice, Louis, *Modern Poetry*, London, 1938.

Roberts, Michael, *Critique of Poetry*, London, 1934.

Symons, Julian, *The Thirties*, London, 1960.

Julian Bell and John Cornford

Julian Bell: Essays, Poems and Letters, edited by Quentin Bell, London, 1938.

John Cornford: A Memoir, edited by Pat Sloan, London, 1938.

Stansky, Peter, and Arahams, William, *Journey to the Frontier. Julian Bell and John Cornford: their lives and the 1930s*, London, 1966.

John Betjeman

Collected Poems, edited by the Earl of Birkenhead, London, 1958; 2nd. ed., 1962.

Roy Campbell

Collected Poems, 3 vols., London, 1949–60.

Light on a Dark Horse, London, 1951.
An autobiography.

William Empson

Collected Poems, London, 1955.

Seven Types of Ambiguity, London, 1930; 2nd. ed., 1947.

Alvarez, A., *The Shaping Spirit*, London, 1958.
Contains an essay on Empson.

Wain, John, *Preliminary Essays*, London, 1957.
Contains an essay on Empson.

The Review 6–7, June 1963.
A double number devoted to Empson.

C. Day Lewis
Collected Poems, London, 1954.
The Buried Day, London, 1960.
An autobiography.

Louis MacNeice
Collected Poems, London, 1967.
Edited impeccably by E. R. Dodds.
The Strings Are False, London, 1965.
An autobiography down to 1940.
Press, John, *Louis MacNeice*, London, 1965.

Stephen Spender
Collected Poems 1928–1953, London, 1955.
World Within World, London, 1951.
An autobiography.

13

DYLAN THOMAS

INTRODUCTION

According to T. S. Eliot, 'the more perfect the artist, the more completely separate in him will be the man who suffers and the mind which creates; the more perfectly will the mind digest and transmute the passions which are its material.'[1] Judged by this criterion, Dylan Thomas was a highly imperfect artist, for his achievement as a poet and his personality as a man were so inextricably linked that we can scarcely understand the one without studying the other. There was a third Dylan Thomas to whom we need not devote much attention – the roistering Bohemian who drank and fornicated his way round the lecture circuits of the United States, and whose exploits titillated that large semi-literate public which, though indifferent to poetry, relishes scabrous details about the intimate affairs of poets.

Despite the plethora of articles about Thomas, reminiscences of his friends and acquaintances, elaborate glosses on his verse, and an admirably documented biography by Constantine FitzGibbon, *The Life of Dylan Thomas* (1965), the mystery of his inner life remains dark and insoluble:

> In the lost boyhood of Judas
> Christ was betrayed.[2]

It seems likely that the pattern of his emotional development was dictated by certain childhood experiences, or even ordained by his genetical endowment. The finest of his poems are illuminated by the radiance in which childhood memories are bathed; and, less happily, there runs through his life a streak of infantilism, which must have stunted and distorted his emotional growth and, consequently, his poetic achievement. The nickname which Bernard Spencer bestowed on him, 'the ugly suckling', testifies to this element in Thomas's life and work. The crucial question is the extent to which he was able to make valid poetry out of his aberrations.

The obsession with death, which is the most striking feature of his work, almost certainly went back to his childhood and became intensified in adolescence. His fascinated preoccupation with the process of birth and the monstrous excitement of sex are by-products of his horror of death. For a while the natural resilience of youth kept the

[1] *Selected Essays*, 1951, p. 18. [2] AE, '*Germinal*'.

horror at bay. In 1935 he and Geoffrey Grigson spent a summer holiday in Donegal where, in Wordsworthian fashion, they called to the echoing mountains, 'We are the Dead.' All too soon this gay defiance turned into a haunting consciousness of death; the drinking and the lechery, which were desperate attempts to blot out this knowledge, plunged him into guilt and misery.

Birth and copulation were for Thomas merely stages on the way to death. The child in the womb knows its destiny:

> My heart knew love, my belly hunger;
> I smelt the maggot in my stool.[3]
>
> Twenty-four years remind the tears of my eyes
> (Bury the dead for fear that they walk to the
> grave in labour.)
> In the groin of the natural doorway I crouched
> like a tailor
> Sewing a shroud for a journey
> By the light of the meat-eating sun.
> Dressed to die, the sensual strut begun . . .[4]

His art was a contemplation of his long dying:

> I sit and watch the worm beneath my nail
> Wearing the quick away.[5]

As he himself observed, his poems are 'statements on the way to the grave'.[6]

Yet it would be wrong to conclude that Thomas's sole poetic theme is death, or the unified process of birth, copulation and death. In poems such as 'The Conversation of Prayer', 'The Hunchback in the Park', 'Poem in October', 'Over Sir John's Hill', the horror of death is transcended, a poem is made which has freed itself from the whirlpool of its author's obsessive fantasies. It is, of course, true that even these poems derive some of their poignant beauty from Thomas's unremitting awareness of death. He celebrated the wonder of creation all the more splendidly because he knew that it would be swallowed up in universal doom. We find it hard to believe in the booming rhetoric of 'And death shall have no dominion', whereas we respond to the ambiguity, the total acceptance of mortality, implicit in 'After the first death, there is no other'.

Thomas was in no sense a political poet, although he was not indifferent to the degrading misery of the Welsh unemployed during the

3 'Before I Knocked'. 4 'Twenty-four years'.

5 'If I were tickled by the rub of love'.

6 Constantine FitzGibbon, *The Life of Dylan Thomas*, 1965, p. 158.

1930s, and retained till his death an anarchistic contempt for the established order. Even his most overtly political poem, 'The hand that signed the paper', probably refers to some imaginary situation, or to a remote historical incident such as the execution of Charles I. I have heard it suggested that it was inspired by the Hoare-Laval pact of 1935, but according to FitzGibbon it was composed on 17 August 1933.[7]

Nor was he deeply concerned with the fate of individual human beings, or the relationships of man with man. The child of 'A Refusal to Mourn' is London's daughter; the centenarian who died in an air raid is a symbolic figure; even in 'After the Funeral', Ann Jones is less a beloved aunt than an ikon to be marvelled at and adored. Unlike Yeats, who magnifies his friends into figures of mythical stature but never robs them of their individual humanity, Thomas depersonalizes the characters in his poems, emptying them of their quirky complexity in order that there may be no impediment to the cosmic forces that take possession of them.

Some of his closest friends insist that he was primarily a religious poet. Vernon Watkins calls him 'a Blakean Christian, but even that would be only an approximation'.[8] In *Dylan: Druid of the Broken Body* (1964), Aneirin Talfan Davies argues that Thomas was gradually moving towards a Catholic, sacramental view of life, abandoning the *ethos* of the Welsh Chapel for the liturgy of the Mass. But the evidence of his poems suggests that, while he responded to the pagan elements in Christianity, to the cosmic grandeur of Christian eschatology, and to the ritual of Christian worship, he remained totally indifferent to the moral economy of Christianity, and utterly incapable of practising any form of self-discipline. Even so, one should not wave aside as the rhetorical gesture of a *poseur* the explicit statement by Thomas in the *Note* to his *Collected Poems*: 'I read somewhere of a shepherd who, when asked why he made, from within fairy rings, ritual observances to the moon to protect his flocks, replied: "I'd be a damn' fool if I didn't!" These poems, with all their crudities, doubts, and confusions, are written for the love of Man and in praise of God, and I'd be a damn' fool if they weren't.'

Thomas once jestingly referred to himself as 'the Rimbaud of Cwmdonkin Drive',[9] although he enjoyed no more than a nodding acquaintance with Rimbaud's work in translation. He shared with Rimbaud at least three characteristics; a fantastic precociousness, a fanatical belief in the alchemy of the Word, and a willingness to embrace destruction.

Few poets have laboured more fiercely at their craft or been more

[7] Constantine FitzGibbon, *The Life of Dylan Thomas*, 1965, p. 191.
[8] ibid, p. 262, f.n.1. [9] *Letters to Vernon Watkins*, 1957, p. 104.

self-conscious about the process 'of constructing a formally water-tight compartment of words'.[10] There is indeed something morbid and terrifying in his endless reworking of material, his permutations of adjective and noun, the virtuosity of his stanzaic patterns, the elaborateness of his rhyming schemes. His sheer cleverness and verbal dexterity come out clearly in a parody of William Empson, the only surviving fragment of a work undertaken in collaboration with John Davenport, which would have contained many such parodies of his contemporaries. First printed in *Horizon*, VI, 3, July 1942, it was omitted from his *Collected Poems* and has been almost forgotten. Its title is 'Request to Leda: Homage to William Empson':

Not your winged lust but his must now change suit.
The harp-waked Casanova takes no range.
The worm is (pin-point) rational in the fruit.

Not girl for bird (gourd being man) breaks root.
Taking no plume for index in love's change
Not your winged lust but his must now change suit.

Desire is phosphorous: the chemic bruit
Lust bears like volts, who'll amplify, and strange
The worm is (pin-point) rational in the fruit.

Dylan Thomas seems to have received no lasting satisfaction from the practice of his art. As a young man he confessed to Pamela Hansford Johnson his fear that he was not a poet, only a freak user of words,[11] and it may be that the strain engendered by this fear damaged much of his poetry. In a letter to Vernon Watkins dated 20 April 1936 we find him lamenting his inability to 'get any real liberation, any diffusion or dilution or anything, into the churning bulk of the words'.[12] It is arguable that he lost the desire to go on living because he knew that his talent was exhausted, that he would never write the libretto for Stravinsky's proposed opera about the Creation, that *Under Milk Wood* was not the prelude to a new phase of imaginative writing but a final confession of poetic bankruptcy.

The most devastating indictment of Dylan Thomas as man and poet is to be found in Geoffrey Grigson's review of Constantine Fitz-Gibbon's *The Life of Dylan Thomas* printed in *The Guardian*, 15

[10] Dylan Thomas, Reply to 'An Enquiry', *New Verse*, 11, October 1934, p. 8.
[11] See below, pp. 223–4. [12] *Letters to Vernon Watkins*, 1957, p. 25.

October 1965. After referring to their calling 'We are the Dead' to the mountains in Donegal, Grigson proceeds:

> A game, and Thomas at 20 was neither so avid nor afraid nor corrupt. But it was a death game all appropriate to him. By this time he had written or roughed out most of his poems. Before long the incorruptible Norman Cameron, who both indulged Dylan and loathed him (not a rare combination), would be writing 'The Dirty Little Accuser' – 'That insolent little ruffian, that crapulous lout'; within 10 years his own wife, too, would be saying coldly, in his hearing, 'Dylan's corrupt. Corrupt right through and through' . . .
>
> Mr. FitzGibbon says, well, this is all a pity, but look through and through to the wonder and shine of the poems, indestructible in the merely incidental mess. He sees how the poems revert to childhood, and to the once encircling maternal warmth; but as critic or appreciator of verse he appears equipped with little else than a by now exceedingly tiresome capacity for exclamation. He deals a romantic hand of mutually adhesive cards, dog-eared, and marked 'innocence', 'boy-poet', 'lost paradise', 'magic', 'craftsmanship', 'poetic truth', etc.

On its own terms this indictment is unanswerable, the Good Pharisee's eager casting of enough stones to build a whited sepulchre. William Empson's review in *The New Statesman* a fortnight later is, despite its author's strong anti-Christian beliefs, a Christian judgment on a man in whom many of his friends discerned a fundamental gaiety, innocence, humility and generosity.

Whatever verdict we may feel inclined to pass on his life and work we can hardly deny that he was a flawed and tragic figure whose gradual disintegration must arouse terror and compassion. The marvel is that he managed to salvage from the wreckage a score of extraordinary poems, verbal constructs of masterly cunning. Vernon Watkins has asserted that he and Thomas are both religious poets, who 'could never write a poem dominated by time, as Hardy could'.[13] Yet although Thomas regarded Yeats as the greatest poet of the century, his favourite poet of the past hundred years was Hardy. Perhaps like Chopin, who used to play Bach before giving a recital, Dylan Thomas was drawn towards Hardy by the attraction of opposites. He is deficient in precisely those qualities with which Hardy is so richly endowed – a deep affectionate humanity, a love for the individual, suffering man and woman, a warm sympathy for birds, beasts, insects, and flowers, a calm delight in the gentler pleasures of life, a strong sense of belonging to a community linked by ties of blood, friendship and moral obligation.

In 1934, according to John Pudney and Ruthven Todd, he talked endlessly and obsessively about Beddoes.[14] Like Beddoes, he is a poet

[13] *Letters to Vernon Watkins*, 1957, pp. 17–18.

[14] Constantine FitzGibbon, *The Life of Dylan Thomas*, 1965, p. 158.

of Gothic horror, the laureate of the worm, symbol of sex and of bodily corruption. He belongs to that company of artists who destroy themselves and who make art in spite of or because of their self-destruction. The most gifted example of such artists in our time is Hart Crane, with whom Thomas has certain affinities, notably an extreme violence of imagery, a sacrifice of prose logic in order to attain concentration and intensity, a despairing search for some kind of wholeness, a committal of the self to death: 'turning on his bed, he awoke to speak, sometimes in tears, of his wife, of the misery of his existence, and of his wish to die. "I want to go to the Garden of Eden", he said, "to die . . . to be forever unconscious."' [15]

CRITICISM

The body, its appearance, death, and disease, is a fact, sure as the fact of a tree. It has its roots in the same earth as the tree. The greatest description I know of our own 'earthiness' is to be found in John Donne's Devotions, where he describes man as earth of the earth, his body earth, his hair a wild shrub growing out of the land. All thoughts and actions emanate from the body. Therefore the description of a thought or action – however abstruse it may be – can be beaten home by bringing it onto a physical level. Every idea, intuitive or intellectual, can be imaged and translated in terms of the body, its flesh, skin, blood, sinews, veins, glands, organs, cells or senses.

Through my small bonebound island I have learnt all I know, experienced all, and sensed all. All I write is inseparable from the island. As much as possible, therefore, I employ the scenery of the island to describe the scenery of my thoughts, the earthquake of the body to describe the earthquake of the heart.

Dylan Thomas, letter to Pamela Hansford Johnson, early November, 1933. *Selected Letters of Dylan Thomas*, edited by Constantine Fitzgibbon, 1966,[16] p. 48.

I am getting more obscure day by day. It gives me now a *physical* pain to write poetry. I feel all my muscles contract as I try to drag out, from the whirlpooling words around my everlasting ideas of the importance of death on the living, some connected words that will explain how the starry system of the dead is seen, ordered as in the grave's sky, along the orbit of a foot or a flower. But when the words do come, I pick them so thoroughly of their *live* associations that only the *death* in the words remains. And I could scream, with real, physical pain, when a line of mine is seen naked on paper and seen to be as meaningless as a Sanskrit limerick . . . My lines, *all* my lines,

[15] J. M. Brinnin, *Dylan Thomas in America*, 1956, p. 227.

[16] Hereafter referred to as *Selected Letters*.

are of the tenth intensity. They are not the words that express what I want to express; they are the only words I can find that come near to expressing a half. And that's no good. I'm a freak user of words, not a poet. That's really the truth. No self-pity there. A freak *user* of words, not a poet, That's terribly true.

Dylan Thomas, letter to Pamela Hansford Johnson, 9 May 1934, *Selected Letters*, p. 122.

Poetry is the rhythmic, inevitably narrative, movement from an overclothed blindness to a naked vision that depends in its intensity on the strength of the labour put into the creation of the poetry. My poetry is, or should be, useful to me for one reason: it is the record of my individual struggle from darkness towards some measure of light, and what of the individual struggle is still to come benefits by the sight and knowledge of the faults and fewer merits in that concrete record. My poetry is, or should be, useful to others for its individual recording of that same struggle with which they are necessarily acquainted...

What is hidden should be made naked. To be stripped of darkness is to be clean, to strip of darkness is to make clean. Poetry, recording the stripping of the individual darkness, must, inevitably, cast light upon what has been hidden for too long, and, by so doing, make clean the naked exposure. Freud cast light on a little of the darkness he had exposed. Benefiting by the sight of the light and the knowledge of the hidden nakedness, poetry must drag further into the clean nakedness of light more even of the hidden causes than Freud could realize.

Dylan Thomas, reply to 'An Enquiry', *New Verse*, 11, October, 1934, pp. 7–8. Reprinted in Constantine FitzGibbon, *The Life of Dylan Thomas*, 1965, pp. 161–2.

You asked me to tell you about my theory of poetry. Really I haven't got one. I like things that are difficult to write and difficult to understand; I like 'redeeming the contraries' with secretive images; I like contradicting my images, saying two things at once in one word, four in two and one in six. But what I like isn't a theory even if I do stabilize by dogma my own personal affections, Poetry, heavy in tare though nimble, should be as orgastic and organic as copulation, dividing and unifying, personal but not private, propagating the individual in the mass and the mass in the individual. I think it should work from words, from the substance of words and the rhythm of substantial words set together, not towards words. Poetry is a medium, not a stigmata on paper.

Dylan Thomas, letters to Charles Fisher, February 1935, *Selected Letters*, p. 151.

A poem by myself *needs* a host of images, because its centre is a host of images. I make only one image – though 'make' is not the word; I let, perhaps an image be 'made' emotionally in me and then apply to it what intellectual and critical forces I possess – let it breed another, let that image contradict the first, make, of the third image bred out of the other two together, a fourth contradictory image, and let them all, within my imposed formal limits, conflict. Each image holds within it the seed of its own destruction, and my dialectical method, as I understand it, is a constant building up and breaking down of the images that come out of the central seed, which is itself destructive and constructive at the same time...

Out of the inevitable conflict of images – inevitable, because of the creative, recreative, destructive and contradictory nature of the motivating centre, the womb of war – I try to make that momentary peace which is a poem.

Dylan Thomas, letter to Henry Treece, 23 March 1938.
Henry Treece, *Dylan Thomas: Dog Among the Fairies*, 1949, p. 47 f.n.

[Treece does not date the letter. The date is supplied in *Selected Letters*, p. 189. A fuller version of this letter is printed there, pp. 189–92, but certain passages on pp. 191–2 do not make sense as printed.]

An interesting example ... was offered to us recently in Mr. Emlyn Williams' reading from Dickens and Dylan Thomas. At first sight there does not seem to be much similarity between the writing of the Victorian Liberal and the writing of the post-war libertine. Yet through the mediation of the artist, fundamental parallel attitudes emerged: gigantic laughter at Tartuffe-ism, delight in the fecundity of communal life, the fascination of grotesquerie; and through the whole interpretation, a feeling for surging, building rhythms and coelenterate organization which signified an enduring, vital optimism.

Genesius Jones, *Approach to the Purpose*, 1964, p. 27.

POEMS

Before I knocked

Before I knocked and flesh let enter,
With liquid hands tapped on the womb,
I who was shapeless as the water
That shaped the Jordan near my home
Was brother to Mnetha's daughter
And sister to the fathering worm.

I who was deaf to spring and summer,
Who knew not sun nor moon by name,
Felt thud beneath my flesh's armour,
As yet was in a molten form,
The leaden stars, the rainy hammer
Swung by my father from his dome.

I knew the message of the winter,
The darted hail, the childish snow,
And the wind was my sister suitor;
Wind in me leaped, the hellborn dew;
My veins flowed with the Eastern weather;
Ungotten I knew night and day.

As yet ungotten, I did suffer;
The rack of dreams my lily bones
Did twist into a living cipher,
And flesh was snopped to cross the lines
Of gallow crosses on the liver
And brambles in the wringing brains.

My throat knew thirst before the structure
Of skin and vein around the well
Where words and water make a mixture
Unfailing till the blood runs foul;
My heart knew love, my belly hunger;
I smelt the maggot in my stool.

And time cast forth my mortal creature
To drift or drown upon the seas
Acquainted with the salt adventure
Of tides that never touch the shores.
I who was rich was made the richer
By sipping at the vine of days.

I, born of flesh and ghost, was neither
A ghost nor man, but mortal ghost.
And I was struck down by death's feather.
I was a mortal to the last
Long breath that carried to my father
The message of his dying christ.

You who bow down at cross and altar,
Remember me and pity Him
Who took my flesh and bone for armour
And doublecrossed my mother's womb.

A Refusal to Mourn the Death, by Fire, of a Child in London

Never until the mankind making
Bird beast and flower
Fathering and all humbling darkness
Tells with silence the last light breaking
And the still hour
Is come of the sea tumbling in harness

And I must enter again the round
Zion of the water bead
And the synagogue of the ear of corn
Shall I let pray the shadow of a sound
Or sow my salt seed
In the least valley of sackcloth to mourn

The majesty and burning of the child's death.
I shall not murder
The mankind of her going with a grave truth
Nor blaspheme down the stations of the breath
With any further
Elegy of innocence and youth.

Deep with the first dead lies London's daughter,
Robed in the long friends,
The grains beyond age, the dark veins of her mother,
Secret by the unmourning water
Of the riding Thames.
After the first death, there is no other.

Fern Hill

Now as I was young and easy under the apple boughs
About the lilting house and happy as the grass was green,
    The night above the dingle starry,
        Time let me hail and climb
    Golden in the heydays of his eyes,
And honoured among wagons I was prince of the apple towns
And once below a time I lordly had the trees and leaves
        Trail with daisies and barley
    Down the rivers of the windfall light.

And as I was green and carefree, famous among the barns
About the happy yard and singing as the farm was home,
    In the sun that is young once only,
        Time let me play and be
    Golden in the mercy of his means,
And green and golden I was huntsman and herdsman, the calves
Sang to my horn, the foxes on the hills barked clear and cold,
        And the sabbath rang slowly
    In the pebbles of the holy streams.

All the sun long it was running, it was lovely, the hay
Fields high as the house, the tunes from the chimneys, it was air
    And playing, lovely and watery
        And fire green as grass.
    And nightly under the simple stars
As I rode to sleep the owls were bearing the farm away,
All the moon long I heard, blessed among stables, the night-jars
    Flying with the ricks, and the horses
        Flashing into the dark.

And then to awake, and the farm, like a wanderer white
With the dew, come back, the cock on his shoulder; it was all
    Shining, it was Adam and maiden,
        The sky gathered again
    And the sun grew round that very day.
So it must have been after the birth of the simple light
In the first, spinning place, the spellbound horses walking warm
    Out of the whinnying green stable
        On to the fields of praise.

And honoured among foxes and pheasants by the gay house
Under the new made clouds and happy as the heart was long,
    In the sun born over and over,
        I ran my heedless ways,
    My wishes raced through the house high hay
And nothing I cared, at my sky blue trades, that time allows
In all his tuneful turning so few and such morning songs
    Before the children green and golden
        Follow him out of grace,

Nothing I cared, in the lamb white days, that time would
take me
Up to the swallow thronged loft by the shadow of my hand,
In the moon that is always rising,
Nor that riding to sleep
I should hear him fly with the high fields
And wake to the farm forever fled from the childless land.
Oh as I was young and easy in the mercy of his means,
Time held me green and dying
Though I sang in my chains like the sea.

SELECT BIBLIOGRAPHY

Works by Dylan Thomas

Collected Poems, London and New York, 1952.

Under Milk Wood, London, 1954; New York, 1959.

Letters to Vernon Watkins, London and New York, 1957.

Selected Letters, edited by Constantine FitzGibbon, London, 1966.

Some Biographical and Critical Studies

Ackerman, John, *Dylan Thomas: His Life and Work*, London and New York, 1964.

Brinnin, John Malcolm, *Dylan Thomas in America*, Boston, 1955; London, 1956.

FitzGibbon, Constantine, *The Life of Dylan Thomas*, London, 1965.
A full-scale biography, of particular value for its account of Thomas's family background and youth.

Fraser, G. S., *Dylan Thomas*, London, 1957; 3rd. ed., 1965.

Jones, T. H., *Dylan Thomas*, Edinburgh, 1963.

Maud, Ralph N., *Entrances to Dylan Thomas's Poetry*, Pittsburgh, 1963; Lowestoft, 1964.
The best critical discussion of Thomas's poetry.

Olson, Elder, *The Poetry of Dylan Thomas*, Chicago, 1954.
A learned, elaborate discourse which tries to unravel some of Thomas's most baffling poems.

Read, Bill, *The Days of Dylan Thomas*, London, 1965.
This pictorial biography is of value for its photographs.

Tedlock, E. W., ed., *Dylan Thomas: The Legend and the Poet*, London, 1960.
Contains a number of important biographical and critical essays on Thomas.

Moynihan, William T., *The Craft and Art of Dylan Thomas*, Ithaca (New York) and London, 1966.

14

POETS OF THE SECOND WORLD WAR AND OF THE 1940s

INTRODUCTION

A legend fostered by the 'Movement' poets of the 1950s portrays the 1940s as a decade in which all sound poetic values were debauched, while fecund images proliferated in surrealist luxuriance, swamping good sense and coherent poetic structure. A few poets escaped the general infection, but public taste succumbed completely to the virus.

These generalizations are based upon a limited and distorted view of the 1940s, and can be legitimately applied only to one particular school of literature which flourished for a short period during the Second World War. Three anthologies edited by J. F. Hendry and Henry Treece, *The New Apocalypse* (1940),[1] *The White Horseman* (1941), and *The Crown and the Sickle* (1944), were designed to illustrate 'a new Romantic tendency, whose most obvious elements are love, death, an adherence to myth and an awareness of war'.[2] It was a heady brew. The most prominent of the New Apocalyptics, apart from the editors, were G. S. Fraser, Nicholas Moore, Tom Scott, and Vernon Watkins, all of whom, except Watkins, were in their mid-twenties. Even at the time the whole enterprise seemed a trifle portentous and grandiloquent: one of Treece's books is called *Towards a Personal Armageddon*, and G. S. Fraser, normally a level-headed critic, made wildly inflated claims for his colleagues, especially for the work of Nicholas Moore, 'the only poet of the century (with the one notable exception of Yeats) who has written love poems which I find at all moving',[3] and whose mind Fraser judged to be 'more interesting than Blake's'.[4] Treece's 'Ballad of the Prince' was described as 'the first great anthropomorph of contemporary poetry'.

Yet these anthologies and the view of poetry which they propagated were taken seriously by a very few people for a very brief period. Even the chief Apocalyptics rapidly got off their high white horse.[5] Moore,

[1] This anthology was edited by Hendry alone; the other two were edited jointly with Treece.

[2] Henry Treece, Preface to *The Crown and the Sickle*, 1944.

[3] *The White Horseman*, 1941, p. 22.

[4] ibid, p. 24.

[5] Nor were they always 'Apocalyptic'. See Treece's 'Lincolnshire Bomber Station', below, p. 243.

Hendry, and Treece published little verse after the end of the 1940s (although Treece became well-known as an historical novelist); G. S. Fraser devoted most of his energy to literary criticism; Watkins and Scott, while remaining visionary poets, disentangled themselves from their Apocalyptic associations. Norman MacCaig, another contributor, brought out no collection between *Far Cry* (1943) and *Riding Lights* (1955), a volume bearing little resemblance to his earlier productions.

The best of the war poets were neither influenced by the Apocalyptics, nor swamped by the foaming neo-Romantic tide in which the Apocalyptic movement was rapidly submerged. Keith Douglas, for example, was a harsh, even brutal, writer, who had, before leaving school, hammered out a style that was proof against the lures of literary fashion. His art reached an early maturity during the months of fighting in the Western Desert, as though all irrelevances and decorative falsities had been burned and scoured away by the fury of war and the abrasive heat of the sands. Like Isaac Rosenberg, whom he greatly admired, his poetry is fiercely metaphysical, a means of grappling with ultimate truth. The notion that a poet is, above all, a man dedicated to set down what is true, inspired Douglas from his undergraudate days at Oxford until his death in Normandy.

It is this conviction which links him with another fine poet, Alun Lewis, who died on active service in Burma. Lewis is a more lyrical poet than Douglas, a brooding, meditative writer, less intensely concentrated upon the search for the metaphysical meaning of life and death, more responsive to the emotional needs of other human beings, more aware of man in society. Douglas savagely dissects the men and women in war-time Cairo as types of social corruption, whereas Lewis observes with compassion the lives of Indian peasants, bound, like their ancestors, to the parched soil. Yet, despite their dissimilar temperaments, both constantly valued above all things fidelity to the truth. Douglas's letter to J. C. Hall is a succinct expression of his *credo*;[6] two extracts from Lewis's letters to his wife reveal his affinity with Douglas: 'Do you see how a poem is made – or fails? By perpetually trying, by closer and closer failing, by seeking and not finding, *and still seeking*, by a robustness in the core of sadness.'[7] 'My longing is more and more for one thing only, integrity, and I discount the other qualities in people far too ruthlessly if they lack that fundamental sincerity and wholeness.'[8]

Some of Douglas's poems appeared in *Personal Landscape*, a periodi-

[6] See below, pp. 235–6.

[7] Letter written November–December 1942. *Letters from India*, 1946, p. 29.

[8] Letter dated 11 October 1943, ibid, pp. 70–1.

cal published in Cairo during the war, the moving spirits behind it being Lawrence Durrell, Bernard Spencer, and Terence Tiller.[9] Geographically, intellectually and emotionally, it was a far cry from the Apocalyptics. The tone of *Personal Landscape* was erudite, sophisticated, allusive; its contributors were acutely conscious of being travellers and exiles, whose paths were crossing for a moment on the shores of the Eastern Mediterranean. This awareness of the Mediterranean world in all its beauty, violence, cosmopolitan amorality and historical complexity is one of the distinctive strands in the poetry of the 1940s. Most poets of the 1930s resembled Auden in their almost complete indifference to the physical allure and symbolic potency of the Mediterranean, rather as the poets of the 1950s affected to despise or to mock at the hedonistic and aesthetic impulses of their immediate predecessors who had fallen under the spell of that ancient shore.

The war, by dispersing young poets throughout the world, broke the continuity of literary life and compelled certain talents to develop in isolation. Thus Roy Fuller, who had published a volume in 1939, first became prominent in the war years by virtue of poems inspired by his experiences in East Africa. Fuller makes nonsense of easy generalizations about literary history; for, writing in the 1940s, he exhibits none of the qualities supposedly prevalent at the time, and resembles neither the Apocalyptics nor the contributors to *Personal Landscape*. Instead, we have a poet who interprets the tensions of a world at war and the baffling incongruities of the East African scene with the aid of Marxist and Freudian exegesis. Here is no revolt against the 1930s, but on the contrary an intelligent extension of Auden's approach to the world.

Yet the feeling that in the 1940s there occurred a deliberate reaction against the previous decade is not wholly illusory. It was during the 1940s that the reputations of Edith Sitwell and of Dylan Thomas were at their peak, and that Robert Graves and Edwin Muir first attracted serious critical approval. Moreover the 1940s saw the emergence as influential poets of George Barker, David Gascoyne, Kathleen Raine, and Vernon Watkins, although every one of them had started printing verse during the 1930s.

These four poets and their followers shared certain assumptions about the nature of poetry which differed from the axioms generally accepted in the previous decade. They were all affected by the doctrines and techniques of surrealism; they all believed that poetry was not primarily concerned with man in society, political aspirations or social commentary, but with the celebration of spiritual truth; all were romantic visionaries, whose view of the world was ritualistic and

[9] A good account of *Personal Landscape* is given by Lawrence Durrell in 'Bernard Spencer', *The London Magazine*, III, 10, January 1964, pp. 42–7.

religious, even though none of them, except Watkins, was an orthodox Christian. Their employment of myth and symbol, drawn from a wide variety of sources, often esoteric and recondite, was designed to emphasize the sacred character of poetry and to stress the fact that the poet is not a lawgiver, a moralist, a teacher or an entertainer, but a bard and a seer. The tone of their verse was appropriately elevated and incantatory, as they proclaimed the sacred mysteries of vatic poetry:

> I speak of the whispering gallery
> Of all Dionysian poetry
> Within whose precincts I have heard
> An apotheosis of the word
>
> As down those echoing corridors
> The Logos rode on a white horse;
> Till every No that sense could express
> Turned to a transcendental Yes.[10]

Kathleen Raine's vision of the world is derived from her study of Neo-Platonism, which is for her not an academic system but the source of perennial wisdom. She has excluded from her *Collected Poems* (1956) 'nearly all poems that include any trace of ecclesiastical symbolism or sentiment . . . love poems of a personal nature . . . poems descriptive of events in place and time as such, mostly from the war years, that seem now as dead as any other journalism.' The austerity and purity of her Neo-Platonic faith are reflected in her poems:

> It was David Gascoyne who said to me that nature remains always in the Year One – the phrase that I used as the title for my last book of poems. The ever-recurring forms of nature mirror eternal reality; the never-recurring productions of human history reflect only fallen men, and are therefore not suitable to become a symbolic vocabulary for the kind of poetry I have attempted to write.[11]

David Gascoyne made a reputation in the 1930s when very young as an interpreter of surrealism and as the author of surrealist poems. His two most substantial volumes, *Poems 1937–1942* (1943) and *A Vagrant* (1950), though bearing traces of his earlier devotion to surrealism, are metaphysical and religious explorations of man's nature and destiny. His universe is one of anguish, guilt, and terror, a place where man, tormented by desire and by the horror of Nothingness, turns for sal-

[10] George Barker, 'Letter to a Young Poet'.
[11] Kathleen Raine, Introduction to *Collected Poems*, 1956, p. xiv–xv.

vation to the 'Christ of Revolution and of Poetry' (or to some other powerful myth) in an endeavour to gain certainty and release. The weakness of Gascoyne's poetry is that the exalted rhetoric at times appears to swell up in a void unsupported by any intellectual structure, unsustained by any coherent emotional life. When, however, the intensity of his imagination is grounded in controlled passion, and matched by his power to order his poetic medium, the resulting poems are endowed with splendid force, penetration, and energy.

George Barker, like Gascoyne, was well known in the Thirties, being the youngest poet included by Yeats in *The Oxford Book of Modern Verse*. It was, however, in the 1940s that his strange *mélange* of rhapsodic mysticism, lavish eroticism, sprawling rhodomontade, and lyrical purity attracted fervent admiration and equally fervent abuse. No poet has ever made more lofty claims for Poetry than Barker, or adopted a more unflinchingly sacerdotal tone when extolling its mysteries. Whatever his theme may be, an elegy for the victims of the war in Spain, death by drowning, an erotic relationship, or the tombs of the Medicis, one is always aware of Barker's hieratic voice conducting the ceremony. His pronouncements on Poetry are invariably couched in oracular cadences, a characteristic example being his short essay entitled 'The Miracle of Images'.[12]

Here, one might argue, is the key to the poetry of the Forties – mystical reverence for the Image. And yet, cheek by jowl with Barker's rhetorical invocation, one discovers Norman Nicholson's 'The Image in my Poetry', which is a cautious, closely-argued analysis of the function of imagery in poetry.[13] Nicholson's sense of place, his involvement in the daily round of Millom, the Cumberland town where he has always lived, gives his poetry an earthy, deep-rooted quality which is not usually associated with the poetry of the 1940s. And, having said this, one thinks of other poets writing then who cannot be pigeonholed – W. S. Graham, John Heath-Stubbs, Laurie Lee, F. T. Prince, Anne Ridler, W. R. Rodgers, and E. J. Scovell, to name a few.

In the late forties and early fifties many poets and critics felt that poetry had come to a dead end, or at least a resting-place. This is the burden of Geoffrey Grigson's Introduction to his *Poetry of the Present* (1949), a verdict confirmed by Alan Ross in the closing pages of his survey *Poetry 1945–1950* (1950), where he remarks that 'at the moment there is neither a single major influence over modern poetry nor a contemporary movement'. Roy Fuller recalls that as late as 1951/1952 'there was still no recognizable crop of good post-war poets',[14] a point

[12] See below, p. 238
[13] *Orpheus*, II, 1949, pp. 120–3.
[14] 'Between Generations', *The London Magazine*, VI, 11, November 1959, p. 18.

noted by Thom Gunn when surveying his own development.[15] After the war nobody came forward to fill the gap left by Auden's departure, nor, with the disappearance of *Poetry London*, was there any dominant little magazine which might have emulated the achievement of *New Verse* in the 1930s and stamped its mark on the decade.

The forties remain a shadowy period wherein all is tentative, elusive, and ambivalent. Reviewing Durrell's *The Ikons*, Cyril Connolly observes that the poems 'are in the manner of the Forties, arcanely objective blank-verse statements, which the reader is expected to construe.'[16] This contradicts with a vengeance the orthodox view of the decade as a period of deliquescence, given over to Apocalyptics regurgitating images of sex and violence from the subconscious. It may be that all attempts to discern a simple pattern in the ebb and flow of poetry end inevitably in a distorted vision; and that the stress of war and its aftermath during the 1940s revealed unmistakably that element in our lives, and in the life of poetry, which a young Greek poet who died in England a few months before the end of the war took to be the principle of all existence: 'the ageless ambiguity of things'.[17]

CRITICISM

Writing which is poetry must say what the writer has himself to say, not what he has observed others to say with effect, nor what he thinks will impress his hearers because it has impressed him hearing it. Nor must he waste any more words over it than a mathematician: every word must work for its keep, in prose, blank verse, or rhyme.

And poetry is to be judged not by what the poet has tried to say; only by what he has said.

Keith Douglas, 'On the Nature of Poetry', *Augury: An Oxford Miscellany of Verse and Prose*, edited by Alex M. Hardie and Keith C. Douglas, 1940. Reprinted in *Collected Poems of Keith Douglas*, edited by John Waller, G. S. Fraser and J. C. Hall, 1966, pp. 148–9.

I am surprised you should still expect me to produce musical verse. A lyric form and a lyric approach will do even less good than a journalese approach to the subjects we have to discuss now. I don't know if you have come across the word Bullshit – it is an army word and signifies humbug and unnecessary detail. It symbolizes what I think must be got rid of – the mass of irrelevancies, of 'attitudes', 'approaches', propaganda, ivory towers, etc., that stands between us and our prob-

[15] Ian Hamilton, 'Four Conversations', *The London Magazine*, IV, 8, November 1964, p. 69.
[16] *The Sunday Times*, 6 November 1966, p. 49.
[17] Demetrios Capetanakis, 'Abel'.

lems and what we have to do about them. To write on the themes which have been concerning me lately in lyric and abstract form would be immense bullshitting ...

But my object (and I don't give a damn about my duty as a poet) is to write true things, significant things in words each of which works for its place in a line. My rhythms, which you find enervated, are carefully chosen to enable the poems to be *read* as significant speech: I see no reason to be either musical or sonorous about things at present. When I do, I shall be so again, and glad to. I suppose I reflect the cynicism and the careful absence of expectation (it is not quite the same as apathy) with which I view the world ... I never tried to write about war (that is battles and things, not London can Take it), with the exception of a satiric picture of some soldiers frozen to death, until I had experienced it. Now I will write of it, and perhaps one day cynic and lyric will meet and make me a balanced style. Certainly you will never see the long metrical similes and galleries of images again ...

To be sentimental or emotional now is dangerous to oneself and to others. To trust anyone or to admit any hope of a better world is criminally foolish, as foolish as it is to stop working for it. It sounds silly to say work without hope, but it can be done; it's only a form of insurance; it doesn't mean work hopelessly.

Keith Douglas, letter to J. C. Hall, 10 August 1943, ibid., pp. 149–50.

He has not simply added poems to poetry, or evolved a sophistication. He is a renovator of language. It is not that he uses words in jolting combinations, or with titanic extravagance, or curious precision. His triumph lies in the way he renews the simplicity of ordinary talk, and he does this by infusing every word with a burning exploratory freshness of mind – partly exhilaration at speaking the forbidden thing, partly sheer casual ease of penetration. The music that goes along with this, the unresting variety of intonation and movement within his patterns, is the natural path of much confident, candid thinking ...

The war brought his gift to maturity, or to a first maturity. In a sense, war was his ideal subject: the burning away of all human pretensions in the ray cast by death. This was the vision, the unifying generalization that shed the meaning and urgency into all his observations and particulars: not truth is beauty only, but truth kills everybody. The truth of a man is the doomed man in him or his dead body ...

Douglas had no time, and perhaps no disposition, to cultivate the fruity deciduous tree of How to Live. He showed in his poetry no concern for man in society. The murderous skeleton in the body of a girl, the dead men being eaten by dogs on the moonlit desert, the dead man behind the mirror, these items of circumstantial evidence are steadily out-arguing all his high spirits and hopefulness.

Ted Hughes, Introduction to *Selected Poems: Keith Douglas*, 1964, pp. 12–13.

And although I'm more and more engrossed with the single poetic theme of Life and Death, for there doesn't seem to be any question more directly relevant than this one of what survives of all the beloved, I find myself quite unable to express at once the passion of Love, the coldness of Death (Death is cold) and the fire that beats against resignation, acceptance. Acceptance seems so spiritless, protest so vain. In between the two I live.

Alun Lewis, letter to his wife, April 1943, *Letters from India*, 1946, p. 49.

I've felt a number of things deeply out here; perhaps the jungle has moved me more deeply than anything else, the green wilderness where one has nothing but one's sense of direction and there is no alarm because there is the Sun and there is one's shadow and there is time – but when I wrote a poem about the jungle I found it had become a criticism of the Western world which in a measure I understand, but of the jungle I had said nothing. That happens nowadays with most of me. And I will have to abandon the vast for the particular, the infinite for the finite, the heart for the eye...

I've taken a sardonic title for the poems from *Job* 39. 'Ha! Ha! among the Trumpets.' You know the beautiful chapter. The liberty of the wild ass, the lovelessness of the ostrich, the intrepidity of the horse. These are the particulars. The infinite, of which I can never be sure, is God the Maker. I prefer the ostrich's eggs warming in the sun. I avoid speculations and haven't been touched by intuitions. No attempt has been made to convince me – neither by man nor God. And I'm as restless and fidgety as a man on a deserted platform.

Alun Lewis, letter to Robert Graves, 23 January 1944. Foreword by Robert Graves to *Ha! Ha! Among the Trumpets*, by Alun Lewis, 1945, pp. 10–11.

The discoveries of Freud, and the work of the Surrealists (valuable as experiment, if not valuable in its results) have convinced the Apocalyptics that every poet has enough to write about in the contents of his own mind, and that the struggle to be classic, social, relevant, and so on, is unnecessary; because if a poet describes honestly his private perspective on the world, his private universe, human minds are sufficiently analogous to each other for that private universe to become (ultimately though certainly not immediately) a generally accessible human property.

G. S. Fraser, 'Apocalypse in Poetry', *The White Horseman*, 1941, p. 29.

The image is what the imagination ascertains about the hitherto unimaginable. The image is what Michelangelo saw lying hidden in a piece of dirt. The image is what Jehovah forbids made of himself because when the image has been given to a thing or an idea then the idea or the thing has been subjugated. The image is made up of words, words are made up of the alphabet, and the alphabet is the twenty-six stations of the cross to the Logos. For this reason the image, occurring somewhere halfway between the Logos and the poem, operates, practically, in much the same way as the saint operates theologically or the eye optically or the kiss erotically. I do not quite see what we could do without it...

The unknown can very seldom be embodied properly or best in images taken without distortion from existence as we normally know it, because into such known images the unknown could not, by definition, easily or properly fit.

George Barker, 'The Miracle of Images', *Orpheus*, II, 1949, pp. 133–6.

Others rather than themselves deduced the shaky principles of a school out of the poems of Barker and Thomas. It has been a new Imagist school, in which the images were not to be concise, clean, neat; but condensed and infinitely suggestive...

Then the coming back, the reinfection of verse by several concurrent diseases which Eliot, then Auden and MacNeice and others, one thought, had killed, in their particular form, for ever. A weakening then of the penicillin in which one had trusted . . .

Images, images, images, not as an Elizabethan would have had an image, but over-ripe verbalisms indicating mystery or the sense of adolescence in a profound pretentiousness, accompanied in the extra-poetic prose, in the prose by poets and about poetry, with banalities and platitudes of an uncommon order, crying out their silliness loudly, one may be thankful to recall, obviously, and recognisably. Thus, in letters and painting the two wars have had contradictory effects. The First War shocked several writers and painters into a sudden humanity devoid of sham, and left a few of them changed and receptive. The Second War shocked other writers and painters out of themselves or out of healthier modes into mystifyings or commonplaces moribundly imaged and dressed. One war killed much sham; the other revived it, as a refuge, at least in frail and noisy talents.

Geoffrey Grigson, Introduction to *Poetry of the Present*, 1949, pp. 21–2.

POEMS

KEITH DOUGLAS
(1920–44)

Simplify me when I'm Dead

Remember me when I am dead
and simplify me when I'm dead.

As the processes of earth
strip off the colour and the skin:
take the brown hair and blue eye

and leave me simpler than at birth,
when hairless I came howling in
as the moon entered the cold sky.

Of my skeleton perhaps,
so stripped, a learned man will say
'He was of such a type and intelligence,' no more.

Thus when in a year collapse
particular memories, you may
deduce, from the long pain I bore

the opinions I held, who was my foe
and what I left, even my appearance
but incidents will be no guide.

Time's wrong-way telescope will show
a minute man ten years hence
and by distance simplified.

Through that lens see if I seem
substance or nothing: of the world
deserving mention or charitable oblivion,

not by momentary spleen
or love into decision hurled,
leisurely arrived at an opinion.

Remember me when I am dead
and simplify me when I'm dead.

Dead Men

To-night the moon inveigles them
to love: they infer from her gaze
her tacit encouragement.
To-night the white dresses and the jasmin scent
in the streets. I in another place
see the white dresses glimmer like moths. Come

to the west, out of that trance, my heart –
here the same hours have illumined
sleepers who are condemned or reprieved
and those whom their ambitions have deceived;
the dead men whom the wind
powders till they are like dolls: they to-night

rest in the sanitary earth perhaps
or where they died, no one has found them
or in their shallow graves the wild dog
discovered and exhumed a face or a leg
for food: the human virtue round them
is a vapour tasteless to a dog's chops.

All that is good of them, the dog consumes.
You would not know now the mind's flame is gone
more than the dog knows: you would forget
but that you see your own mind burning yet
and till you stifle in the ground will go on
burning the economical coal of your dreams.

Then leave the dead in the earth, an organism
not capable of resurrection, like mines,
less durable than the metal of a gun,
a casual meal for a dog, nothing but the bone
so soon. But to-night no lovers see the lines
of the moon's face as the lines of cynicism.

And the wise man is the lover
who in his planetary love resolves
without the traction of reason or time's control
and the wild dog finding meat in a hole
is a philosopher. The prudent mind resolves
on the lover's or the dog's attitude forever.

ALUN LEWIS
(1915–44)

The Mahratta Ghats

The valleys crack and burn, the exhausted plains
Sink their black teeth into the horny veins
Straggling the hills' red thighs, the bleating goats
– Dry bents and bitter thistles in their throats –
Thread the loose rocks by immemorial tracks.
Dark peasants drag the sun upon their backs.

High on the ghat the new turned soil is red,
The sun has ground it to the finest red,
It lies like gold within each horny hand.
Siva has spilt his seed upon this land.

Will she who burns and withers on the plain
Leave, ere too late, her scraggy herds of pain,
The cow-dung fire and the trembling beasts,
The little wicked gods, the grinning priests,
And climb, before a thousand years have fled,
High as the eagle to her mountain bed
Whose soil is fine as flour and blood-red?

But no! She cannot move. Each arid patch
Owns the lean folk who plough and scythe and thatch
Its grudging yield and scratch its stubborn stones.
The small gods suck the marrow from their bones.

Who is it climbs the summit of the road?
Only the beggar bumming his dark load.
Who was it cried to see the falling star?
Only the landless soldier lost in war.

And did a thousand years go by in vain?
And does another thousand start again?

F. T. PRINCE
(b. 1912)

Soldiers Bathing

The sea at evening moves across the sand.
Under a reddening sky I watch the freedom of a band
Of soldiers who belong to me. Stripped bare
For bathing in the sea, they shout and run in the warm air;
Their flesh, worn by the trade of war, revives
And my mind towards the meaning of it strives.

All's pathos now. The body that was gross,
Rank, ravenous, disgusting in the act or in repose,
All fever, filth and sweat, its bestial strength
And bestial decay, by pain and labour grows at length
Fragile and luminous. 'Poor bare forked animal,'
Conscious of his desires and needs and flesh that rise and fall,
Stands in the soft air, tasting after toil
The sweetness of his nakedness: letting the sea-waves coil
Their frothy tongues about his feet, forgets
His hatred of the war, its terrible pressure that begets
A machinery of death and slavery,
Each being a slave and making slaves of others: finds that he
Remembers lovely freedom in a game,
Mocking himself, and comically mimics fear and shame.

He plays with death and animality;
And reading in the shadows of his pallid flesh, I see
The idea of Michelangelo's cartoon
Of soldiers bathing, breaking off before they were half done
At some sortie of the enemy, an episode
Of the Pisan wars with Florence. I remember how he showed
Their muscular limbs that clamber from the water,
And heads that turn across the shoulder, eager for the slaughter,
Forgetful of their bodies that are bare,
And hot to buckle on and use the weapons that are lying there.
– And I think too of the theme another found
When, shadowing men's bodies on a sinister red ground,
Another Florentine, Pollaiuolo,
Painted a naked battle: warriors straddled, hacked the foe,
Dug their bare toes into the ground and slew
The brother-naked man who lay between their feet and drew
His lips back from his teeth in a grimace.

They were Italians who knew war's sorrow and disgrace
And showed the thing suspended, stripped: a theme
Born out of the experience of a war's horrible extreme
Beneath a sky where even the air flows
With lacrimae Christi. For that rage, that bitterness, those blows,
That hatred of the slain, what could they be
But indirectly or directly a commentary
On the Crucifixion, And the picture burns
With indignation and pity and despair by turns,
Because it is the obverse of the scene

Where Christ hangs murdered, stripped, upon the Cross.
    I mean,
That is the explanation of its rage.

And we too have our bitterness and pity that engage
Blood, spirit, in this war. But night begins,
Night of the mind: who nowadays is conscious of our sins?
Though every human deed concerns our blood,
And even we must know, what nobody has understood,
That some great love is over all we do,
And that is what has driven us to this fury, for so few
Can suffer all the terror of that love:
The terror of that love has set us spinning in this groove
Greased with our blood.

                                        These dry themselves and dress,
Combing their hair, forget the fear and shame of nakedness.
Because to love is frightening we prefer
The freedom of our crimes. Yet, as I drink the dusky air,
I feel a strange delight that fills me full,
Strange gratitude, as if evil itself were beautiful,
And kiss the wound in thought, while in the west
I watch a streak of red that might have issued from Christ's breast.

HENRY TREECE
(1912–66)

Lincolnshire Bomber Station

Across the road the homesick Romans made
The ground-mist thickens to a milky shroud;
Through flat, damp fields call sheep, mourning their dead
In cracked and timeless voices, unatterably sad,
Suffering for all the world, in Lincolnshire.

And I wonder how the Romans liked it here;
Flat fields, no sun, the muddy misty dawn,
And always, above all, the mad rain dripping down,
Rusting sword and helmet, wetting the feet
And soaking to the bone, down to the very heart...

MICHAEL RIVIERE
(b. 1919)

Oflag Night Piece

There, where the swifts flicker along the wall
And the last light catches, there in the high schloss
(How the town grows dark) all's made impregnable:
They bless each window with a double cross
Of iron; weave close banks of wire and train
Machine guns down on them; and look – at the first star
Floodlight the startled darkness back again...
All for three hundred prisoners of war.
Yet now past them and the watch they keep,
Unheard, invisible, in ones and pairs,
In groups, in companies – alarms are dumb,
A sentry loiters, a blind searchlight stares –
Unchallenged as their memories of home
The vanishing prisoners escape to sleep.

ROY FULLER
(b. 1912)

Autumn 1942

Season of rains: the horizon like an illness
Daily retreating and advancing: men
Swarming on aircraft: things that leave their den
And prowl the suburbs: cries in the starlit stillness

Into the times' confusion such sharp captions
Are swiftly cut, as symbols give themselves
To poets, though the convenient nymphs and elves
They know fall sadly short of their conceptions.

I see giraffes that lope, half snake, half steed,
A slowed-up film; the soft bright zebra race,
Unreal as rocking horses; and the face –
A solemn mandarin's – of the wildebeest.

And sometimes in the mess the men and their
Pathetic personal trash become detached
From what they move on; and my days are patched
With newspapers about the siege-like war.

Should I be asked to speak the truth, these are
What I should try to explain, and leave unsaid
Our legacy of failure from the dead,
The silent fate of our provincial star.

But what can be explained? The animals
Are what you make of them, are words, are visions,
And they for us are moving in dimensions
Impertinent to use or watch at all.

And of the men there's nothing to be said:
Only events, with which they wrestle, can
Transfigure them or make them other than
Things to be loved or hated and soon dead.

It is the news at which I hesitate,
That glares authentically between the bars
Of style and lies, and holds enough of fears
And history, and is not too remote.

And tells me that the age is thus: chokes back
My private suffering, the ghosts of nature
And of the mind: it says the human features
Are mutilated, have a dreadful lack.

It half convinces me that some great faculty,
Like hands, has been eternally lost and all
Our virtues now are the high and horrible
Ones of a streaming wound which heals in evil.

LAWRENCE DURRELL
(b. 1912)

Nemea

A song in the valley of Nemea:
Sing quiet, quite quiet here.

Song for the bride of Argos
Combing the swarms of golden hair:
Quite quiet, quiet there.

Under the rolling comb of grass,
The sword outrusts the golden helm.

Agamemnon under tumulus serene
Outsmiles the jury of skeletons:
Cool under cumulus the lion queen:

Only the drum can celebrate,
Only the adjective outlive them.

A song in the valley of Nemea:
Sing quiet, quiet, quiet here.

Tone of the frog in the empty well,
Drone of the bald bee on the cold skull,

Quiet, Quiet, Quiet.

VERNON WATKINS
(1906–67)

The Heron

The cloud-backed heron will not move:
He stares into the stream.
He stands unfaltering while the gulls
And oyster-catchers scream.
He does not hear, he cannot see
The great white horses of the sea,
But fixes eyes on stillness
Below their flying team.

How long will he remain, how long
Have the grey woods been green?
The sky and the reflected sky,
Their glass he has not seen,
But silent as a speck of sand
Interpreting the sea and land,
His fall pulls down the fabric
Of all that windy scene.

Sailing with clouds and woods behind,
Pausing in leisured flight,
He stepped, alighting on a stone,
Dropped from the stars of night.
He stood there unconcerned with day,
Deaf to the tumult of the bay,
Watching a stone in water,
A fish's hidden light.

Sharp rocks drive back the breaking waves,
Confusing sea with air.
Bundles of spray blown mountain-high
Have left the shingle bare.
A shipwrecked anchor wedged by rocks,
Loosed by the thundering equinox,
Divides the herded waters,
The stallion and his mare.

Yet no distraction breaks the watch
Of that time-killing bird.
He stands unmoving on the stone;
Since dawn he has not stirred.
Calamity about him cries,
But he has fixed his golden eyes
On water's crooked tablet,
On light's reflected word.

GEORGE BARKER
(b. 1913)

Turn on your side and bear the day to me

Turn on your side and bear the day to me
Beloved, sceptre-struck, immured
In the glass wall of sleep. Slowly
Uncloud the borealis of your eye
And show your iceberg secrets, your midnight prizes
To the green-eyed world and to me. Sin
Coils upward into thin air when you awaken
And again morning announces amnesty over
The serpent-kingdomed bed. Your mother
Watched with as dove an eye the unforgiveable night
Sigh backward into innocence when you
Set a bright monument in her amorous sea.
Look down, Undine, on the trident that struck
Sons from the rock of vanity. Turn in the world
Sceptre-struck, spellbound, beloved,
Turn in the world and bear the day to me.

DAVID GASCOYNE
(b. 1916)

Winter Garden

The season's anguish, crashing whirlwind, ice,
Have passed, and cleansed the trodden paths
That silent gardeners have strewn with ash.
The iron circles of the sky
Are worn away by tempest;
Yet in this garden there is no more strife:
The Winter's knife is buried in the earth.
Pure music is the cry that tears
The birdless branches in the wind.
No blossom is reborn. The blue
Stare of the pond is blind.

And no-one sees
A restless stranger through the morning stray
Across the sodden lawn, whose eyes
Are tired of weeping, in whose breast
A savage sun consumes its hidden day.

NORMAN NICHOLSON
(b. 1914)

On Duddon Marsh

This is the shore, the line dividing
The dry land from the waters, Europe
From the Atlantic; this is the mark
That God laid down on the third day.
Twice a year the high tide sliding,
Unwrapping like a roll of oil-cloth, reaches
The curb of the mud, leaving a dark
Swipe of grease, a scaled-out hay

Of wrack and grass and gutterweed. Then
For full three hundred tides the bare
Turf is unwatered except for rain;
Blown wool is dry as baccy; tins
Glint in the sedge with not a sight of man
For two miles round to drop them there.
But once in spring and once again
In autumn, here's where the sea begins.

NORMAN MACCAIG
(b. 1910)

Ego

Stare at the stars, the stars say. Look at me,
Whispers the water and protests the tree;
The rose is its own exclamation and
Frost touches with an insinuating hand.
Yet they prefigure to my human mind
Categories only of a human kind.

I see a rose, that strange thing, and what's there
But a seeming something coloured on the air
With the transparencies that make up me,
Thickened to existence by my notice. Tree
And star are ways of finding out what I
Mean in a text composed of earth and sky.

What reason to believe this, any more
Than that I am myself a metaphor
That's noticed in the researches of a rose
And self-instructs a star? Time only knows
Creation's mad cross-purposes and will
Destroy the evidence to keep them secret still.

SELECT BIBLIOGRAPHY

General

The White Horseman: Prose and Verse of the New Apocalypse, edited by J. F. Hendry and Henry Treece, London, 1941.
The best-known of the three Apocalyptic anthologies.

Personal Landscape: An Anthology of Exile, edited by Lawrence Durrell, Bernard Spencer, and Robin Fedden, London, 1945.

Poems from New Writing, edited by John Lehmann, London, 1946.

Poetry of the Present, edited by Geoffrey Grigson, London, 1949.

The Poetry of War, edited by Ian Hamilton, London, 1965.

The Terrible Rain, edited by Brian Gardner, London, 1966.

Poetry of the Forties, edited by Robin Skelton, Harmondsworth, 1968.

Press, John, *Rule and Energy*, London and New York, 1963.
A survey of poetry from the Second World War to the end of the 1950s.

Raine, Kathleen, *Defending Ancient Springs*, London, 1967.
Contains essays on Vernon Watkins and David Gascoyne.

George Barker

Collected Poems, London, 1957.

The True Confession of George Barker, London, 1965.
Consists of two Books. Book I was first published in 1950.

Keith Douglas
Collected Poems, edited by John Waller, G. S. Fraser and J. C. Hall, London, 1966.
A revised and enlarged edition of *Collected Poems*, London, 1951.

Roy Fuller
Collected Poems, London, 1962.
Buff, London, 1965.
New Poems, London, 1968.

David Gascoyne
Collected Poems, edited by Robin Skelton, London, 1965.

Alun Lewis
Selected Poetry and Prose, edited by Ian Hamilton, London, 1966.

Kathleen Raine
Collected Poems, London, 1956.
The Hollow Hill, London, 1965.

15

THE MOVEMENT AND POETS OF THE 1950s

INTRODUCTION

Early in the 1950s there were signs that a new generation of poets was about to appear, for whom the heroes of the 1930s were remote historical figures and the fashionable idols of the 1940s sinister corrupters of poetic taste. Oscar Mellor's Fantasy Press books and pamphlets, John Wain's series of readings on the Third Programme, a few volumes printed by the Reading School of Art, and the anthology *Springtime*, edited by G. S. Fraser and Iain Fletcher (1953), were among the early manifestations of this new spirit. Then came the launching of a periodical called *Listen*, produced by George Hartley, who also published volumes by Philip Larkin and by John Holloway; and various articles appeared in *The Spectator* and *The Times Literary Supplement* suggesting that a new literary movement was under way. Since nobody was quite clear what it stood for, it was commonly referred to as 'The Movement'.

It seemed to a number of intelligent observers that two main lines of poetry were discernible:

> One stems from the early Eliot, passes through the poets of the Thirties (especially Auden and Empson) and ends with our young academic poets, the University Wits (Kingsley Amis and Donald Davie, for example). The second began with bits of Yeats, bits of Pound and a good deal of outside help from the French Symbolists and Rilke. It takes in Dylan Thomas and *The New Apocalypse* to end in what might be called our New Symbolists (Kathleen Raine and others).[1]

A few months later an anonymous writer attempted to define the characteristics of this first line: 'Poets like Mr. Donald Davie or Mr. Thom Gunn are only less hostile to the political preoccupations of the Thirties than to the lush, loose fashionable writing of the Forties and Fifties.'[2] This article provoked a lively correspondence; and in a letter to *The Spectator* printed on 15 October 1954 Denis Donoghue argued that 'the characteristic work of the new poets has, and deliberately sets out to attain, the virtues of late eighteenth-century poetry, in parti-

[1] Anthony Hartley, 'Critic Between the Lines', *The Spectator*, 8 January 1954.
[2] 'In The Movement', *The Spectator*, 1 October 1954.

cular of Goldsmith, Denham, Johnson and Cowper.'[3] To what extent are these generalizations accurate?

The attitude of the Movement poets to the 1930s was ambivalent. Donald Davie's poem, 'Remembering the Thirties',[4] has been generally misinterpreted as a cruel piece of mockery, even though its irony is sharply turned against Davie's own generation. As originally printed, the poem bore as its epigraph a quotation from Paul Tillich: 'Courage is an ethical reality, but it is rooted in the whole breadth of existence and ultimately in the structure of being itself.' Read in conjunction with the final verse, this epigraph should have alerted Davie's readers to the poem's many reservations, qualifications and courtesies.

Moreover, one of the formative influences upon the Movement was William Empson, about whom John Wain wrote, at the end of the forties, a long, enthusiastic article which he reprinted in *Preliminary Essays* (1957). G. S. Fraser had anticipated some of Wain's points in a review of *The Gathering Storm* printed in *Poetry London* at the beginning of the decade, but nobody had paid much heed. During the interval the climate of opinion had shifted, so that the younger poets were prepared to accept Wain's contention that Empson 'has, after all, written at least a dozen poems which pass every known test of greatness; and who has done more?'[5]

It is often stated that the Movement poets were unequivocally hostile to Edith Sitwell and to Dylan Thomas. While it is true that they would allow no merit to Edith Sitwell, they carefully distinguished between Thomas's work and the debasing legend which had sprung up around his life and personality: 'The death of Dylan Thomas was very sad, and it is clear that some of the poems he wrote are going to be remembered for a very long time . . . But the saddest thing about it, to my mind, was the fulsome ballyhoo it evoked on both sides of the Atlantic.'[6]

There was one poet who had throughout the 1940s maintained most of the values associated with Auden and his coevals – Roy Fuller. He admired and was admired by the Movement, his dry, astringent tone, his ironical disgust at the spectacle of human folly, his self-scrutiny and austere gloom all being congenial to his younger contemporaries. Appropriately enough, he ushered in the decade with a tart poem of welcome, 'The Fifties':

[3] Denham in fact lived from 1615 to 1669.

[4] See above, p. 208.

[5] John Wain, *Preliminary Essays*, 1957, p. 180.

[6] Donald Davie, letter printed in *The London Magazine*, I, 2, March 1954, p. 75. For a discerning tribute to Thomas by another Movement poet, see John Wain, *Anthology of Modern Poetry*, 1963, pp. 28–32.

The wretched summers start again
With lies and armies ready for
Advancing on that fast terrain.

As for the influence of the eighteenth-century poets, the only member of the Movement to have acknowledged such a debt is Donald Davie:

A pasticheur of late-Augustan styles,
I too have sung the sofa and the hare,
Made nightmare ride upon a private air,
And hearths, extinguished, send a chill for miles.[7]

There was, however, a general consensus of agreement about the use of traditional metres and conventional stanzaic forms. Once again Davie may serve as a spokesman for the group: 'The metrical and other habits of English verse seem to me to be in no sense "arbitrary", but rather to be rooted in the nature of English as a spoken and written language; I see no other explanation of the fact that the rules which, say, Mr. Amis and Mr. Graves observe are the rules which have governed ninety per cent of English poetry for more than 500 years.'[8]

To what extent the Movement was more than a lively journalistic invention is not easy to decide. Thom Gunn and Philip Larkin take the view that the whole affair was largely a joke, and that the Movement had no real existence,[9] which is precisely the attitude that Davie finds deplorably evasive.[10] It is undeniable that Robert Conquest's anthology, *New Lines* (1956), provided much the same kind of platform for the poets of the fifties that *New Signatures* (1932) had offered to the poets of the thirties.

It is probably true that the poets in this anthology were united by 'a negative determination to avoid bad principles'[11] rather than by any positive programme. To label them New University Wits or Neo-Empsonians, to trace some common resemblances between poets as diverse as Elizabeth Jennings, Kingsley Amis, and John Holloway, would be a pointless exercise. The most one can say is that the nine contributors to the anthology shared a common tone, a suspicion of large rhetorical gestures, a belief that the intellect and the moral judgment must play a decisive part in the shaping of a poem. The addiction to defensive irony and the fear of unregulated, unscrutinized emotion were sometimes elevated into moral principles. Davie's 'Rejoinder to

7 'Homage to William Cowper'. 8 *Delta*, 8, Spring 1956, p. 8.
9 Ian Hamilton, 'Four Conversations', *The London Magazine*, IV, 8, November 1964, p. 69, and p. 72.
10 Donald Davie, 'Remembering the Movement', *Prospect*, Summer 1959, pp. 13–16.
11 Robert Conquest, Introduction to *New Lines*, 1956, p. xv.

a Critic' is an attempt to justify this caution, this bitter realization that strong feelings and enthusiasm, however generous their origin, are all too easily perverted into evil courses. Yet the charge that the Movement poets are deficient in passion can hardly survive a reading of Larkin, Holloway, and Enright or, indeed, a careful study of *New Lines*. Davie himself in 'Dream Forest' names as 'Types of ideal virtue' Brutus, Pushkin, and Strindberg, none of them famous for timidity, emotional anaemia or rational calculation.

It is ironical that Philip Larkin, the most widely admired of all the Movement poets, should have published his first volume, *The North Ship* (1945) in the mid-Forties, a period reviled by the Movement as marking the nadir of twentieth-century verse.[12] In his witty Introduction to the 1966 edition of *The North Ship* he remarks that in the early 1940s he was infatuated with the dangerously potent music of Yeats, and that his poetic talent was preserved from ruin by his discovery in early 1946 of Hardy's verse. He adds to this edition a poem 'written a year or so later, which, though not noticeably better than the rest, shows the Celtic fever abated and the patient sleeping soundly'.[13] But the poem is an enormous advance on Larkin's earlier work, exhibiting for the first time the characteristics of his mature poetry – a fine, though unobtrusive, power of evoking an atmosphere, and the subtleties of an emotional relationship; a muted wit; a masterly control of tone; a lyrical poignancy tempered with irony:

> Waiting for breakfast, while she brushed her hair,
> I looked down at the empty hotel yard
> Once meant for coaches. Cobblestones were wet,
> But sent no light back to the loaded sky,
> Sunk as it was with mist down to the roofs.
> Drainpipes and fire-escape climbed up
> Past rooms still burning their electric light:
> I thought: Featureless morning, featureless night.

It is difficult to believe that a mere switch of literary allegiance could have brought about so remarkable a change. Perhaps even a poet cannot trace the process by which he transmutes the obscure passions of his buried life into the clarity and formal perfection of the artefact.

Larkin's poems present with a rare accuracy the outward appearance and the social climate of suburban England in the 1950s. His verse is suffused with a compassionate melancholy, a sense of the sadness and the transience of things, an awareness of the random quality inherent

[12] Talking about the Movement, Larkin has observed that 'I wasn't mentioned at the beginning. The poets of the group were Wain, Gunn, Davie and, funnily enough, Alvarez'. *The London Magazine*, IV, 8, November 1964, p. 72.

[13] *The North Ship*, 1966, p. 10.

in human existence. He accepts resignedly all the implications of his atheism, pronouncing in level tones his verdict on our lives:

> Life is first boredom, then fear.
> Whether or not we use it, it goes,
> And leaves what something hidden from us chose,
> And age, and then the only end of age.[14]

It would be misleading to claim that all the best poets of the 1950s were represented in *New Lines*, or that the Movement comprised everything that was vital in the poetry of the decade. As at all times, there were a few poets working quietly in solitude, indifferent to current literary disputes, immune to changes in fashion.

R. S. Thomas's first two volumes, *The Stones of the Field* (1946), and *An Acre of Land* (1952), were printed by small, little-known firms in Wales, and it was not until 1955 that he made his mark with *Song at the Year's Turning*, a selection of poems written between 1942 and 1954. Although he clearly owes nothing to the Movement poets his work exhibits many of the virtues which they admired. He presents with a bleak, unsparing directness the small world of the Welsh hill-country where he laboured as a priest. The hill-farmers wrestle with the soil, much as he struggles with the recalcitrant wills of his parishioners and with his own divided nature. The background to his poems is almost always the Welsh landscape in winter, the cold sky, the bare branches, the snow; and behind the physical world there lurks, invisible but omnipresent, the God who moves so mysteriously and seems to ordain cruel destinies for men:

> But the God
> We worship fashions the world
> From such torment, and every creature
> Decorates it with its tribute of blood.[15]

A much younger poet, Ted Hughes, published his first collection, *The Hawk in the Rain*, in 1957. It is interesting to compare him with his Cambridge contemporary, Thom Gunn, who is usually associated with the Movement, though he is several years younger than his fellow-contributors to *New Lines*. Both are anatomists of violence; but whereas Gunn is primarily concerned with its operation in society and in the workings of the human will, Hughes broods on violence as a principle of the universe and, in particular, of the animal kingdom. Gunn, as befits a student of Donne, is capable of writing superb metaphysical poetry in which energy is generated by the sheer force and intricate exactitude of the argument. His weakness is that the objects living in

[14] 'Dockery and Son'. [15] 'Ah!'

the physical world (including human beings) are often reduced to mere bloodless counters in a metaphysical game. Hughes, on the contrary, presents with marvellous solidity and precision the essential nature as well as the outward appearance of birds, beasts and fishes. Nobody since D. H. Lawrence has done this so powerfully as Hughes; and one feels that, like Lawrence, Hughes is overwhelmingly right when he is communicating his naked apprehensions of physical reality. When he tries to find a metaphysical sanction for what he intuitively experiences, the result is less convincing.

In his review of *New Lines* and in the controversy which followed, Charles Tomlinson voiced his dissatisfaction with the precepts and the practice of the Movement.[16] After some years during which he was admired in the States but virtually ignored in his own country, Tomlinson gradually won recognition in Britain. His poetry, which has the energizing crispness of frosty weather, is notable for clarity of outline and precision, and for its enactment of Tomlinson's responsiveness to the inexhaustible variety and power of the visible world as perceived by an alert sensibility. He believes that Symbolism was the major poetic achievement in the late nineteenth century, admiring not only the French Symbolists but the work of Tyutchev and of Machado, whom he has translated in collaboration with Henry Gifford. One of his major complaints against his British contemporaries is that they have not even tried to assimilate the Symbolist achievement, but have lazily retreated to the old Georgian backwater, where Betjeman descants on the beauties of a Gothic revival spire, while Larkin broods on the gloomy vistas of Cemetery Road.

There are other poets who deserve more than a passing mention. Thomas Blackburn, whose early verse draws on myth and legend in order to illuminate his own perplexities, has steadily become more direct in the exploration of his inner tensions, until nowadays he starts from some domestic incident or private grief and proceeds to endow it with a mythical or legendary significance. Geoffrey Hill, who has published only two small volumes, writes poetry of extraordinary concentration and purity, which though often bafflingly difficult is always possessed of great assurance and authority. Burns Singer and Edward Lowbury, two fine undervalued poets, have wrestled with the metaphysical problems of time, death, metamorphosis, and nothingness. It may be more than a coincidence that Jon Silkin's most haunting poem, 'Death of a Son', should be concerned, like Blackburn's 'Hospital for Defectives', with the inexplicable tragedy of mental deficiency.

We are perhaps too close to the 1950s to distinguish clearly between the fashionable trends and the lasting achievements of the decade. One

[16] See below, pp. 259–60. Eliot's strictures on the Georgians (see above, pp. 117–18) are applicable to much of the Movement's poetry.

could argue that the Movement does not merit the degree of importance accorded to it in this brief survey, and that its adherents won for themselves a disproportionate amount of attention by their shrewd manipulation of publicity. But at least it restored to poetry a few virtues which had been in abeyance and, by introducing a challenging, even a hectoring, note into the criticism of poetry, stimulated a number of good poets into scrutinizing the principles of their art. Remembering the fifties, we should be grateful to the Movement for its destructive irreverence as well as for the good poems which it fostered.

CRITICISM

These new 'formalists' fall into two groups. The first is a small homogeneous body, a 'school', known generally as 'the Empsonians'. How far Mr. Empson is gratified by this, I cannot say. The recipe for this type of poetry is simple. Read five hundred lines of Dryden until you have the 'noble, frank, and manly' rhythm pat; choose any theme more proper to critical prose; garnish with two chic philosophical terms, three classical references (*minor* writers, please!) and half a dozen rather naughty ones; deluge in an *espagnole* of Total Knowingness, and serve up in *villanelle* or *terza rima*.

Hilary Corke, 'The Bad Old Style', *Encounter*, IV, 6, June 1955, p. 22.

[For Empson's views on the Empsonians, see above, p. 207.]

The chief characteristics of the 'Movement', we are often told, are neatness and lucidity. But are these so new in our time? To mention just one name from many, what about the late Norman Cameron? Surely any professional poet, grouped or ungrouped, dated or dateless, ought to be able, *when he chooses*, to be neat or lucid, or both; just as any professional draughtsman should be able to command, when he needs them, the old-fasioned tricks of perspective. But what distinguishes the 'Movement' as a group from a poet like Robert Graves is that the latter's neatness is always a means to an end. As individuals then, we must welcome some of these New Liners, but as a group or a Movement, well, let them go. And behold, they go – with what docile arrogance, with what lowered but polished sights; roped together, alert for falling slates, they scale their suburban peaks – the Ascent of C3. And the banner with the strange device will soon droop on the cairn of red bricks. 'Snaffle and Curb' – but see Roy Campbell about that.

Louis MacNeice, 'Lost Generations?', review of *Poetry Now*, edited by G. S. Fraser, and *Mavericks*, edited by Howard Sergeant and Dannie Abse, *The London Magazine*, IV, 4, April 1957, p. 54.

If one had briefly to distinguish this poetry of the fifties from its predecessors, I believe the most important general point would be that it submits to no great systems of theoretical constructs nor agglomerations of unconscious commands. It is free from both mystical and logical compulsions and – like modern philosophy – is empirical in its attitude to all that comes. This reverence for the real person or event is, indeed, a part of the general intellectual ambience (in so far as that is not blind or retrogressive) of our time. One might, without stretching matters too far, say that George Orwell with his principle of real, rather than ideological honesty, exerted, even though indirectly, one of the major influences on modern poetry.

Robert Conquest, Introduction to *New Lines*, 1956, pp. xiv–xv.

. . . Yeats's own declared belief that to write 'a little song about a rose' a poet must have 'hard philosophic bones under the skin' (he meant, of course, real philosophy, Plato and Plotinus, not Russell and Ayer).

Kathleen Raine, letter to *The New Statesman*, 8 February 1958, p. 170.

A philosophy so unfashionable as Platonism is unlikely to find favour with a generation raised on a diet of materialism, positivism, and the like (can these be called *love of wisdom*?).

Kathleen Raine, letter to *The Times Literary Supplement*, 25 May 1956, p. 313.

There seems to be a school of young poets who have never heard of Muse or daimon, and who write only from personal experience. Inspiration is one thing, personal memory quite another; and as Blake never tired of pointing out, memory is not a Muse.

Kathleen Raine, letter to *The Times Literary Supplement*, 8 June 1956, p. 345.

I write poems to preserve things I have seen/thought/felt . . . both for myself and for others, though I feel that my prime responsibility is to the experience itself, which I am trying to keep from oblivion for its own sake. Why I should do this I have no idea, but I think the impulse to preserve lies at the bottom of all art . . .

As a guiding principle I believe that every poem must be its own sole freshly-created universe, and therefore have no belief in 'tradition' or a common myth-kitty or casual allusions in poems to other poems or poets, which last I find unpleasantly like the talk of literary understrappers letting you see they know the right people.

Philip Larkin, *Poets of the 1950s*, edited by D. J. Enright, 1955, pp. 77–8.

I would say that I have been most influenced by the poetry that I've enjoyed – and this poetry has not been Eliot or Pound or anybody who is normally regarded as 'modern' – which is a sort of technique word, isn't it? The poetry I've enjoyed has been the kind of poetry you'd associate with me – Hardy pre-eminently, Wilfred Owen, Auden, Christina Rossetti, William Barnes; on the whole, people to whom technique seems to matter less than content, people who accept the forms they have inherited but use them to express their own content...

What I do feel a bit rebellious about is that poetry seems to have got into the hands of a critical industry which is connected with culture in the abstract, and this I do rather lay at the door of Eliot and Pound . . . I think a lot of this 'myth-kitty' business has grown out of that, because first of all you have to be terribly educated, you have to read everything to know these things, and secondly you've got somehow to work them in to show that you are working them in. But to me the whole of the ancient world, the whole of classical and biblical mythology means very little, and I think that using them today not only fills poems full of dead spots but dodges the writer's duty to be original.

Philip Larkin, Ian Hamilton, 'Four Conversations', *The London Magazine*, IV, 8, November 1964, pp. 71–2.

The lack of experiences in, I think, all Mr. Conquest's poets is their general failure to see things anew, to register any *nouveau frisson*, if one can attempt to strip Hugo's congratulatory phrase to Baudelaire of its more romantic nuances. They show a singular want of the vital awareness of the continuum outside themselves, of the mystery bodied over against them in the created universe, which they fail to experience with any degree of sharpness or to embody with any instress or sensuous depth...

A poet's sense of objectivity, however, of that which is beyond himself and beyond his mental conceit of himself, and his capacity to realise that objectivity within the artefact is the gauge of his artistry and the first prerequisite of all artistic genius.

Charles Tomlinson, 'The Middlebrow Muse', review of *New Lines*, edited by Robert Conquest, *Essays in Criticism*, VII, 2, April 1957, p. 215.

It is [Donald Davie's] contention that only by means of a 'self-imposed loss of nerve' can poetry be renewed after the verbal debauchery of the forties. It is mine that it can only be renewed by poets whose sensory organization is alive, who are aware to the fingertips of the universe around them and who have broken through that suburban mental ratio which too many of the movement poets attempt to impose on their experience.

Charles Tomlinson, 'The Middle Brow Muse', *Essays in Criticism*, VII, 4, October 1957, p. 460.

[A rejoinder to critics of his review.]

HAMILTON: You yourself were writing at the time of the Movement, but it had little effect on you. Could you reconstruct your position at the time?

TOMLINSON: My position was that I felt the Movement to be a symptom of that suffocation which has affected so much English art ever since the death of Byron. I couldn't see why we shouldn't have the romantics, the cubists, the futurists, the Americans, Apollinaire, Picasso and Paul Klee in *our* movement. And one needs to stress visual art, because visual art has stayed major whereas poetry, since the 'grand old men', has dwindled: it has no equivalents for Pollock, de Kooning, or Arshile Gorky.

HAMILTON: You mention all these other artists. People have spoken of there being a danger of too much influence in your work. What do you feel about this?

TOMLINSON: That's Alvarez, not 'people'. You can't have too much influence if you know what to do with it – look at Picasso, or, just as striking, in a different way, the American-Armenian painter, Gorky. The trouble with most critics is that they have such shallow notions of originality. A measure of the real artist is his capacity for discipleship...

It's quite possible a genuine poet might find himself (and modernism) via Laforgue, or for that matter, via Rilke or Leopardi or Vallejo or what you will. As I say, I began with Blake and Whitman myself.

Charles Tomlinson and Ian Hamilton, 'Four Conversations', *The London Magazine*, IV, 8, November 1964, pp. 84–5.

Hardly ever did we seem to write our poems out of an idea of poetry as a way of knowing the world we were in, apprehending it, learning it; instead we conceived of it as an act of private and public therapy, the poet resolving his conflicts by expressing them and proffering them to the reader so that vicariously he should do the same. The most obvious register of this is the striking absence from 'Movement' poetry of outward and non-human things apprehended crisply for their own sakes. I'm not asking for 'nature poetry', but simply for an end to attitudinizing. In 'Movement' poetry the poet is never so surrendered to his experience, never so far gone out of himself in his response, as not to be aware of the attitudes he is taking up.

Donald Davie, 'Remembering the Movement', *Prospect*, Summer 1959, p. 16. [Davie also looks back at the Movement in 'A Postscript', *Purity of Diction in English Verse* (2nd. ed., 1967), pp. 197–202.]

POEMS

PHILIP LARKIN
(b. 1922)

Wants

Beyond all this, the wish to be alone:
However the sky grows dark with invitation-cards
However we follow the printed directions of sex
However the family is photographed under the flagstaff –
Beyond all this, the wish to be alone.

Beneath it all, desire of oblivion runs:
Despite the artful tensions of the calendar,
The life insurance, the tabled fertility rites,
The costly aversion of the eyes from death –
Beneath it all, desire of oblivion runs.

Maiden Name

Marrying left your maiden name disused.
Its five light sounds no longer mean your face,
Your voice, and all your variants of grace;
For since you were so thankfully confused
By law with someone else, you cannot be
Semantically the same as that young beauty:
It was of her that these two words were used.

Now it's a phrase applicable to no one,
Lying just where you left it, scattered through
Old lists, old programmes, a school prize or two,
Packets of letters tied with tartan ribbon –
Then is it scentless, weightless, strengthless, wholly
Untruthful? Try whispering it slowly.
No, it means you. Or, since you're past and gone,

It means what we feel now about you then:
How beautiful you were, and near, and young,
So vivid, you might still be there among
Those first few days, unfingermarked again.
So your old name shelters our faithfulness,
Instead of losing shape and meaning less
With your depreciating luggage laden.

No Road

Since we agreed to let the road between us
Fall to disuse,
And bricked our gates up, planted trees to screen us,
And turned all time's eroding agents loose,
Silence, and space, and strangers – our neglect
Has not had much effect.

Leaves drift unswept, perhaps; grass creeps unmown;
No other change.
So clear it stands, so little overgrown,
Walking that way tonight would not seem strange,
And still would be allowed. A little longer,
And time will be the stronger,

Drafting a world where no such road will run
From you to me;
To watch that world come up like a cold sun,
Rewarding others, is my liberty.
Not to prevent it is my will's fulfilment.
Willing it, my ailment.

DONALD DAVIE
(b. 1922)

On Bertrand Russell's 'Portraits from Memory'

Those Cambridge generations, Russell's, Keynes' . . .
And mine? Oh mine was Wittgenstein's, no doubt:
Sweet pastoral, too, when some-one else explains,
Although my memories leave the eclogues out.

The clod's not bowed by sedentary years,
Yet, set by Thyrsis, he's a crippled man:
How singularly naked each appears,
Beside the other on this bosky plan.

Arrangements of the copse and cloister seem,
Although effective, still Utopian,
For groves find room, behind a leafy screen,
For sage and harvester, but not for man.

I wonder still which of the hemispheres
Infects the other, in this grassy globe;
The chumbling moth of Madingley, that blears
The labourer's lamp, destroys the scarlet robe.

It was the Muse that could not make her home
In that too thin and yet too sluggish air,
Too volatile to live among the loam,
Her sheaves too heavy for the talkers there.

The Fountain

Feathers up fast, and steeples; then in clods
Thuds into its first basin; thence as surf
Smokes up and hangs; irregularly slops
Into its second, tattered like a shawl;
There, chill as rain, stipples a danker green,
Where urgent tritons lob their heavy jets.

For Berkeley this was human thought, that mounts
From bland assumptions to inquiring skies,
There glints with wit, fumes into fancies, plays
With its negations, and at last descends,
As by a law of nature, to its bowl
Of thus enlightened but still common sense.

We who have no such confidence must gaze
With all the more affection on these forms,
These spires, these plumes, these calm reflections, these
Similitudes of surf and turf and shawl,
Graceful returns upon acceptances.
We ask of fountains only that they play,

Though that was not what Berkeley meant at all.

THOM GUNN
(b. 1929)

The Annihilation of Nothing

Nothing remained: Nothing, the wanton name
That nightly I rehearsed till led away
To a dark sleep, or sleep that held one dream.

In this a huge contagious absence lay,
More space than space, over the cloud and slime,
Defined but by the encroachments of its sway.

Stripped to indifference at the turns of time,
Whose end I knew, I woke without desire,
And welcomed zero as a paradigm.

But now it breaks – images burst with fire
Into the quiet sphere where I have bided,
Showing the landscape holding yet entire:

The power that I envisaged, that presided
Ultimate in its abstract devastations,
Is merely change, the atoms it divided

Complete, in ignorance, new combinations.
Only an infinite finitude I see
In those peculiar lovely variations.

It is despair that nothing cannot be
Flares in the mind and leaves a smoky mark
Of dread.
Look upward. Neither firm nor free,

Purposeless matter hovers in the dark.

TED HUGHES
(b. 1930)

Pennines in April

If this county were a sea (that is solid rock
Deeper than any sea) these hills heaving
Out of the east, mass behind mass, at this height
Hoisting heather and stones to the sky
Must burst upwards and topple into Lancashire.

Perhaps, as the earth turns, such ground-stresses
Do come rolling westward through the locked land.
Now, measuring the miles of silence
Your eye takes the strain: through

Landscapes gliding blue as water
Those barrellings of strength are heaving slowly and heave
To your feet and surf upwards
In a still, fiery air, hauling the imagination,
Carrying the larks upward.

Relic

I found this jawbone at the sea's edge:
There, crabs, dogfish, broken by the breakers or tossed
To flap for half an hour and turn to a crust
Continue the beginning. The deeps are cold:
In that darkness camaraderie does not hold:
Nothing touches but, clutching, devours. And the jaws,
Before they are satisfied or their stretched purpose
Slacken, go down jaws; go gnawn bare. Jaws
Eat and are finished and the jawbone comes to the beach:
This is the sea's achievement; with shells,
Vertebrae, claws, carapaces, skulls.

Time in the sea eats its tail, thrives, casts these
Indigestibles, the spars of purposes
That failed far from the surface. None grow rich
In the sea. This curved jawbone did not laugh
But gripped, gripped and is now a cenotaph.

CHARLES TOMLINSON
(b. 1927)

Farewell to Van Gogh

The quiet deepens. You will not persuade
  One leaf of the accomplished, steady, darkening
Chestnut-tower to displace itself
  With more of violence than the air supplies
When, gathering dusk, the pond brims evenly
  And we must be content with stillness.

Unhastening, daylight withdraws from us its shapes
  Into their central calm. Stone by stone
Your rhetoric is dispersed until the earth
  Becomes once more the earth, the leaves
A sharp partition against cooling blue.

Farewell, and for your instructive frenzy
  Gratitude. The world does not end tonight
And the fruit that we shall pick tomorrow
  Await us, weighing the unstripped bough.

Winter-piece

You wake, all windows blind – embattled sprays
grained on the medieval glass.
Gates snap like gunshot
as you handle them. Five-barred fragility
sets flying fifteen rooks who go together
silently ravenous about this winter-piece
that will not feed them. They alight
beyond, scavenging, missing everything
but the bladed atmosphere, the white resistance.
Ruts with iron flanges track
through a hard decay
where you discern once more
oak-leaf by hawthorn, for the frost
rewhets their edges. In a perfect web
blanched along each spoke
and circle of its woven wheel,
the spider hangs, grasp unbroken
and death-masked in cold. Returning
you see the house glint-out behind
its holed and ragged glaze,
frost-fronds all streaming.

R. S. THOMAS
(b. 1913)

The Cry

Don't think it was all hate
That grew there; love grew there, too,
Climbing by small tendrils where
The warmth fell from the eyes' blue

Flame. Don't think even the dirt
And the brute ugliness reigned
Unchallenged. Among the fields
Sometimes the spirit, enchained

So long by the gross flesh, raised
Suddenly there its wild note of praise.

In Church

Often I try
To analyse the quality
Of its silences. Is this where God hides
From my searching? I have stopped to listen,
After the few people have gone,
To the air recomposing itself
For vigil. It has waited like this
Since the stones grouped themselves about it.
These are the hard ribs
Of a body that our prayers have failed
To animate. Shadows advance
From their corners to take possession
Of places the light held
For an hour. The bats resume
Their business. The uneasiness of the pews
Ceases. There is no other sound
In the darkness but the sound of a man
Breathing, testing his faith
On emptiness, nailing his questions
One by one to an untenanted cross.

THOMAS BLACKBURN
(b. 1916)

Hospital for Defectives

By your unnumbered charities
A miracle disclose,
Lord of the Images, whose love,
The eyelid and the rose,
Takes for a language, and today
Tell to me what is said
By these men in a turnip field
And their unleavened bread.

For all things seem to figure out
The stirrings of your heart,
And two men pick the turnips up
And two men pull the cart;
And yet between the four of them
No word is ever said
Because the yeast was not put in
Which makes the human bread.

But three men stare on vacancy
And one man strokes his knees;
What is the meaning to be found
In such dark vowels as these?

Lord of the Images, whose love,
The eyelid and the rose,
Takes for a metaphor, today
Beneath the warder's blows,
The unleavened man did not cry out
Or turn his face away;
Through such men in a turnip field
What is it that you say?

GEOFFREY HILL
(b. 1932)

Requiem for the Plantagenet Kings

For whom the possessed sea littered, on both shores,
Ruinous arms; being fired, and for good,
To sound the constitution of just wars,
Men, in their eloquent fashion, understood.

Relieved of soul, the dropping-back of dust,
Their usage, pride, admitted within doors;
At home, under caved chantries, set in trust,
With well-dressed alabaster and proved spurs
They lie; they lie; secure in the decay
Of blood, blood-marks, crowns hacked and coveted,
Before the scouring fires of trial-day
Alight on men; before sleeked groin, gored head,
Budge through the clay and gravel, and the sea
Across daubed rock evacuates its dead.

BURNS SINGER
(1928–64)

Sonnets for a Dying Man, XXIII

Is it perhaps a telephone unanswered,
A sun in trouble, or a star on heat,
The B.B.C. truncating bits of Hansard,
Or is a ghost howling beneath the street?

I do not know what it can be you hear.
I know that you are listening, and I try,
By listening also, not to interfere
With your supreme unshared perplexity.
What words can say to me the words have said
Out there where nothing happens since you are
No longer there for things to happen to
And there's no way of telling what is true
You cannot find me any image for
Our knowledge of our ignorance of the dead.

EDWARD LOWBURY
(b. 1913)

Nothing

Her sixth midsummer eve keeps Ruth awake.
The silent house is full of yellow light –
Put out, from time to time, by prowling clouds;
The dripping tap, an unsuspected heart
Somewhere inside the house, seems to grow louder;
Street noises have an unfamiliar ring.
She cannot shut her ears, but even her eyelids
Let through the silent play of light and shade.

At last she leaves her bed and creeps downstairs,
Trembling a little; whispers, 'I'm afraid.'
'Afraid of what?' 'Of Nothing.' When we laugh,
Saying 'That means you're not afraid,' she cries,
And says, more loudly, 'I'm afraid of Nothing!'
Says it again, till suddenly we see it –
Nothing outside the windows; Nothing after
The longest day; Nothing inside the house;
Nothing where everything seemed set for ever.

SELECT BIBLIOGRAPHY

General
Springtime, edited by G. S. Fraser and Iain Fletcher, London, 1953.
New Lines, edited by Robert Conquest, London, 1956.
New Lines 2, edited by Robert Conquest, London, 1963.
Mavericks, edited by Howard Sergeant and Dannie Abse, London, 1957.
The New Poetry, edited by A. Alvarez, Harmondsworth, 1962; 2nd. ed., 1966.

Fraser, G. S., *Vision and Rhetoric*, London, 1959.
Contains two chapters on the 1950s.
Grubb, Frederick, *A Vision of Reality*, London, 1965.
Contains a section on the 1950s.
Press, John, *Rule and Energy*, London, 1963.
Rosenthal, M. L., *The New Poets*, New York, 1967.

Donald Davie
Brides of Reason, Swinford, 1955.
A Winter Talent, London, 1957.
The Forests of Lithuania, Hull, 1959.
A Sequence for Francis Parkman, Hull, 1961.
Events and Wisdoms, London, 1964.
Purity of Diction in English Verse, London, 1952; 2nd. ed., 1967.
Articulate Energy, London, 1955; 2nd. ed., 1967.
These two critical works, although concerned with poetry in general, throw indirect light on the aesthetic principles of the Movement.

Thom Gunn
Fighting Terms, Swinford, 1954; reissued, London, 1962.
The Sense of Movement, London, 1957.
My Sad Captains, London, 1961.
Positives, London, 1967.
Verses by Thom Gunn, photographs by Ander Gunn.
Touch, London, 1967.

Ted Hughes
The Hawk in the Rain, London, 1957.
Lupercal, London, 1960.
Wodwo, London, 1967.

Philip Larkin
The North Ship, London, 1945; reissued, London, 1966.
The Less Deceived, Hull, 1955.
The Whitsun Weddings, London, 1964.

Charles Tomlinson
The Necklace, Swinford, 1955; reissued, London, 1966.
Seeing is Believing, London, 1960.
A Peopled Landscape, London, 1963.
American Scenes, London, 1966.

INDEX

INDEX

Page numbers in bold type indicate poems quoted in the sections entitled POEMS